The book is dedicated to my lovely
and talented wife, Angela Walker.

ABOUT THE AUTHOR

Matt Walker is currently an IT security architect working for Hewlett-Packard on NASA's desktop support contract. An IT security and education professional for more than 20 years, he has served as the director of the Network Training Center and the curriculum lead/senior instructor for Cisco Networking Academy on Ramstein Air Base, Germany, and as a network engineer for NASA's Secure Network Systems (NSS), designing and maintaining secured data, voice, and video networking for the agency. Matt also worked as the instructor supervisor and senior instructor at Dynetics, Inc., in Huntsville, Alabama, providing onsite certification awarding classes for ISC2, Cisco, and CompTIA, and after two years he came right back to NASA as the IT security manager for UNITeS, SAIC, at Marshall Space Flight Center. He has written and contributed to numerous technical training books for NASA, Air Education and Training Command, and the U.S. Air Force, as well as commercially, and he continues to train and write certification and college-level IT and IA security courses. Matt holds numerous commercial certifications, including CEHv7, CPTS, CNDA, CCNA, and MCSE.

About the Technical Editor

Brad Horton currently works as an information security specialist with the U.S. Department of Defense. Brad has worked as a security engineer, commercial security consultant, penetration tester, and information systems researcher in both the private and public sectors.

This has included work with several defense contractors, including General Dynamics C4S, SAIC, and Dynetics, Inc. Mr. Horton currently holds the Certified Information Systems Security Professional (CISSP), Certified Ethical Hacker (CEH), Certified Information Systems Auditor (CISA), and a recently expired Cisco Certified Network Associate (CCNA) trade certifications. Brad has a bachelor's degree in commerce and business administration from the University of Alabama, a master's degree in management of information systems from the University of Alabama in Huntsville (UAH), and a graduate certificate in information assurance from UAH. When not hacking, Brad can be found at home with his family or on a local golf course.

The views and opinions expressed in all portions of this publication belong solely to the author and/or editor and do not necessarily state or reflect those of the Department of Defense or the United States Government. References within this publication to any specific commercial product, process, or service by trade name, trademark, manufacturer, or otherwise, do not necessarily constitute or imply its endorsement, recommendation, or favoring by the United States Government.

CEH™
Certified Ethical Hacker
Hacker Practice Exams
Second Edition

Matt Walker

New York • Chicago • San Francisco
Athens • London • Madrid • Mexico City
Milan • New Delhi • Singapore • Sydney • Toronto

ISBN: Book p/n 978-0-07-183870-2 and CD p/n 978-0-07-183871-9
of set 978-0-07-183873-3

MHID: Book p/n 0-07-183870-8 and CD p/n 0-07-183871-6
of set 0-07-183873-2

Sponsoring Editor	**Technical Editor**	**Composition**
Stephanie Evans	Brad Horton	Cenveo Publisher Services
Editorial Supervisor	**Copy Editor**	**Illustration**
Jody McKenzie	Kim Wimpsett	Cenveo Publisher Services
Project Manager	**Proofreader**	**Art Director, Cover**
Kritika Kaushik,	Paul Tyler	Jeff Weeks
Cenveo® Publisher Services	**Production Supervisor**	
Acquisitions Coordinator	George Anderson	
Mary Demery		

CONTENTS

ACKNOWLEDGMENTS

I, like most of you, had hardly ever read the acknowledgment portion of a book before. When I bought a book, I just wanted to get to the meat of the thing and see what I could drag out of it—either intellectually or entertainment-wise—and couldn't give a care about what the author thought about those who helped put it all together. Then, of all things, I *wrote* a book.

Now, I read the acknowledgment of *every* book I purchase. Why? Because having gone through the trials and tribulations of writing, editing, arguing, planning, researching, rewriting, screaming at a monitor, and restarting the whole thing all over again, I understand why they're so important. I know what it means when the writer says they "couldn't have done it without *fill-in-the-blank*." Trust me, if it's written there, then the author truly means they *couldn't have done it without them*. My *fill-in-the-blanks* deserve more than just a mention in an acknowledgments section, though, because they really did make it all possible, and I most assuredly couldn't have done it without them.

My undying gratitude and heartfelt thanks go out to Tim Green, Stephanie Evans, Mary Demery, Jigyasa Bhatia, Kritika Kaushik, and the entire team at McGraw-Hill Education. Once again, they provided me with the chance to do something I dearly love and were very patient with me in putting this all together. Life always seems to throw a lot of things at us, and I had a lot of stuff coming my way during this little adventure. If you've read the opening to the companion CEH All-in-One book, then you know how much regard I have for all involved with this.

Lastly, I can't thank our technical editor, Brad Horton, enough. Brad makes a difficult process—technically scrubbing everything to make sure it's all in good order—not only bearable but downright fun. His edits were spot on and were always designed to make this project the absolute best it could be. He not only pointed out corrections when I messed something up but added immeasurably to the real-world aspects of this book. I simply could not, *would not*, have done this without him. It's an honor to work with him and a great blessing in my life to call him a friend.

INTRODUCTION

Hello there, Dear Reader, and welcome to the practice exams for Certified Ethical Hacker, version 8. If you're the proud owner of previous editions of this book or its companion All-in-One book, *CEH Certified Ethical Hacker All-in-One Exam Guide*, welcome back! If not and you're just picking this book up for the first time to see whether it's for you, settle in for a moment and let's cover a few really important items.

Some of you may be curious about what a "hacking" study guide looks like or you may be thinking about attempting a new certification or career choice. Some of you may have already taken that decision leap and started down the path, now looking for the next resource to help you along the journey. And some of you reading this may even be simply looking for some credentials for your career—most of this group are true professionals who already know how to do this job and are just finally ready to get the certification knocked out, while a small few are simply looking for a résumé bullet (one more certification you can put on your e-mail signature line to impress others).

Regardless of where you stand in your career or your desires for this certification, there are a couple of things I need to clear the air about—right up front before you commit to purchasing and reading this book. First (before I get to the bad stuff), I firmly believe this book will assist you in attaining your CEH certification. The entire team involved in this effort has spent a lot of time, energy, thought, research, and bourbon on producing what we think is the best companion resource guide on the market. I'm proud of it and proud to have been associated with the professionals who helped put it together.

That said, if you're looking for a silver bullet—a virtual copy of the exam so you can simply memorize, go take the test, and forget about it—please stop reading now and go take your chances elsewhere. Part of the ethics of attaining, and maintaining, a CEH credential is the nondisclosure agreement all candidates sign before attempting the exam. I, and everyone else involved in this project, have taken great pains to provide you with examples of questions designed to test your knowledge of the subject at hand, not to provide you with questions to memorize. Those who are looking for that, and use that method to attain the certification, belittle and cheapen the hard work the community puts into this, and I would be sickened to know of any of them using this work for that purpose.

If you want to pass this exam and have the respect and benefits that come along with holding the certification, then you better damn well know how to do the job. The memorization/test-taking junkies out there may get an interview or two with this certification on their résumé, but trust me—they'll be discovered as frauds before they ever get to round 2. This community knows the difference between a contender and a pretender, so don't try to take shortcuts. Learn the material. Become an expert in it. Then go take the exam. If you're not willing to put in the effort, maybe you should pick up another line of study. Like professional dodge ball. Or the janitorial arts. To quote a really bad 1980s testosterone movie, "There's always Barber School."

With all that out of the way, and now that we're talking to the *real* candidates for this certification, once again I firmly believe this book will help you in your attempt to attain the certification. As always, however, I must caution the rest of you: Relying on a single book—*any* single book—to pass this exam is a recipe for disaster. Yes, this is a great resource, and you should definitely buy it (*right now—don't wait!*); however, you simply will not pass this exam without the time and benefit that can come only from experience. As a matter of fact, EC-Council now requires candidates sitting for the exam to have at least two years of IT security–related experience. Bolster your study in this book with practice, practice, and more practice. You'll thank me for it later.

Lastly, keep in mind this certification isn't a walk in the park. Certified Ethical Hacker (CEH) didn't gain the reputation and value it has by being easy to attain. Its worth has elevated it as one of the top certifications a technician can attain and is now part of DoD 8570's call for certification on DoD networks. In short, this certification *actually means something* to employers because they know the effort it takes to attain it.

The exam itself—now on version 8—is a 4-hour, 125-question grueling marathon that will leave you exhausted when you click the Finish button. EC-Council has provided a handbook on the certification and exam (as of this writing, located at https://cert. eccouncil.org/wp contents/uploads/CEH-Candidate-Handbook-v1.6-31012012. pdf) that provides all you'll need to know about qualifications, content, and other information about the exam and certification. I've included some highlights from this handbook here, detailing the exam and what you'll need:

- **Test details** The exam is a proctored (in other words, in-person at an authorized testing facility) 4-hour, 125-question test. It's computer based and allows you to skip and mark questions to revisit at the end. Your exam score is tabulated immediately after completion, so be sure to review everything before clicking Finish. A passing score is 70 percent, which means you need to answer at least 88 of them correctly. You can find authorized Prometric or VUE test facilities at their respective web sites (www.prometric.com/ec-council and www .vue.com/eccouncil, respectively).

- **Test content** Version 8 of the CEH exam, per EC-Council, is designed to test six tasks and seven knowledge categories. Tasks listed for the exam include System Development and Management, System Analysis and Audits, Security Testing/Vulnerabilities, Reporting, Mitigation, and Ethics. Knowledge categories tested on the exam include Background, Analysis/Assessment, Security, Tools/ Systems/Programs, Procedures/Methodology, Regulation/Policy, and Ethics. Each section has a weighted value and an appropriate number of questions offered to cover the material. Most of the exam points and weighting comes from system attacks and tool knowledge.

- **Eligibility** Per EC-Council, you must either attend its official training (an official CEH instructor-led training [ILT], computer-based training [CBT], or online live training) or submit an exam eligibility form (along with a $100 nonrefundable fee) proving you've been in the security field for at least two years. In either case, once you've been approved to sit for the exam, EC-Council will forward a code to you that must be presented at the Authorized Prometric or VUE Testing Center on the date of the exam.

- **Forms** Before sitting for the exam, you'll be required to sign nondisclosure forms and candidate agreement forms (indicating you promise to be ethical in your hacking). If you're taking the exam without attending training, you'll also need to submit the CEH eligibility form to certmanager@eccouncil.org. The eligibility form requires your colleagues' and boss's signature, and you'll need to include a copy of a valid government-approved identification. EC-Council will contact your boss for a follow-up interview to complete the process and verify your eligibility. All forms and submission instructions (fax numbers and e-mail addresses) are available within the handbook.

- **Test retake policy** If a candidate fails the first attempt, there is no waiting period—you can immediately retake it if you want. On the second, third, and fourth failures, you must wait 14 days before a re-attempt. The only other restriction on this is you are not allowed to attempt the exam 5 times within a 12-month period.

- **Getting your certification** Per the handbook, after successfully attaining at least a minimum score, you will be issued your CEHv8 credential and will receive your CEHv8 welcome kit within four to eight weeks. The CEH credential is valid for three-year periods but can be renewed each period by successfully earning EC-Council Continued Education (ECE) credits. All EC-Council correspondence will be sent to the e-mail address provided during your exam registration. If your e-mail address changes, it is your responsibility to notify certadmin@eccouncil.org; failing that, you will not be able to receive ECE credits for your work.

Best of luck to you, Dear Reader. I sincerely hope your exam goes well for you and your career is filled with great experiences. Be honest, do a good job, and make every day and action work toward a better world.

In This Book

We've organized this book so that each chapter consists of a battery of practice exam questions representing part of the knowledge and skills you need to know to pass the Certified Ethical Hacker exam. This book was designed to mirror the organization of the *CEH Certified Ethical Hacker All-in-One Exam Guide, Second Edition*, and it serves as an excellent companion.

Pre-assessment Test

This book features a pre-assessment test as Appendix A. The pre-assessment test will gauge your areas of strength and weakness and allow you to tailor your studies based on your needs. We recommend you take this pre-assessment test before starting the questions in Chapter 1.

Objective Map

Following this introduction, you will find an objective map. This map has been constructed in the form of a table to allow you to reference the various topics covered in this book, the chapter in which it is covered, and the specific questions pertaining to each topic.

Practice Exams

Of the 500-plus questions included in this book, more than 350 are on the accompanying CD-ROM in a customizable test engine. You can create practice exams by chapter or objective, or you can take multiple full-length practice exams. For more information, please see Appendix B.

Objective Map

The purpose of the following objective map is to identify objective coverage throughout this practice exams book. This checklist may help you focus on your assessed needs, if you so choose.

Objective	Chapter No.	Question No.
Chapter 1: Getting Started: Essential Knowledge		
Understand basic elements of information security	1	1, 4, 11, 13, 22, 24
Describe the five stages of ethical hacking	1	2, 7, 14
Identify essential terminology associated with ethical hacking	1	3, 5, 15, 17, 18
Identify fundamentals of security policies	1	6, 8, 10, 12, 16
Define ethical hacker and classifications of hackers	1	9, 20
Define the types of system attacks	1	19, 21, 23, 25
Chapter 2: Reconnaissance: Information Gathering for the Ethical Hacker		
Define footprinting	2	6, 8, 25
Describe information gathering methodology	2	2, 3, 5, 10, 17, 18, 19, 24
Understand the use of whois, ARIN, and nslookup	2	1, 12, 14, 26
Describe DNS record types	2	7, 9, 11, 13, 15, 16, 20, 21, 22
Define and describe Google hacking	2	4, 23

Getting Started: Essential Knowledge

This chapter includes questions from the following topics:
- Identify components of TCP/IP computer networking
- Understand basic elements of information security
- Understand incident management steps
- Identify fundamentals of security policies
- Identify essential terminology associated with ethical hacking
- Define ethical hacker and classifications of hackers
- Describe the five stages of ethical hacking
- Define the types of system attacks

Even if you've never read the book, I'm certain you know all about *Alice in Wonderland*. Maybe you saw the original Disney cartoon version of the tale, or perhaps you watched a retelling of it in a local play. No matter what your exposure to the story (and I hope your only experience with the story is not that dreadful version starring Johnny Depp in 2010), or even if you missed all of it, you've probably heard the endless references in conversation from the tale. Things like "chasing it down the rabbit hole," "mad as a hatter," and "off with their heads!" are all tied to the story and find their way into our day-to-day lives.

One quote from the book is especially apropos to where we find ourselves right now, Dear Reader: at the beginning. Oftentimes when we have a huge task ahead of us, we falter and are gripped with indecision about where to begin. After all, with so much to do, we can become paralyzed and overwhelmed, not knowing which step to take first. And here, to help with that small problem comes the King of Wonderland himself with some great advice: "Begin at the beginning, and go on till you come to the end. Then stop."

Look, I know you're wanting to dive right in and get to the juicy stuff, but if you don't start at the beginning and cover all the mundane, boring things, you'll wind up doing yourself a disservice and may never find yourself at the end. No, this stuff isn't the sexy hacking questions you're just dying to get to, but this is stuff you *really* need to know, and you'll definitely be tested on it. The good news with this part of your exam is that this is the easy stuff. It's almost pure memorization and definitions—with no wacky formulas or script nuances to figure out. And don't worry, it's not nearly as bad as you think it's going to be.

 STUDY TIPS   When it comes to studying this chapter, where mostly definitions and rote memorization is all that is required for the exam, repetition is the key. Tables with words on one side and corresponding definitions on the other can be pretty effective—and don't discount the old-school flash cards either. When studying, try to find some key words in each definition you can associate with the term. That way, when you're looking at a weird test question on the exam, a key word will pop out and help provide the answer for you. And for goodness sake, please try not to confuse real world with the exam—trust what you get out of this book and your other study material, and don't read too much into the questions.

Some of the most confusing questions for you in this section will probably come from the CIA triad, the methodology steps, security policies, and security control mechanisms. Be careful with *confidentiality* versus *integrity* (watch out for that pesky *authentication* word as well), know the methodology like the back of your hand, and use logic in figuring out preventive versus corrective controls. And when it comes to policy questions, just remember that the process of elimination can sometimes be helpful in narrowing the options down to the correct answer. Concentrate on key words for definition, and you should be fine.

Additionally, and at the risk of generating derision from the "Thank you, Captain Obvious" crowd, here's another piece of advice I have for you: Spend your time on the things you don't already know (trust me, I'm on to something here). Many exam prospects and students spend way too much valuable time repeating portions they already know instead of concentrating on the things they don't. If you understand the definitions regarding white hat and black hat, don't bother reviewing them. Instead, spend your time concentrating on areas that aren't so "commonsense" to you.

And, finally, keep in mind that this certification is provided by an international organization. Therefore, you will sometimes see some fairly atrocious grammar on test questions here and there, especially in this section of the exam. Don't worry about it—just keep focused on the main point of the question and look for your key words.

1. A security team is implementing various security controls across the organization. After several configurations and applications, a final agreed-on set of security controls are put into place; however, not all risks are mitigated by the controls. Of the following, which is the next best step?

    A. Continue applying controls until all risk is eliminated.

    B. Ignore any remaining risk as "best effort controlled."

    C. Ensure that any remaining risk is residual or low and accept the risk.

    D. Remove all controls.

2. A Certified Ethical Hacker (CEH) follows a specific methodology for testing a system. Which step comes after footprinting in the CEH methodology?

    A. Scanning

    B. Enumeration

    C. Reconnaissance

    D. Application attack

3. Which of the following best describes a newly discovered flaw in a software application?

    A. Input validation flaw

    B. Shrink-wrap vulnerability

    C. Insider vulnerability

    D. Zero-day

4. Which type of security control is met by encryption?

    A. Preventive

    B. Detective

    C. Offensive

    D. Defensive

    E. Corrective

5. You've been hired as part of a pen test team. During the brief, you learn the client wants the pen test attack to simulate a normal user who finds ways to elevate privileges and create attacks. Which test type does the client want?

    A. White box

    B. Gray box

    C. Black box

    D. Hybrid

6. Which of the following is defined as ensuring the enforcement of organizational security policy does not rely on voluntary user compliance by assigning sensitivity labels on information and comparing this to the level of security a user is operating at?

   A. Mandatory access control

   B. Authorized access control

   C. Role-based access control

   D. Discretionary access control

7. You begin your first pen test assignment by checking out IP address ranges owned by the target as well as details of their domain name registration. Additionally, you visit job boards and financial websites to gather any technical information online. What activity are you performing?

   A. Security assessment

   B. Vulnerability assessment

   C. Active footprinting

   D. Passive footprinting

8. Of the following choices, which best defines a formal written document defining what employees are allowed to use organization systems for, what is not allowed, and what the repercussions are for breaking the rules?

   A. Information audit policy (IAP)

   B. Information security policy (ISP)

   C. Penetration testing policy (PTP)

   D. Company compliance policy (CCP)

9. An ethical hacker is given no prior knowledge of the network and has a specific framework in which to work. The agreement specifies boundaries, nondisclosure agreements, and a completion date definition. Which of the following is true?

   A. A white hat is attempting a black-box test.

   B. A white hat is attempting a white-box test.

   C. A black hat is attempting a black-box test.

   D. A black hat is attempting a gray-box test.

10. Which of the following is a detective control?

   A. Audit trail

   B. CONOPS

C. Procedure

D. Smartcard authentication

E. Process

11. As part of a pen test on a U.S. government system, you discover files containing Social Security numbers and other sensitive personally identifiable information (PII) information. You are asked about controls placed on the dissemination of this information. Which of the following acts should you check?

A. FISMA

B. Privacy Act

C. PATRIOT Act

D. Freedom of Information Act

12. Joe is performing an audit to validate the effectiveness of the organization's security policies. During his tests, he discovers that a user has a dial-out modem installed on a PC. Which security policy should be checked to see whether modems are allowed?

A. Firewall policy

B. Acceptable use policy

C. Remote access policy

D. Telework policy

13. A hacker is attempting to gain access to a target inside a business. After trying several methods, he gets frustrated and starts a denial-of-service attack against a server attached to the target. Which security control is the hacker affecting?

A. Confidentiality

B. Integrity

C. Availability

D. Authentication

14. In which phase of the ethical hacking methodology would a hacker discover available targets on a network?

A. Reconnaissance

B. Scanning and enumeration

C. Gaining access

D. Maintaining access

E. Covering tracks

15. Which of the following are potential drawbacks to a black-box test? (Choose all that apply.)

    A. The client does not get a full picture of an external attacker focused on their systems.

    B. The client does not get a full picture of an internal attacker focused on their systems.

    C. This test takes the longest amount of time to complete.

    D. This test takes the shortest amount of time to complete.

16. Which of the following best defines a logical or technical control?

    A. Air conditioning

    B. Security tokens

    C. Fire alarms

    D. Security policy

17. Which of the following would not be considered passive reconnaissance?

    A. Dumpster diving for valuable, discarded information

    B. Thoroughly examining financial sites for clues on target inventory and other useful information

    C. Ping sweeping a range of IP addresses found through a DNS lookup

    D. Using a search engine to discover competitive intelligence on the organization

18. As part of the preparation phase for a pen test that you are participating in, the client relays their intent to discover security flaws and possible remediation. They seem particularly concerned about external threats and do not mention internal threats at all. When defining scope, the threat of internal users is not added as part of the test. Which test is this client ignoring?

    A. Gray box

    B. Black box

    C. White hat

    D. Black hat

19. In which phase of the attack would a hacker set up and configure "zombie" machines?

    A. Reconnaissance

    B. Covering tracks

    C. Gaining access

    D. Maintaining access

20. Which of the following best describes an ethical hacker?

   A. An ethical hacker never knowingly or unknowingly exceeds the boundaries of the scope agreement.

   B. An ethical hacker never performs a denial-of-service attack on a target machine.

   C. An ethical hacker never proceeds with an audit or test without written permission.

   D. An ethical hacker never performs social engineering on unsuspecting members of the target organization.

21. Which of the following describes activities taken in the conclusion phase of a penetration test?

   A. Reports are prepared detailing security deficiencies.

   B. Vulnerability assessment is conducted.

   C. Security control audits are performed.

   D. Contract and scope agreement is created.

22. Which of the following should a security professional use as a possible means to verify the integrity of a data message from sender to receiver?

   A. Strong password requirements for encryption of the file

   B. Access controls on all network devices

   C. Hash algorithm

   D. Strong password requirements on operating system login

23. You are examining security logs snapshotted during a prior attack against the target. The target's IP address is 135.17.22.15, and the attack originated from 216.88.76.5. Which of the following correctly characterizes this attack?

   A. Inside attack

   B. Outside attack

   C. Black-box attack

   D. Spoofing

24. A machine in your environment uses an open X-server to allow remote access. The X-server access control is disabled, allowing connections from almost anywhere and with little to no authentication measures. Which of the following are true statements regarding this situation? (Choose all that apply.)

   A. An external vulnerability can take advantage of the misconfigured X-server threat.

   B. An external threat can take advantage of the misconfigured X-server vulnerability.

C. An internal vulnerability can take advantage of the misconfigured X-server threat.

D. An internal threat can take advantage of the misconfigured X-server vulnerability.

25. While performing a pen test, you find success in exploiting a machine. Your attack vector took advantage of a common mistake—the Windows 7 installer script used to load the machine left the administrative account with a default password. Which attack did you successfully execute?

A. Application level

B. Operating system

C. Shrink wrap

D. Social engineering

E. Misconfiguration

1. C
2. A
3. D
4. A
5. B
6. A
7. D
8. B
9. A
10. A
11. B
12. C
13. C
14. B
15. B, C
16. B
17. C
18. A
19. D
20. C
21. A
22. C
23. B
24. B, D
25. B

1. A security team is implementing various security controls across the organization. After several configurations and applications, a final agreed-on set of security controls are put into place; however, not all risks are mitigated by the controls. Of the following, which is the next best step?

   A. Continue applying controls until all risk is eliminated.

   B. Ignore any remaining risk as "best effort controlled."

   C. Ensure that any remaining risk is residual or low and accept the risk.

   D. Remove all controls.

   ☑ **C.** Remember at the beginning of this chapter when I said the process of elimination may be your best bet in some cases? Well, even if you aren't well-versed in risk management and security control efforts, you could narrow this down to the correct answer. It is impossible to remove all risk from any system and still have it usable. I'm certain there are exceptions to this rule (maybe super-secret machines in underground vaults buried deep within the earth, running on geothermal-powered batteries, without any network access at all and operated by a single operator who hasn't seen daylight in many years), but in general the goal of security teams has always been to reduce risk to an acceptable level.

   ☒ **A** is incorrect because, as I just mentioned, it's impossible to reduce risk to absolute zero and still have a functional system. Remember the Security, Functionality, and Usability triangle? As you move toward more Security, you move further away from Functionality and Usability.

   ☒ **B** is incorrect because it's just silly. If you're a security professional and your response to a risk—any risk—is to ignore it, I can promise you won't be employed for long. Sure, you can point out that it's low or residual and that the chance for actual exploitation is next to nonexistent, but you can't ignore it. Best effort is for kindergarten trophies and IP packet delivery.

   ☒ **D** is incorrect because removing all controls is worse than ignoring the risk. If you remove everything, then *all* risks remain. Remember, the objective is to balance your security controls to cover as much risk as possible, while leaving the system as usable and functional as possible.

2. A Certified Ethical Hacker (CEH) follows a specific methodology for testing a system. Which step comes after footprinting in the CEH methodology?

   A. Scanning

   B. Enumeration

   C. Reconnaissance

   D. Application attack

☑ **A.** CEH methodology is laid out this way: reconnaissance (footprinting), scanning and enumeration, gaining access, escalating privileges, maintaining access, and covering tracks. While you may be groaning about scanning and enumeration both appearing as answers, they're placed here in this way on purpose. This exam is not only testing your rote memorization of the methodology but how the methodology actually works. Remember, after scoping out the recon on your target, your next step is to scan it. After all, you have to know what targets are there first before enumerating information about them.

☒ **B** is incorrect because, although it is mentioned as part of step 2, it's actually secondary to scanning. Enumerating is used to gather more in-depth information about a target you already discovered by scanning. Things you might discover in scanning are IPs that respond to a ping. In enumerating each "live" IP, you might find open shares, user account information, and other goodies.

☒ **C** is incorrect because *reconnaissance* and *footprinting* are interchangeable in CEH parlance. An argument can be made that footprinting is a specific portion of an overall recon effort; however, in all CEH documentation, these terms are used interchangeably.

☒ **D** is incorrect because it references an attack. As usual, there's almost always one answer you can throw out right away, and this is a prime example. We're talking about step 2 in the methodology, where we're still figuring out what targets are there and what vulnerabilities they may have. Attacking, at this point, is folly.

3. Which of the following best describes a newly discovered flaw in a software application?

   A. Input validation flaw

   B. Shrink-wrap vulnerability

   C. Insider vulnerability

   D. Zero-day

   ☑ **D.** A *zero-day* threat is an attack or exploit on a vulnerability that the vendor, developer, system owner, and security community didn't even know existed. When these arise, developers of the operating system application or system have had no time (zero days) to work on a fix, so even though we all know there is a security flaw, there's not a whole lot we can do about it yet. Oftentimes the bad guys have been aware of it for quite a while, proving the old adage that the biggest security flaw in your system is the one *you don't even know about*: We may have just now discovered the flaw, but it's been in the application since the beginning.

☒ **A** is incorrect because input validation flaws aren't applicable here. While it is true that the newly discovered issue may indeed be an input that is not validated, allowing an attacker to put whatever they want in the field designed to have a serial number entered (for example), there's nothing in this question to indicate that. It's a newly discovered flaw, indicating that we didn't know about it until just now.

☒ **B** is incorrect because while a shrink-wrap vulnerability may actually exist in the real world (after all, an attack against a vulnerability in the shrink-wrapped application is taking advantage of a shrink-wrapped vulnerability), the term just isn't real as far as your exam is concerned. There is a shrink-wrap attack, but it's not a term for a vulnerability.

☒ **C** is incorrect for the same reason as B: The term just doesn't exist. It sounds good and makes for a decent distractor, but it's irrelevant for this question.

4. Which security control role does encryption meet?

   A. Preventive

   B. Detective

   C. Offensive

   D. Defensive

   E. Corrective

   ☑ **A.** This one should be easy. Controls fall into three categories: preventive, detective, and corrective. In this instance, encryption of data is designed to prevent unauthorized eyes from seeing it. Depending on the encryption used, this can provide for confidentiality and nonrepudiation and is most definitely preventive in nature.

   ☒ **B** is incorrect because a detective control is designed to watch for security breaches and detect when they occur. Tripwire running in real time and validating file integrity, alerting when one changes? IDS running on a machine or network to alert when naughty traffic comes by? Both are examples of detective controls.

   ☒ **C** and **D** are incorrect for the same reason: These aren't real terms. They may be actions you want to take as a security professional, but they're not control categories.

   ☒ **E** is incorrect because corrective controls are deigned to fix things after an attack has been discovered and stopped. An example would be a protected backup, ready to bring the system back to life after an attack.

5. You've been hired as part of a pen test team. During the brief, you learn the client wants the pen test attack to simulate a normal user who finds ways to elevate privileges and create attacks. Which test type does the client want?

A. White box

B. Gray box

C. Black box

D. Hybrid

☑ **B.** A gray box test is designed to replicate an inside attacker. Otherwise known as the *partial knowledge* attack (don't forget this term), the idea is to simulate a user on the inside who might know a little about the network, directory structure, and other goodies in your enterprise. You'll probably find this one to be the most enlightening attack in out-briefing your clients in the real world—it's amazing what you can get to when you're a trusted, inside user. As an aside, you'll often find in the real world that *gray-box testing* can also refer to a test where *any* inside information is given to a pen tester—you don't necessarily need to be a fully knowledgeable inside user. In other words, if you have usable information handed to you about your client, you're performing gray-box testing.

☒ **A** is incorrect because a white-box test provides all knowledge to the pen tester up front and is designed to simulate an admin on your network who, for whatever reason, decides to go on the attack. For most pen testers, this test is really just unfair. It's tantamount to sending him into the Roman Colosseum armed with a .50 caliber automatic weapon to battle a gladiator who is holding a knife.

☒ **C** is incorrect because black-box testing indicates no knowledge at all. And if you think about it, the name is easy to correlate and remember: black = no light. Therefore, you can't "see" anything. This is the test most people think about when it comes to hacking. You know nothing and are (usually) attacking from the outside.

☒ **D** is incorrect because, as far as I can tell from the EC-Council's documentation, there is no terminology for a "hybrid-box" test. This is a little tricky because the term *hybrid* is used elsewhere—for attacks and other things. If you apply a little common sense here, this answer is easy to throw out. If you know everything about the target, it's white. If you know nothing, it's black. If you're in the middle, it's gray. See?

6. Which of the following is defined as ensuring the enforcement of organizational security policy does not rely on voluntary user compliance by assigning sensitivity labels on information and comparing this to the level of security a user is operating at?

A. Mandatory access control

B. Authorized access control

C. Role-based access control

D. Discretionary access control

☑ **A.** Access control is defined as the selective restraint of access to a resource, and there are several overall mechanisms to accomplish this goal. Mandatory access control (MAC) is one type that constrains the ability of a subject to access or perform an operation on an object by assigning and comparing "sensitivity labels." Suppose a person (or a process) attempts to access or edit a file. In MAC, a label is placed on the file indicating its security level. If the entity attempting to access it does not have that level, or higher, access is denied. With mandatory access control, security is centrally controlled by a security policy administrator, and users do not have the ability to override security settings.

This should not be confused with role-based access control (RBAC) systems, which may actually use MAC to get the job done. The difference is in whether the information itself has a labeled description or whether the person accessing it has their own label. For example, in a classified area, the information classified as Top Secret will have a label on it identifying it as such, while you, as an auditor, will have your own clearance and need-to-know label allowing you to access certain information. MAC is a property of an object; RBAC is a property of someone accessing an object.

☒ **B** is incorrect because while authorized access control may sound great, it's not a valid term.

☒ **C** is incorrect because role-based access control can use MAC or discretionary access control to get the job done. In RBAC, the goal is to assign a role, and any entity holding that role can perform the duties associated with it. Users are not assigned permissions directly; they acquire them through their role (or roles). The roles are assigned to the user's account, and each additional role provides its own unique set of permissions and rights.

☒ **D** is incorrect because discretionary access control (DAC) allows the data owner, the user, to set security permissions for the object. If you're on a Windows machine right now, you can create files and folders and then set sharing and permissions on them as you see fit. MAC administrators in the Department of Defense may shudder at that thought now.

7. You begin your first pen test assignment by checking out IP address ranges owned by the target as well as details of their domain name registration. Additionally, you visit job boards and financial websites to gather any technical information online. What activity are you performing?

   A. Security assessments

   B. Vulnerability assessment

   C. Active footprinting

   D. Passive footprinting

☑ **D.** This question is another potential stumbling block on the test. The desire is to look at the question and think, "Wow, I'm typing things and using the Internet to gather information, so I'm *actively* working on the target." The key when it comes to *active* versus *passive* recon is to think of your probability of being caught doing it. For example, the activities of checking Internet pages, performing Google searches, and looking up DNS entries aren't necessarily going to alert anyone. These are things everyone does every day anyway. Walking into the offices and checking locked doors or trying to elicit information from people out in the parking lot probably will get you caught.

Two other things on this topic you'll need to keep in mind are social engineering and what you're actually touching during your information gathering. Social engineering can be tricky because it can be both passive and active recon. Dumpster diving is considered passive (despite that in the real world it's really easy to get caught doing it), whereas walking in and talking to users *can* be considered active. Pay attention to the circumstances on these types of questions.

What's more, when it comes to active and passive recon, sometimes a question can be answered based on the target network itself: If you touch it, you're active; if you don't, you're passive. Think of it this way: Imagine the network you're paid to examine is actually a big wire that's electrified with 10,000 volts. If you walk around it, look over the fence, and take pictures, you're passively gathering information. Touch that wire, though, and you become active. *Real* active. Active footprinting involves touching the target network, and it can bleed over into the scanning and enumeration phase.

☒ **A** is incorrect because *security assessments* is a broad term that can indicate actual pen tests or basic security audits. Pen tests are designed to discover, exploit, and report on security vulnerabilities within a target. A security audit doesn't necessarily intentionally exploit any vulnerability; it just finds them and points them out.

☒ **B** is incorrect because it has nothing to do with what is being described in the question. A *vulnerability assessment* lists potential vulnerabilities and considers the potential impact of loss from a successful attack against any of them. In CEH parlance—and on your test—this term is more often than not used as a distractor. If you do see it on an exam, remember it is designed as more of a measurement technique and not an attack vector.

☒ **C** is incorrect because active footprinting indicates you're touching the target network itself. In the question, you (as the attacker) never actually touch the target. You are availing yourself of all that competitive intelligence lying around. Remember, competitive intelligence is freely available for anyone to get and is often used by competitors seeking an advantage in the marketplace. It's not only legal to pull and analyze this information, it's *expected*, and it does not require any active reconnaissance at all to acquire.

8. Of the following choices, which best defines a formal written document defining what employees are allowed to use organization systems for, what is not allowed, and what the repercussions are for breaking the rules?

   A. Information audit policy (IAP)

   B. Information security policy (ISP)

   C. Penetration testing policy (PTP)

   D. Company compliance policy (CCP)

   ☑ **B.** The Information Security Policy (ISP) holds all sorts of information, but a big part of it is defining what is allowed, what's not allowed, and what will happen if you disobey the rules. A subset of this (and generally what gets people all tricked up in this kind of question) is the Acceptable Use Policy. Generally speaking, users have to sign an Acceptable Use Policy before they're given access. It has to be very clear and concise, and usually references the ISP for all the details a user may need to know.

   ☒ **A** is incorrect because the Information Audit Policy defines what is audited, how long it's retained, and who has access to the audit logs.

   ☒ **C** is incorrect because, if it's even valid for your organization, a Pen Test Policy defines the frequency, scope and guidelines of testing requirements for the organization.

   ☒ **D** is incorrect because, there is no such thing as a Company Compliance Policy.

9. An ethical hacker is given no prior knowledge of the network and has a specific framework in which to work. The agreement specifies boundaries, nondisclosure agreements, and a completion date definition. Which of the following is true?

   A. A white hat is attempting a black-box test.

   B. A white hat is attempting a white-box test.

   C. A black hat is attempting a black-box test.

   D. A black hat is attempting a gray-box test.

   ☑ **A.** I love these types of questions. Not only is this a two-for-one question, but it involves identical but confusing descriptors, causing all sorts of havoc. The answer to attacking such questions—and you *will* see them, by the way—is to take each section one at a time. Start with what kind of hacker he is. He's hired under a specific agreement, with full knowledge and consent of the target, thus making him a white hat. That eliminates C and D right off the bat. Second, to address what kind of test he's performing, simply look at what he knows about the system. In this instance, he has no prior knowledge at all, thus making it a black-box test.

☒ **B** is incorrect because although the attacker is one of the good guys (a white hat, proceeding with permission and an agreement in place), he is not provided with full knowledge of the system. In fact, it's quite the opposite—according to the question he knows absolutely nothing about it, making this particular "box" as black as it can be. A white-box target indicates one that the attacker already knows everything about. It's lit up and wide open.

☒ **C** is incorrect right off the bat because it references a black hat. Black-hat attackers are the bad guys—the ones proceeding without the target's knowledge or permission. They usually don't have inside knowledge of their target, so their attacks often start "black box."

☒ **D** is incorrect for the same reason just listed: This attacker has permission to proceed and is operating under an agreement; therefore, he can't be a black-box attacker. Additionally, this answer went the extra mile to convince you it was wrong—and missed on both swings. Not only is this a white-hat attacker, but the attack itself is black box. A gray-box attack indicates at least some inside knowledge of the target.

10. Which of the following is a detective control?

   A. Audit trail

   B. CONOPS

   C. Procedure

   D. Smartcard authentication

   E. Process

   ☑ **A.** A detective control is an effort used to identify problems, errors, or (in the case of post-attack discovery) cause or evidence of an exploited vulnerability. Ideally, detective controls should be in place and working such that errors can be corrected as quickly as possible. Many compliance laws and standards (the Sarbanes–Oxley Act of 2002 is one example) mandate the use of detective controls.

   ☒ **B** is incorrect because a concept of operations (CONOPS) isn't detective in nature. A CONOPS defines what a system is and how it is supposed to be used.

   ☒ **C** is incorrect because a procedure is a document the spells out specific step-by-step instructions for a given situation or process.

   ☒ **D** is incorrect because smartcard authentication is a preventive control, not a detective one. It's designed to provide strong authentication, ideally preventing a problem in the first place.

   ☒ **E** is incorrect because a process can refer to a lot of different things, depending on your definition and viewpoint, but is not detective in nature as a control.

A process, in general, refers to a set of steps or actions directed at accomplishing a goal.

11. As part of a pen test on a U.S. government system, you discover files containing Social Security numbers and other sensitive personally identifiable information (PII) information. You are asked about controls placed on the dissemination of this information. Which of the following acts should you check?

    A. FISMA

    B. Privacy Act

    C. PATRIOT Act

    D. Freedom of Information Act

☑ **B.** The Privacy Act of 1974 protects information of a personal nature, including Social Security numbers. The Privacy Act defines exactly what "personal information" is, and it states that government agencies cannot disclose any personal information about an individual without that person's consent. It also lists 12 exemptions for the release of this information (for example, information that is part of a law enforcement issue may be released). In other questions you see, keep in mind that the Privacy Act generally will define the information that is *not* available to you in and after a test. Dissemination and storage of privacy information needs to be closely controlled to keep you out of hot water.

☒ **A** is incorrect because federal information security management act (FISMA) isn't designed to control the dissemination of PII or sensitive data. Its primary goal is to ensure the security of government systems by promoting a standardized approach to security controls, implementation, and testing. The act requires government agencies to create a security plan for their systems and to have it "accredited" at least once every three years.

☒ **C** is incorrect because the PATRIOT Act is not an effort to control personal information. Its purpose is to aid the U.S. government in preventing terrorism by increasing the government's ability to monitor, intercept, and maintain records on almost every imaginable form of communication. As a side effect, it has also served to increase observation and prevention of hacking attempts on many systems.

☒ **D** is incorrect because the Freedom of Information Act wasn't designed to tell you what to do with information. Its goal is to define how you can get information—specifically information regarding how your governments work. It doesn't necessarily help you in hacking, but it does provide a cover for a lot of information. Anything you uncover that could have been gathered through the Freedom of Information Act is considered legal and should be part of your overall test.

12. Joe is performing an audit to validate the effectiveness of the organization's security policies. During his tests, he discovers that a user has a dial-out modem installed on a PC. Which security policy should be checked to see whether modems are allowed?

 A. Firewall policy

 B. Conduct policy

 C. Remote access policy

 D. Telework policy

 ☑ C. Yes, Dear Reader, I do realize how ridiculous a question like this seems, and I am absolutely sure there is no way you missed it. Sometimes things are really that obvious. Organizations usually have tons of different policies that cover all sorts of different things. The remote access policy, covering things like what is an allowable method to access the network remotely, is the best option provided here.

 ☒ A is incorrect because a firewall policy deals with corporate firewalls—how they're used, where they're placed, and how their rules get approved and implemented. Despite that every movie Hollywood puts out begins and ends network security with a firewall, it has absolutely nothing to do with this user bypassing everything with a modem.

 ☒ B is incorrect because, as far as I know, there is no such thing as a conduct policy. I suppose an acceptable use policy would be the closest thing to it, but conduct policy simply doesn't exist and wouldn't be correct here if it did.

 ☒ D is incorrect because, again, I'm not altogether sure this is a real term. A telework policy, if it existed at all, would be to define the roles and responsibilities of employees working from home or remote locations. A good distractor? Absolutely. The best answer here? Not even close.

13. A hacker is attempting to gain access to a target inside a business. After trying several methods, he gets frustrated and starts a denial-of-service attack against a server attached to the target. Which security control is the hacker affecting?

 A. Confidentiality

 B. Integrity

 C. Availability

 D. Authentication

 ☑ C. Denial-of-service attacks are always attacks against the availability of the system. Regardless of whatever else the hacker has tried to accomplish against the machine, a successful denial-of-service (DoS) attack removes the availability of the machine. Remember, availability refers to the communications systems and data being ready for use when legitimate users need them. Many methods are used for availability, depending on whether the discussion is about a system, network resource, or the data itself. However, they all attempt to ensure one thing: When the system or data is needed, it can be accessed by the appropriate personnel. Attacks against availability always fall into the denial-of-service realm.

☒ **A** is incorrect because the attacker is not affecting the machine's ability to discern his true identity. As a matter of fact, it seems the confidentiality controls in place on the machine are working well. Remember, confidentiality addresses the secrecy and privacy of information and refers to the measures taken to prevent the disclosure of information or data to unauthorized individuals or systems.

☒ **B** is incorrect because the attacker didn't get frustrated and attempt to change or alter any data; he simply decided to cut off access to it. Remember, integrity refers to the methods and actions taken to protect the information from unauthorized alteration or revision—whether the data is at rest or in transit.

☒ **D** is incorrect because the hacker appears to be having problems authenticating at the machine, which boasts well for the security personnel devoted to protecting it. Authentication is a subset of the larger confidentiality factor.

14. In which phase of the ethical hacking methodology would a hacker discover available targets on a network?

   A. Reconnaissance

   B. Scanning and enumeration

   C. Gaining access

   D. Maintaining access

   E. Covering tracks

   ☑ **B.** The scanning and enumeration phase is where you'll use things such as ping sweeps to discover available targets on the network. This step occurs *after* reconnaissance. In this step, tools and techniques are actively applied to information gathered during recon to obtain more in-depth information on the targets. For example, reconnaissance may show a network subnet to have 500 or so machines connected inside a single building, whereas scanning and enumeration would discover which ones are Windows machines and which ones are running FTP.

   ☒ **A** is incorrect because the reconnaissance phase is nothing more than the steps taken to gather evidence and information on the targets you want to attack. Activities that occur in this phase include dumpster diving and social engineering. Another valuable tool in recon is the Internet. Look for any of these items as key words in answers on your exam. Of course, in the real world you may actually gather so much information in your recon you'll already be way ahead of the game in identifying targets and whatnot, but when it comes to the exam, stick with the hard-and-fast boundaries they want you to remember and move on.

☒ **C** is incorrect because the gaining access phase is all about attacking the machines themselves. You've already figured out background information on the client and have enumerated the potential vulnerabilities and security flaws on each target. In this phase, you break out the big guns and start firing away. Key words you're looking for here are the attacks themselves: Accessing an open and nonsecured wireless access point, manipulating network devices, writing and delivering a buffer overflow, and performing SQL injection against a web application are all examples.

☒ **D** is incorrect because this phase is all about back doors and the steps taken to ensure you have a way back in. For the savvy readers out there who noticed I skipped a step here (escalating privileges), well done. Key words you'll look for on this phase (maintaining access) are back doors, zombies, and rootkits.

☒ **E** is incorrect because this phase is all about cleaning up when you're done and making sure no one can see where you've been. Clearing tracks involves steps to conceal success and avoid detection by security professionals. Steps taken here consist of removing or altering log files, hiding files with hidden attributes or directories, and even using tunneling protocols to communicate with the system.

15. Which of the following are potential drawbacks to a black-box test? (Choose all that apply.)

   A. The client does not get a focused picture of an external attacker dedicated on their systems.

   B. The client does not get a focused picture of an internal attacker dedicated on their systems.

   C. This test takes the longest amount of time to complete.

   D. This test takes the shortest amount of time to complete.

   ☑ **B** and **C**. Black-box tests are conducted to simulate an outside attacker. The problem with this test, if done solely on its own, is twofold. First, it concentrates solely on what most people think of as the biggest threat: an outside attacker. You know—some guy in a dark room surrounded by green tinted monitors who has decided to break into the enterprise network. This totally ignores one of the biggest threats to the network in the first place—the disgruntled insider. Additionally, because of its very nature, a black-box test takes longer than any other type to complete. If you think about it, this makes sense.

☒ **A** is incorrect because the *point* of the black-box test is to simulate the external attacker. It's designed to simulate an outside, unknown attacker; takes the most amount of time to complete; and is usually (by far) the most expensive option.

☒ **D** is incorrect because black-box testing takes the longest amount of time to complete. The reason for this is obvious: With white- or gray-box testing, you've already got a leg up on your black-box brethren, in that you already have some insider information. With black-box testing, you need to go through all the phases of the CEH methodology.

16. Which of the following best defines a logical or technical control?

    A. Air conditioning

    B. Security tokens

    C. Fire alarms

    D. Security policy

    ☑ **B.** A logical (or technical) control is one used for identification, authentication, and authorization. They can be embedded inside operating systems, applications, or database management systems. A security token (such as RSA's SecureID) can provide a number that changes on a recurring basis that a user must provide during authentication or may provide a built-in number on a USB device that must be attached during authentication. A physical control is something, well, physical in nature, such as a lock or key or maybe a guard.

    ☒ **A** and **C** are incorrect because air conditioning and fire alarms both fall into the category of physical control.

    ☒ **D** is incorrect because a security policy isn't a logical or technical control.

17. Which of the following would *not* be considered passive reconnaissance?

    A. Dumpster diving for valuable, discarded information

    B. Thoroughly examining financial sites for clues on target inventory and other useful information

    C. Ping sweeping a range of IP addresses found through a DNS lookup

    D. Using a search engine to discover competitive intelligence on the organization

    ☑ **C.** When it comes to active versus passive recon, remember the two golden rules. First rule: If it's something that exposes you to more risk in being caught, the recon is active. Second rule: If you touch the target, the recon is active. For example, walking up to locked doors and checking them or going into the building to attempt social engineering on the user are both active measures. Dumpster diving, "quiet" social engineering, and using Google to find information on the target are all examples of passive reconnaissance (a.k.a. passive footprinting). And lastly, ping sweeping is done in the scanning and enumeration phase, not during reconnaissance, so this answer should have been an easy one for you to eliminate.

☒ **A** is incorrect because dumpster diving is one of the prime examples of passive recon. It's simple and doesn't expose you to too much risk of being caught. It also doesn't require you to interact with your target at all.

☒ **B** is incorrect because examining competitive intelligence is free and readily available and should be gathered as part of your passive reconnaissance. Other avenues for this type of recon include job boards, social networking sites, and the company's own website. Pull a copy down and explore it. You'll be amazed what you can find passively.

☒ **D** is incorrect because this is also a prime example of passive reconnaissance. During passive recon, you are expected to use all avenues of the Internet to find information on your target. In addition to the other avenues mentioned here, don't neglect the blogosphere—that wonderful world of blogging that has sprung up over the past few years. Sometimes people post the strangest stuff on their blogs, and sometimes that posted material is just the ticket you need to successfully complete your task.

18. As part of the preparation phase for a pen test you are participating in, the client relays their intent to discover security flaws and possible remediation. They seem particularly concerned about external threats and do not mention internal threats at all. When defining scope, the threat of internal users is not added as part of the test. Which test is this client ignoring?

A. Gray box

B. Black box

C. White hat

D. Black hat

☑ **A.** Once again, this is a play on words the exam will throw at you. Note the question is asking about a *test type*, not the attacker. Reviewing CEH documentation, you'll see there are three types of tests—white, black, and gray—with each designed to test a specific threat. White tests the internal threat of a knowledgeable systems administrator or an otherwise elevated privilege level user. Black tests external threats with no knowledge of the target. Gray tests the average internal user threat to expose potential security problems inside the network.

☒ **B** is incorrect because black-box testing is designed to simulate the external threat, which is exactly what this client is asking for. Black-box testing takes the most amount of time to complete because it means a thorough romp through the five stages of an attack (and removes any preconceived notions of what to look for) and is usually the most expensive option. Another drawback to this type of test is that it focuses solely on the threat *outside* the organization and does not take into account any trusted users on the inside.

☒ **C is incorrect** because a hat color refers to the attacker himself. True, the client is hiring a white hat in this instance to perform the test; however, the hat does not equate to the test. White hats are the "good guys"—ethical hackers hired by a customer for the specific goal of testing and improving security. White hats don't use their knowledge and skills without prior consent.

☒ **D is incorrect** because this question refers to the test itself, not the type of attacker. Black hats are the "bad guys" and are otherwise known as *crackers*. They illegally use their skills either for personal gain or for malicious intent, seeking to steal or destroy data or to deny access to resources and systems. Black hats do *not* ask for permission or consent.

19. In which phase of the attack would a hacker set up and configure "zombie" machines?

A. Reconnaissance

B. Covering tracks

C. Gaining access

D. Maintaining access

☑ **D. Zombies** are basically machines the hacker has confiscated to do his work for him. If the attacker is really good, the owners of the zombie machines don't even know their machines have been drafted into the war.

☒ **A is incorrect** because the reconnaissance phase is all about gaining knowledge and information on a target. In reconnaissance you're learning about the target itself—what system types they may have in use, what operating hours they run, whether they use a shredder, and what personal information about their employees is available are all examples. Think of reconnaissance as the background information on a good character in a novel; it may not be completely necessary to know before you read the action scenes, but it sure makes it easier to understand why the character behaves in a certain manner during the conflict phase of the book. Setting up zombie systems goes far beyond the boundaries of gathering information.

☒ **B is incorrect** because this phase is where attackers attempt to conceal their success and avoid detection by security professionals. This can involve removing or altering log files, hiding files with hidden attributes or directories, and using tunneling protocols to communicate with the system.

☒ **C is incorrect** because in this phase attacks are leveled against the targets enumerated during the scanning and enumeration phase. Key words to look for in identifying this phase are the attacks themselves (such as buffer overflow and SQL injection). Finally, be careful about questions relating to elevating privileges. Sometimes this is counted as its own phase, so pay close attention to the question's wording in choosing your answer.

20. Which of the following best describes an ethical hacker?

    A. An ethical hacker never knowingly or unknowingly exceeds the boundaries of the scope agreement.

    B. An ethical hacker never performs a denial-of-service attack on a target machine.

    C. An ethical hacker never proceeds with an audit or test without written permission.

    D. An ethical hacker never performs social engineering on unsuspecting members of the target organization.

    ☑ C. I know you're tired of seeing this question. I'm tired of asking it. But you get the point now, right? This is important, and you *will* see it on the exam. The only real difference between those bad-guy crackers out there and us, the ethical hackers, is *written permission*. Bad guys want to steal and destroy stuff. They don't care about rules and don't bother to ask for permission. They will ruthlessly attack every avenue they can possibly think of in order to break into the target, and they don't care how far down the rabbit hole it takes them. The only difference between them and us is that we agree to do it only under certain controlled circumstances and guidelines. If, for one second, you think an ethical hacker won't take advantage of every single tool, loophole, loose lip, or technique available without regard to how bad it makes someone in the target organization feel, you are in the wrong field. We're just as dirty as the other guys; we just do it with permission.

    ☒ A is incorrect because, although the ethical hacker shouldn't ever knowingly exceed the scope or boundaries of his test, it's sometimes done unknowingly. Heck, sometimes there's almost no way around it, and it often occurs without the tester knowing about it until later. In several famous cases a pen test has gone awry and hit things outside the target organization. This doesn't mean the tester was unethical, however. It just happens.

    ☒ B is incorrect because your client may specifically ask you to perform a DoS attack. Oftentimes, they'll explicitly ask you *not* to perform a DoS attack, but the point is the same regardless: We will test everything we're told to, just as a bad guy would do in trying to affect or gain access to a resource.

    ☒ D is incorrect because social engineering is a big part of a true pen test. After all, the users are the weakest link in the chain, right? If you don't test them, you're not performing a full test. Because social engineering is on the table for the bad guys, it's on the table for us, too.

21. Which of the following describes activities taken in the conclusion phase of a penetration test?

    A. Reports are prepared detailing security deficiencies.

    B. Vulnerability assessment is conducted.

    C. Security control audits are performed.

    D. Contract and scope agreement is created.

    ☑ **A.** Pen tests consist of three major phases: preparation, assessment, and conclusion. The conclusion phase is where you wrap everything up and present your findings to the customer. The only tricky thing about this question is overthinking it. While you're testing and discovering things, you're documenting everything that's happening. Therefore, you could easily make an argument that, in a way, you're preparing reports during the *assessment* phase. Don't overthink this one—reports are done in the conclusion phase.

    ☒ **B** is incorrect because vulnerability assessment and all attacks and audits occur during the assessment phase of a pen test.

    ☒ **C** is incorrect because security control audits occur during the assessment phase of a pen test. Remember, all the action occurs in the middle, surrounding by planning for the action (preparation phase) and presenting it to the customer (conclusion phase).

    ☒ **D** is incorrect because contract and scope agreement are hammered out in the preparation phase. This is where you determine how far you can go, what the client actually wants to find out, and where they don't want you to be.

22. Which of the following should a security professional use as a possible means to verify the integrity of a data message from sender to receiver?

    A. Strong password requirements for encryption of the file

    B. Access controls on all network devices

    C. Hash algorithm

    D. Strong password requirements on operating system login

    ☑ **C.** A hash is the preferred method most often used for verifying the integrity of a file. Basically, before you send the file, you run it through a hash algorithm (such as MD5 or SHA-1) that generates a number. When it's received, you do the same. If the numbers match, *voilà!*

    ☒ **A** is incorrect because it's referencing confidentiality controls. Almost every time you see *password* referenced, you should think confidentiality, not integrity.

    ☒ **B** is incorrect because it's also referencing confidentiality controls. Access controls are exactly what they sound like: controls put in place to control access to something. In the context of network devices, they control things such as administrative access to the IOS.

☒ **D** is incorrect because it's also referencing confidentiality controls. Once again, passwords equate to confidentiality controls.

23. You are examining security logs snapshotted during a prior attack against the target. The target's IP address is 135.17.22.15, and the attack originated from 216.88.76.5. Which of the following correctly characterizes this attack?

    A. Inside attack

    B. Outside attack

    C. Black-box attack

    D. Spoofing

    ☑ **B.** This is an example of one of those little definition questions you'll see on the exam and will be thankful for. An *inside attack* generates from inside the network boundary, whereas an *outside attack* comes from outside the border. Granted, anyone with any networking knowledge at all knows it's impossible to tell, solely from an IP address, whether one is inside or outside a company's network boundary. All sorts of things, such as VPNs, multiple nets, and subsidiaries, could make life miserable in figuring out where the inside versus outside line is. If you're faced with this on the exam, though, just take it at face value. Trust me on this.

    ☒ **A** is incorrect because the attack came from a different network—fully outside the enterprise's virtual walls. The only time this can become a tricky question is when subnetting is involved, in which case the question will have to point out where the enterprise network footprint stops.

    ☒ **C** is incorrect because we simply have no idea what type of attack—black, gray, or white—this is. True, it's starting from outside the network, leading us to believe it a black-box attack, but that's not necessarily true, and there certainly isn't enough information here to make that call.

    ☒ **D** is incorrect because spoofing has to do with an attempt to fake a machine's identity (usually through MAC or IP). The question doesn't specify whether this is in play, so it can't be the answer you're looking for.

24. A machine in your environment uses an open X-server to allow remote access. The X-server access control is disabled, allowing connections from almost anywhere and with little to no authentication measures. Which of the following are true statements regarding this situation? (Choose all that apply.)

    A. An external vulnerability can take advantage of the misconfigured X-server threat.

    B. An external threat can take advantage of the misconfigured X-server vulnerability.

C. An internal vulnerability can take advantage of the misconfigured X-server threat.

D. An internal threat can take advantage of the misconfigured X-server vulnerability.

☑ **B and D.** This is an easy one because all you have to understand are the definitions of threat and vulnerability. A *threat* is any agent, circumstance, or situation that could potentiality cause harm or loss to an IT asset. In this case, the implication is the threat is an individual (hacker) either inside or outside the network. A *vulnerability* is any weakness, such as a software flaw or logic design, that could be exploited by a threat to cause damage to an asset. In both these answers, the vulnerability—the access controls on X-server are not in place—can be exploited by the threat, whether internal or external.

☒ **A and C** are both incorrect because they list the terms backward. Threats take advantage of vulnerabilities and exploit them, not the other way around.

25. While performing a pen test, you find success in exploiting a machine. Your attack vector took advantage of a common mistake—the Windows 7 installer script used to load the machine left the administrative account with a default password. Which attack did you successfully execute?

A. Application level

B. Operating system

C. Shrink wrap

D. Social engineering

E. Misconfiguration

☑ **B.** Operating system (OS) attacks target common mistakes many people make when installing operating systems—accepting and leaving all the defaults. Examples usually include things such as administrator accounts with no passwords, ports left open, and guest accounts left behind. Another OS attack you may be asked about deals with versioning. Operating systems are never released fully secure and are consistently upgraded with hotfixes, security patches, and full releases. The potential for an old vulnerability within the enterprise is always high.

☒ **A** is incorrect because application-level attacks are centered on the actual programming codes of an application. These attacks are usually successful in an overall pen test because many people simply discount the applications running on their OS and network, preferring to spend their time hardening the OSs and network devices. Many applications on a network aren't tested for vulnerabilities as part of their creation and, as such, have many vulnerabilities built in.

☒ **C** is incorrect because shrink-wrap attacks take advantage of the built-in code and scripts most *off-the-shelf applications* come with. These attacks allow hackers to take advantage of the very things designed to make installation and administration easier. These shrink-wrapped snippets make life easier for installation and administration, but they also make it easier for attackers to get in.

☒ **D** is incorrect because social engineering isn't relevant at all in this question. There is no human element here, so this one can be thrown out.

☒ **E** is incorrect because misconfiguration attacks take advantage of systems that are, on purpose or by accident, not configured appropriately for security. For example, suppose an administrator wants to make things as easy as possible for the users and, in keeping with security and usability being on opposite ends of the spectrum, leaves security settings at the lowest possible level, enabling services, opening firewall ports, and providing administrative privileges to all users. It's easier for the users but creates a target-rich environment for the hacker.

Reconnaissance: Information Gathering for the Ethical Hacker

This chapter includes questions from the following topics:

- Define active and passive footprinting
- Identify methods and procedures in information gathering
- Understand the use of whois, ARIN, and nslookup
- Describe DNS record types
- Define and describe Google hacking
- Use Google hacking in footprinting

Criminology (the study of the nature, causes, control, and prevention of criminal behavior) is a fascinating subject, and while we're concentrating on the virtual world in this book, it's amazing how much footprinting is done in the *physical* criminal world as well. Most of us have already heard a million times the standard things we're supposed to do to make our homes less desirable as a target for the bad guys. Things such as keeping your house well lit, installing timers on lights and TVs to make the house appear "lived in" all the time, and installing a good alarm system are so common in these discussions that we tend to nod off in boredom when a security expert starts talking about them. But did you know most common burglars prefer to work during the daytime, when it's most likely you're not at home at all? Did you know most don't give a rip about your alarm system because they plan on being inside for eight to ten minutes or less? And did you know that most timer systems for lights don't change a thing in the bad guy's mind because there's usually sound associated with people being home?

For the sake of example, take an imaginary ride with me around my subdivision here in Satellite Beach, Florida, and we'll try thinking like a criminal footprinting a neighborhood for targets. Maybe we'll start by just driving around the neighborhood to ascertain who the nosy neighbors are and what houses make the most promising opportunities. This house on our right is in a cul de sac and provides more privacy and less police patrol traffic than those on the main drag. That house over there? Yeah, it looks like the yard hasn't been mowed for a while, so maybe they aren't home or they just don't pay as close attention to home details as the other houses do. The owners of that two-story over there have a dog, so we'll probably avoid that one. But look here: This house has a giant box leaned against the garbage can showing the brand-new 65-inch LED TV the owner has just purchased. We should probably write this address down for a closer look later. And the house across the pond there with the sliding glass door? It definitely has potential.

As fascinating as footprinting a building might seem, were you aware that *you*, as a person, could be footprinted in the physical world as well? According to several studies on the matter, criminals are good at sensing weakness based just on *the way you walk*. In one such study, 47 inmates at a maximum-security prison were surveyed, and the findings showed that social predators are very good at picking victims based on their gait, posture, and stride. The study provided the inmates with a film of 12 people (eight women and four men, some of whom had been attacked before) walking down a street and asked them to rate each person as a potential victim. The ratings were then compared against each person's actual history. Surprisingly (or maybe not so surprisingly), the people who the criminals picked as likely victims were usually the same ones who had been victimized in the past. Inmates described the men and women they saw as targets as "walking like an easy target...slow, with short strides." What distinguished the likely victims from the rest of the pedestrians? Things like posture, body language, pace, length of stride, and awareness of their environment. Nonverbal communication works wonderfully well, and a person's level of self-confidence can be identified just by the style of walk. Walk with your head down at a slow or unorganized, meandering pace, and you're screaming to the world you lack self-confidence. Walk fast, fluidly, and with a purpose, and you're less likely to be a target.

I could go on and on here (I really like this subject and could chat about it forever), but this book is about the virtual world, and I'm prepping you to be an ethical hacker, not a policeman working a beat. This chapter is also all about reconnaissance and footprinting—in the virtual world—and is all about the methods and tools to gather information about your targets before you even try to attack them.

 STUDY TIPS   There are tons of questions from this particular segment of hacking, namely because it's so important to gather good intelligence before starting an attack. Sure, you can sometimes get lucky and strike quickly, but oftentimes he who puts in the work during footprinting reaps the biggest rewards.

The biggest area of focus you'll probably see on your actual exam will revolve around DNS. Know your record types like the back of your hand, play with whois so you know what you're looking at, and get really familiar with nslookup. The biggest area to trip you up will most likely come in the form of active versus passive reconnaissance. I can't help you much there other than to remind you that sometimes the exam and the real world are at opposites.

You'll see a few questions on the other stuff too. Know your e-mail headers well, and by all means start practicing your Google hacking right now—you'll definitely need it. Most Google hacking questions will require you to know exact syntax, so be careful in your study and practice.

1. The result of a whois search on a target is listed here:

```
Registrant:
        AnyBusiness Inc.
        1377 somewhere street
New York, NY 10013
        US
Phone: +13219667786
        Email: noemailhere@anybus.com


    Domain Name: anybusiness.com
        Created on..............: Mon, Jul 07, 1997
        Expires on..............: Sat, Jul 06, 2013
        Record last updated on..: Mon, Jul 02, 2012

    Administrative Contact:
        anybusiness.com
        P. O. Box 8799 615 N. Riverside Dr
        Somewhere, FL 32903
        US
        Phone: +1.3215550587
        Email: admin@anybus.com

    Technical  Contact:
        Mark Sensei
        187 Someplace drive
        Indialantic, FL 32903
        US
        Phone: +1.3215550879
        Email: M.sensei@gmail.com

DNS Servers:
        ns2.anybus.com
        ns1.anybus.com
```

Which of the following is a true statement regarding this output?

A. Anybusiness.com was registered using GoDaddy.com.

B. The technical contact for this website may have entered personal information at registration.

C. There is no information within this output useful for a zone transfer.

D. The administrative and technical contacts are the same.

2. A pen test team member sends an e-mail to an address that she knows is not valid inside an organization. Which of the following is the best explanation for why she took this action?

A. To possibly gather information about internal hosts used in the organization's e-mail system

B. To start a denial-of-service attack

C. To determine an e-mail administrator's contact information

D. To gather information about how e-mail systems deal with invalid addressed messages

3. From the partial e-mail header provided, which of the following represents the true originator of the e-mail message?

Return-path: <SOMEONE@anybiz.com>

Delivery-date: Wed, 13 Apr 2011 00:31:13 +0200

Received: from mailexchanger.anotherbiz.com([220.15.10.254])

by mailserver.anotherbiz.com running ExIM with esmtp

id xxxxxx-xxxxxx-xxx; Wed, 13 Apr 2011 01:39:23 +0200

Received: from mailserver.anybiz.com ([158.190.50.254] helo=mailserver.anybiz.com)

by mailexchanger.anotherbiz.com with esmtp id xxxxxx-xxxxxx-xx

for USERJOE@anotherbiz.com; Wed, 13 Apr 2011 01:39:23 +0200

Received: from SOMEONEComputer [217.88.53.154] (helo=[SOMEONEcomputer])

by mailserver.anybiz.com with esmtpa (Exim x.xx)

(envelope-from <SOMEONE@anybiz.com) id xxxxx-xxxxxx-xxxx

for USERJOE@anotherbiz.com; Tue, 12 Apr 2011 20:36:08 -0100

Message-ID: <xxxxxxxx.xxxxxxxx@anybiz.com>

Date: Tue, 12 Apr 2011 20:36:01 -0100

X-Mailer: Mail Client

From: SOMEONE Name <SOMEONE@anybiz.com>

To: USERJOE Name <USERJOE@anotherbiz.com>

Subject: Something to consider

...

A. 220.15.10.254.

B. 158.190.50.254.

C. 217.88.53.154.

D. The e-mail header does not show this information.

4. You are looking for files with the terms *CEH* and *V8* in their titles. Which Google hack is the appropriate one?

A. inurl:CEHinurl:V7

B. allintitle:CEH V7

C. intitle:CEHinurl:V7

D. allinurl:CEH V7

5. You've just kicked off a penetration test against a target organization and have decided to perform a little passive footprinting. One of the first sites you visit is a job board, where the company has listed various openings. What is the primary useful footprinting information to be gained through this particular search?

A. Insight into the HR processes of the company

B. Insight into the operating systems, hardware, and applications in use

C. Insight into corporate security policy

D. None of the above

6. Which of the following activities is not considered passive footprinting?

A. Dumpster diving

B. Reviewing financial sites for company information

C. Clicking links within the company's public website

D. Calling the company's help desk line

7. Examine the following command sequence:

```
C:\> nslookup
Default Server: ns1.anybiz.com
Address: 188.87.99.6
> set type=HINFO
> someserver
Server: resolver.anybiz.com
Address: 188.87.100.5
Someserver.anybiz.com CPU=Intel Quad Chip OS=Linux 2.8
```

Which of the following best describes the intent of the command sequence?

A. The operator is enumerating a system named someserver.

B. The operator is attempting DNS poisoning.

C. The operator is attempting a zone transfer.

D. The operator is attempting to find a name server.

8. You are footprinting information for a pen test. Social engineering is part of your reconnaissance efforts, and some of it will be active in nature. You take steps to ensure that if the social engineering efforts are discovered at this early stage, any trace efforts point to another organization. Which of the following terms best describes what you are participating in?

A. Anonymous footprinting

B. Pseudonymous footprinting

C. Passive footprinting

D. Redirective footprinting

9. You are setting up DNS for your enterprise. Server A is both a web server and an FTP server. You want to advertise both services for this machine as name references your customers can use. Which DNS record type would you use to accomplish this?

   A. NS

   B. SOA

   C. MX

   D. PTR

   E. CNAME

10. A company has a publicly facing web application. Its internal intranet-facing servers are separated and protected by a firewall. Which of the following choices would be helpful in protecting against unwanted enumeration?

    A. Allowing zone transfers to any

    B. Ensuring there are no A records for internal hosts on the public-facing name server

    C. Changing the preference number on all MX records to zero

    D. Not allowing any DNS query to the public-facing name server

11. Within the DNS system a primary server (SOA) holds and maintains all records for the zone. Secondary servers will periodically ask the primary if there have been any updates, and if updates have occurred, they will ask for a zone transfer to update their own copies. Under what conditions will the secondary name server request a zone transfer from a primary?

    A. When the primary SOA record serial number is higher than the secondary's

    B. When the secondary SOA record serial number is higher than the primary's

    C. Only when the secondary reboots or restarts services

    D. Only when manually prompted to do so

12. Examine the following SOA record:

```
@   IN  SOARTDNSRV1.somebiz.com.  postmaster.somebiz.com. (
200408097    ; serial number
                           3600          ; refresh   [1h]
                           600           ; retry     [10m]
                           86400         ; expire    [1d]
7200 )         ; min TTL   [2h]
```

    If a secondary server in the enterprise is unable to check in for a zone update within an hour, what happens to the zone copy on the secondary?

    A. The zone copy is dumped.

    B. The zone copy is unchanged.

C. The serial number of the zone copy is decremented.

D. The serial number of the zone copy is incremented.

13. Which protocol and port number combination is used by default for DNS zone transfers?

    A. UDP 53

    B. UDP 161

    C. TCP 53

    D. TCP 22

14. Examine the following command-line entry:

```
C:\>nslookup
    Default Server:  ns1.somewhere.com
    Address:  128.189.72.5
> set q=mx
>mailhost
```

Which two statements are true regarding this command sequence? (Choose two.)

    A. Nslookup is in noninteractive mode.

    B. Nslookup is in interactive mode.

    C. The output will show all mail servers in the zone somewhere.com.

    D. The output will show all name servers in the zone somewhere.com.

15. Joe accesses the company website, www.anybusi.com, from his home computer and is presented with a defaced site containing disturbing images. He calls the IT department to report the website hack and is told they do not see any problem with the site—no files have been changed, and when accessed from their terminals (inside the company), the site appears normally. Joe connects over VPN into the company website and notices the site appears normally. Which of the following might explain the issue?

    A. DNS poisoning

    B. Route poisoning

    C. SQL injection

    D. ARP poisoning

16. One way to mitigate against DNS poisoning is to restrict or limit the amount of time records can stay in cache before they're updated. Which DNS record type allows you to set this restriction?

    A. NS

    B. PTR

    C. MX

    D. CNAME

    E. SOA

17. Which of the following may be a security concern for an organization?

    A. The internal network uses private IP addresses registered to an Active Directory–integrated DNS server.

    B. An external DNS server is Active Directory integrated.

    C. All external name resolution requests are accomplished by an ISP.

    D. None of the above.

18. Which of the following is a good footprinting tool for discovering information on a publicly traded company's founding, history, and financial status?

    A. SpiderFoot

    B. EDGAR Database

    C. Sam Spade

    D. Pipl.com

19. What method does traceroute use to map routes traveled by a packet?

    A. By carrying a hello packet in the payload, forcing the host to respond

    B. By using DNS queries at each hop

    C. By manipulating the time to live (TTL) parameter

    D. By using ICMP Type 5, code 0 packets

20. Brad is auditing an organization and is asked to provide suggestions on improving DNS security. Which of the following would be valid options to recommend? (Choose all that apply.)

    A. Implementing split-horizon operation

    B. Restricting zone transfers

    C. Obfuscating DNS by using the same server for other applications and functions

    D. Blocking all access to the server on port 53

21. A zone file consists of which records? (Choose all that apply.)

    A. PTR

    B. MX

    C. SN

    D. SOA

    E. DNS

    F. A

    G. AX

22. Examine the following SOA record:

```
@   IN  SOARTDNSRV1.somebiz.com.  postmaster.somebiz.com. (
200408097    ; serial number
                              3600      ; refresh   [1h]
                              600       ; retry     [10m]
                              86400     ; expire    [1d]
7200 )       ; min TTL    [2h]
```

How long will the secondary server wait before asking for an update to the zone file?

A. 1 hour

B. 2 hours

C. 10 minutes

D. 1 day

23. A colleague enters the following into a Google search string:

```
intitle:intranetinurl:intranet+intext:"human resources"
```

Which of the following is most correct concerning this attempt?

A. The search engine will not respond with any result because you cannot combine Google hacks in one line.

B. The search engine will respond with all pages having the word *intranet* in their title and *human resources* in the URL.

C. The search engine will respond with all pages having the word *intranet* in the title and in the URL.

D. The search engine will respond with only those pages having the word *intranet* in the title and URL and with *human resources* in the text.

24. Amanda works as senior security analyst and overhears a colleague discussing confidential corporate information being posted on an external website. When questioned on it, he claims about a month ago he tried random URLs on the company's website and found confidential information. Amanda visits the same URLs but finds nothing. Where can Amanda go to see past versions and pages of a website?

A. Search.com

B. Google cache

C. Pasthash.com

D. Archive.org

25. Which of the following is a primary service of the U.S. Computer Security Incident Response Team (CSIRT)?

   A. CSIRT provides an incident response service to enable a reliable and trusted single point of contact for reporting computer security incidents worldwide.

   B. CSIRT provides a computer security surveillance service to supply a government with important intelligence information on individuals traveling abroad.

   C. CSIRT provides a penetration testing service to support exception reporting on incidents worldwide by individuals and multinational corporations.

   D. CSIRT provides a vulnerability assessment service to assist law enforcement agencies with profiling an individual's property or company's asset.

26. Your client's business is headquartered in Japan. Which regional registry would be the best place to look for footprinting information?

   A. APNIC

   B. RIPE

   C. ASIANIC

   D. ARIN

   E. LACNIC

1. B
2. A
3. C
4. B
5. B
6. D
7. A
8. B
9. E
10. B
11. A
12. B
13. C
14. B, C
15. A
16. E
17. B
18. B
19. C
20. A, B
21. A, B, D, F
22. A
23. D
24. D
25. A
26. A

1. The result of a whois search on a target is listed here:

```
Registrant:
        AnyBusiness Inc.
        1377 somewhere street
New York, NY 10013
        US
Phone: +13219667786
        Email: noemailhere@anybus.com

    Domain Name: anybusiness.com
        Created on..............: Mon, Jul 07, 1997
        Expires on..............: Sat, Jul 06, 2013
        Record last updated on..: Mon, Jul 02, 2012

    Administrative Contact:
        anybusiness.com
        P. O. Box 8799
Somewhere, FL 32937
        US
        Phone: +1.3215550587
        Email: admin@anybus.com

    Technical  Contact:
        Mark Sensei
        187 Someplace drive
        Thistown, FL 32903
        US
        Phone: +1.3212970879
        Email: M.sensei@gmail.com

DNS Servers:
        ns2.anybus.com
        ns1.anybus.com
```

Which of the following is a true statement regarding this output?

A. Anybusiness.com was registered using GoDaddy.com.

B. The technical contact for this website may have entered personal information at registration.

C. There is no information within this output useful for a zone transfer.

D. The administrative and technical contacts are the same.

☑ **B.** The Technical Contact listing displays the technical contact's name, as well as what may be their personal phone number. The address? It's probably where they work, but you never know. This could turn out to be nothing, but it might provide you with an "in" for social engineering efforts later.

☒ **A** is incorrect because the registrant is clearly listed as Anybusiness.com. You'll find these whois searches to be hit-and-miss sometimes. Every once in a while there is a ton of information. Sometimes it's bare-bones basics. Had this been registered with GoDaddy.com, it would look something like this:

```
Registrant:
    Domains By Proxy, LLC
    Registered through: GoDaddy.com, LLC (http://www.godaddy.com)
    Domain Name: anybusiness.COM
```

☒ **C** is incorrect because the target's DNS servers are listed right there at the bottom. If you're going to pull a zone transfer, you'll need to know the DNS servers holding the proper information.

☒ **D** is incorrect because both are clearly different. The administrative contact is listed as a business name—smart idea. The technical contact, however, may be personal in nature.

2. A pen test team member sends an e-mail to an address that she knows is not valid inside an organization. Which of the following is the best explanation for why she took this action?

    A. To possibly gather information about internal hosts used in the organization's e-mail system.

    B. To start a denial-of-service attack

    C. To determine an e-mail administrator's contact information

    D. To gather information about how e-mail systems deal with invalid addressed messages

☑ **A.** The thought process behind this is a lot like banner grabbing or any of a hundred different forced error situations in hacking: Lots of information can be gleaned from responses to an error situation. A bogus internal address has the potential to provide more information about the internal servers used in the organization, including IP addresses and other pertinent details.

☒ **B** is incorrect because a bogus e-mail doesn't necessarily indicate the beginning of a DoS attack.

☒ **C** is incorrect because the e-mail administrator's contact information is not sent on invalid e-mail responses.

☒ **D** is incorrect because we already know how systems deal with bogus e-mail addresses—what we don't know is what servers inside this particular organization carry out those steps.

3. From the partial e-mail header provided, which of the following represents the true originator of the e-mail message?

    Return-path: <SOMEONE@anybiz.com>

    Delivery-date: Wed, 13 Apr 2011 00:31:13 +0200

    Received: from mailexchanger.anotherbiz.com([220.15.10.254])

    by mailserver.anotherbiz.com running ExIM with esmtp

    id xxxxxx-xxxxxx-xxx; Wed, 13 Apr 2011 01:39:23 +0200

Received: from mailserver.anybiz.com ([158.190.50.254] helo=mailserver.
anybiz.com)
by mailexchanger.anotherbiz.com with esmtp id xxxxxx-xxxxxx-xx
for USERJOE@anotherbiz.com; Wed, 13 Apr 2011 01:39:23 +0200
Received: from SOMEONEComputer [217.88.53.154]
(helo=[SOMEONEcomputer])
by mailserver.anybiz.com with esmtpa (Exim x.xx)
(envelope-from <SOMEONE@anybiz.com) id xxxxx-xxxxxx-xxxx
for USERJOE@anotherbiz.com; Tue, 12 Apr 2011 20:36:08 -0100
Message-ID: <xxxxxxxx.xxxxxxxx@anybiz.com>
Date: Tue, 12 Apr 2011 20:36:01 -0100
X-Mailer: Mail Client
From: SOMEONE Name <SOMEONE@anybiz.com>
To: USERJOE Name <USERJOE@anotherbiz.com>
Subject: Something to consider

...

A. 220.15.10.254.

B. 158.190.50.254.

C. 217.88.53.154.

D. The e-mail header does not show this information.

☑ C. E-mail headers are packed with information showing the entire route
the message has taken, and I can guarantee you'll see at least one question
on your exam about them. You'll most likely be asked to identify the true
originator—the machine (person) who sent it in the first place (even though
in the real world with proxies and whatnot to hide behind it may be impossible). This is clearly shown in line 9: Received: from SOMEONEComputer
[217.88.53.154] (helo=[SOMEONEcomputer]). But don't just study and rely
on that one section. Watch the entire trek the message takes and make note
of the IPs along the way.

☒ A and B are incorrect because these IPs do not represent the true originator
of the message. They show e-mail servers that are passing/handling the
message.

☒ D is incorrect because the e-mail header definitely shows the true originator.

4. You are looking for files with the terms *CEH* and *V8* in their titles. Which
Google hack is the appropriate one?

A. inurl:CEHinurl:V7

B. allintitle:CEH V7

C. intitle:CEHinurl:V7

D. allinurl:CEH V7

☑ **B.** The Google search operator *allintitle* searches for pages that contain the string, or strings, you specify. It also allows for the combination of strings in the title, so you can search for more than one term within the title of a page.

☒ **A** is incorrect because the operator *inurl* looks only in the URL of the site, not the page title. In this example, the search might bring you to a page like this: http://anyplace.com/apache_Version/pdfs.html.

☒ **C** is incorrect because the *inurl* operator isn't looking in the page title. Yes, you can combine operators, but these two just won't get this job done.

☒ **D** is incorrect because *allinurl* does not look at page titles; it's concerned only with the URL itself. As with the title searches, this allinurl operator allows you to combine search strings.

5. You've just kicked off a penetration test against a target organization and have decided to perform a little passive footprinting. One of the first sites you visit is a job board, where the company has listed various openings. What is the primary useful footprinting information to be gained through this particular search?

   A. Insight into the HR processes of the company

   B. Insight into the operating systems, hardware, and applications in use

   C. Insight into corporate security policy

   D. None of the above

   ☑ **B.** Jobs boards are great sources of information. You probably wouldn't get much of a response if you called the business up and said, "Hi! I'll be attempting a hack into your network. Would you be so kind as to tell me your server infrastructure and if you're using Microsoft Exchange for your e-mail?" However, go to a job board, and the listing will provide all that for you anyway. If they're asking for system administrator experience on Linux RHEL 8, you're already ahead of the game. Job postings list the set of skills, technical knowledge, and system experience required, so why not use them in preparation?

   ☒ **A** is incorrect because while the HR process may be usable in a long-term attack—for social engineering purposes—you're probably not going to get too much actual policy/process information here, and, frankly, that's not what you'd be looking for.

   ☒ **C** is incorrect because that type of information simply isn't put in a job listing. If it is, they have serious problems a pen test simply isn't going to fix.

☒ **D** is incorrect because ignoring job listings as part of your reconnaissance effort is folly. Why ignore such a gold mine of easily obtainable information? Depending on how deeply they go into describing job duties and knowledge requirements, you might be able to build a pretty good picture of your attack before even leaving the living room (or wherever you do your recon from).

6. Which of the following activities is not considered passive footprinting?

   A. Dumpster diving

   B. Reviewing financial sites for company information

   C. Clicking links within the company's public website

   D. Calling the company's help desk line

   ☑ **D.** This one may be a little tricky, but it's pretty easy if you think about it. Remember active and passive footprinting can be defined by two things: what you touch and how much discovery risk you put yourself in. Social engineering in and of itself is not all passive or active in nature. In the case of dumpster diving, it's considered passive. Pick up a phone and call someone inside the company or talk to people in the parking lot, however, and you've exposed yourself to discovery and are now practicing active footprinting.

   ☒ **A** is incorrect because digging through the trash for useful information is passive footprinting: According to EC-Council and this exam, your discovery risk is negligible, and you're not touching the company's network or personnel. Now, in the real world, rummaging through someone's trash on private property with no authorization and in full view of security personnel is probably going to get you caught and is about as passive as a Tasmanian Devil, but for your exam, ditch your hold on the real world and please remember it's passive.

   ☒ **B** is incorrect because reviewing financial sites for company information is a method of gaining competitive intelligence. As we know, competitive intelligence refers to the information gathered by a business entity about their competitor's customers, products, and marketing. Most of this information is readily available and can be acquired through a host of different means.

   ☒ **C** is incorrect because while you are actively participating in moving around inside the company's website, you are not necessarily putting yourself at discovery risk or touching anything the company doesn't want you to. The public website is placed there for people to use, and the odds of someone picking up your clicks out of the thousands they receive every day anyway are minimal. Granted, if you keep digging through their site and get deep enough (for example, you dig your way to an admin portal on a SAP site), you can, and should, be detected.

7. Examine the following command sequence:

```
C:\> nslookup
Default Server:  ns1.anybiz.com
Address:  188.87.99.6
> set type=HINFO
> someserver
Server:  resolver.anybiz.com
Address:  188.87.100.5
Someserver.anybiz.com CPU=Intel Quad Chip OS=Linux 2.8
```

Which of the following best describes the intent of the command sequence?

A. The operator is enumerating a system named someserver.

B. The operator is attempting DNS poisoning.

C. The operator is attempting a zone transfer.

D. The operator is attempting to find a name server.

☑ **A.** The HINFO record type is one of those really great ideas that was designed to make life easier on everyone yet turned out to be a horrible idea. Defined in RFC 1035, Host Information (HINFO) DNS records were originally intended to provide the type of computer and operating system a host uses (back in the day, you could also put things in like room numbers and other descriptions in the record, too). However, to avoid publicly advertising that information (for obvious reasons), they're simply not used much anymore. And if you find one on a public-facing machine, it's a sure sign of incompetence on the part of the server administrators. In this example, the type is set to HINFO, and a machine name—someserver—is provided.

☒ **B** is incorrect because DNS poisoning is not carried out this way. In this command sequence, the operator is asking for information, not pushing up false entries to a name server.

☒ **C** is incorrect because this is not how nslookup is used to perform a zone transfer. To do that, you would use the *set type=any* command and then *ls –d anybiz.com*. You'll more than likely see that on your exam, too.

☒ **D** is incorrect because checking for name servers in the domain would require the *set type=NS* command.

8. You are footprinting information for a pen test. Social engineering is part of your reconnaissance efforts, and some of it will be active in nature. You take steps to ensure that if the social engineering efforts are discovered at this early stage, any trace efforts point to another organization. Which of the following terms best describes what you are participating in?

A. Anonymous footprinting

B. Pseudonymous footprinting

C. Passive footprinting

D. Redirective footprinting

☑ **B.** Pseudonymous footprinting is a relatively new term in the CEH realm, so you'll probably see it on your exam. It refers to obfuscating your footprinting efforts in such a way that anyone trying to trace it back to you would instead be pointed to a different person (usually to look like a competitor's business). I understand there's probably a large segment out there (like my tech editor) screaming at the page that this word sounds fabricated and shouldn't be here. I won't argue for or against: All I'll say is it's on your exam, so you better memorize it. As a side note for those of you getting ready for a real-world job in pen testing, the scenario presented here may sound like a great idea, but you better be careful in practicing this. In many ways this could be illegal: Pointing to another organization without authorization could make you liable both criminally or civilly.

☒ **A** is incorrect because anonymous footprinting refers to footprinting efforts that can't be traced back to you. These don't redirect a search to someone else; they're just efforts to hide your footprinting in the first place.

☒ **C** is incorrect because passive footprinting is generally gathering competitive intelligence and doesn't put you at risk of discovery anyway.

☒ **D** is incorrect because this term simply doesn't exist. It's here purely as a distractor.

9. You are setting up DNS for your enterprise. Server A is both a web server and an FTP server. You want to advertise both services for this machine as name references your customers can use. Which DNS record type would you use to accomplish this?

A. NS

B. SOA

C. MX

D. PTR

E. CNAME

☑ **E.** We all know—or should know by now—that a hostname can be mapped to an IP using an A record within DNS. CNAME records provide for aliases within the zone on that name. For instance, your server might be named mattserver1.matt.com. A sample DNS zone entry to provide HTTP and FTP access might look like this:

```
NAME                      TYPE    VALUE
-------------------------------------------------
ftp.matt.com.             CNAME   mattserver.matt.com
www.matt.com              CNAME   mattserver.matt.com
mattserver1.matt.com.     A       202.17.77.5
```

☒ **A** is incorrect because a name server (NS) record shows the name servers within your zone. These servers are the ones that respond to your client's requests for name resolution.

☒ **B** is incorrect because the Start of Authority (SOA) entry identifies the primary name server for the zone. The SOA record contains the hostname of the server responsible for all DNS records within the namespace, as well as the basic properties of the domain.

☒ **C** is incorrect because the Mail Exchange (MX) record identifies the e-mail servers within your domain.

☒ **D** is incorrect because a pointer record (PTR) works opposite to an A record. The pointer maps an IP address to a hostname and is generally used for reverse lookups.

10. A company has a publicly facing web application. Its internal intranet-facing servers are separated and protected by a firewall. Which of the following choices would be helpful in protecting against unwanted enumeration?

A. Allowing zone transfers to any

B. Ensuring there are no A records for internal hosts on the public-facing name server

C. Changing the preference number on all MX records to zero

D. Not allowing any DNS query to the public-facing name server

☑ **B.** If your company has a publicly facing website, it follows that a name server somewhere has to answer lookups in order for your customers to find the site. That name server, however, does not need to provide lookup information to internal machines. Of the choices provides, as silly as it seems to point out, ensuring there are no A records (those used to map hostnames to an IP address) on the external name server is a good start.

☒ **A** is incorrect because allowing a zone transfer to anyone asking for it is just plain dumb. It may or may not help an attacker enumerate your internal network (maybe you don't have anything in there to worry about), but it's just a horrendously bad idea.

☒ **C** is incorrect because changing the preference number on an MX record doesn't have a thing to do with enumeration. The preference number (a lower number means first used) determines only which server handles e-mail first.

☒ **D** is incorrect because if your customers can't query for the IP associated with the hostname, how are they supposed to find your website?

11. Within the DNS system a primary server (SOA) holds and maintains all records for the zone. Secondary servers will periodically ask the primary if there have been any updates, and if updates have occurred, they will ask for a zone transfer to update their own copies. Under what conditions will the secondary name server request a zone transfer from a primary?

   A. When the primary SOA record serial number is higher than the secondary's

   B. When the secondary SOA record serial number is higher than the primary's

   C. Only when the secondary reboots or restarts services

   D. Only when manually prompted to do so

   ☑ A. Occasionally you'll get a question like this. It's not necessarily hacking in nature but more about how the DNS system works in general. The serial number on an SOA record is incremented each time the zone file is changed. So, when the secondary checks in with the primary, if the serial number is higher than its own, the secondary knows there has been a change and asks for a full zone transfer.

   ☒ B is incorrect because the serial number increments with each change, not decrements. If the secondary checked in and the numbers were reversed—in other words, the secondary had a serial number higher than the primary—it would either leave its own record unchanged or most likely dump the zone altogether.

   ☒ C is incorrect because a zone transfer does not occur on startup. Additionally, and this is a free test-taking tip here, any time you see the word "only" in an answer, it's usually wrong. In this case, that's definitely true because the servers are configured to check in with each other on occasion to ensure the zone is consistent across the enterprise.

   ☒ D is incorrect because this is just a ridiculous answer. Could you imagine having to manually update every DNS server? I can think of worse jobs, but this one would definitely stink.

12. Examine the following SOA record:

```
@   IN  SOARTDNSRV1.somebiz.com.  postmaster.somebiz.com. (
200408097    ; serial number
                              3600        ; refresh   [1h]
                              600         ; retry     [10m]
                              86400       ; expire    [1d]
7200 )         ; min TTL    [2h]
```

   If a secondary server in the enterprise is unable to check in for a zone update within an hour, what happens to the zone copy on the secondary?

   A. The zone copy is dumped.

   B. The zone copy is unchanged.

C. The serial number of the zone copy is decremented.

D. The serial number of the zone copy is incremented.

☑ **B.** You will definitely see questions about the SOA record. In this question, the key portion you're looking for is the time to live (TTL) at the bottom, currently set to 2 hours (7,200 seconds). This sets the time a secondary server has to verify its records are good. If it can't check in, this TTL for zone records will expire, and they'll all be dumped. Considering, though, this TTL is set to 2 hours and the question states it's been only one hour since update, the zone copy on the secondary will remain unchanged.

☒ **A** is incorrect because the secondary is still well within its window for verifying the zone copy it holds. It dumps the records only when TTL is exceeded.

☒ **C** is incorrect because, first, serial numbers are never decremented; they're always incremented. Second, the serial number of the zone copy is changed only when a connection to the primary occurs and a copy is updated.

☒ **D** is incorrect because while serial numbers are incremented on changes (the secondary copies the number from the primary's copy when transferring records), the serial number of the zone copy is changed only when a connection to the primary occurs and a copy is updated. That has not occurred here.

13. Which protocol and port number combination is used by default for DNS zone transfers?

A. UDP 53

B. UDP 161

C. TCP 53

D. TCP 22

☑ **C.** TCP 53 is the default protocol and port number for zone transfers. DNS actually uses both TCP and UDP to get its job done, and if you think about what it's doing, they make sense in particular circumstances. A name resolution request and reply? Small and quick, so use port 53 on UDP. A zone transfer, which could potentially be large and requires some insurance it all gets there? Port 53 on TCP is the answer.

☒ **A, B,** and **C** are incorrect because they do not represent the default port and protocol combination for a zone transfer.

14. Examine the following command-line entry:

```
C:\>nslookup
   Default Server:  ns1.somewhere.com
   Address:  128.189.72.5
> set q=mx
>mailhost
```

Chapter 2: Reconnaissance: Information Gathering for the Ethical Hacker

Which two statements are true regarding the following command sequence? (Choose two.)

A. Nslookup is in noninteractive mode.

B. Nslookup is in interactive mode.

C. The output will show all mail servers in the zone somewhere.com.

D. The output will show all name servers in the zone somewhere.com.

☑ **B and C.** Nslookup runs in one of two modes—interactive and noninteractive. Noninteractive mode is simply the use of the command followed by an output. For example, nslookup www.google.com will return the IP address your server can find for Google. Interactive mode is started by simply typing nslookup and pressing ENTER. Your default server name will display, along with its IP address, and a carrot (>) will await entry of your next command. In this scenario we've entered interactive mode and set the type to MX, which we all know means "Please provide me with all the mail exchange servers you know about."

☒ **A** is incorrect because we are definitely in interactive mode.

☒ **D** is incorrect because type was set to MX, not NS.

15. Joe accesses the company website, www.anybusi.com, from his home computer and is presented with a defaced site containing disturbing images. He calls the IT department to report the website hack and is told they do not see any problem with the site—no files have been changed, and when accessed from their terminals (inside the company), the site appears normally. Joe connects over VPN into the company website and notices the site appears normally. Which of the following might explain the issue?

A. DNS poisoning

B. Route poisoning

C. SQL injection

D. ARP poisoning

☑ **A.** DNS poisoning makes the most sense here. Joe's connection from home uses a different DNS server for lookups than that of the business network. It's entirely possible someone has changed the cache entries in his local server to point to a different IP than the one hosting the real website—one that the hackers have set up to provide the defaced version. The fact the web files haven't changed and it seems to be displaying just fine from inside the network also bears this out. Also, for those of you paying close attention, in a case like this, it's important to note VPN access. If it turns out Joe's DNS modification is the only one in place, there is a strong likelihood that Joe is being specifically targeted for exploitation—something Joe should take very seriously.

☒ **B** is incorrect because route poisoning has nothing to do with this. Route poisoning is used in distance vector routing protocols to prevent route loops in routing tables.

☒ **C** is incorrect because while SQL injection is, indeed, a hacking attack, it's not relevant here. The fact the website files remain intact and unchanged prove that access to the site through an SQL weakness isn't what occurred here.

☒ **D** is incorrect because ARP poisoning is relevant inside a particular subnet, not outside it (granted, you can have ARP forwarded by a router configured to do so, but it simply isn't the case for this question). ARP poisoning will redirect a request from one machine to another inside the same subnet and has little to do with the scenario described here.

16. One way to mitigate against DNS poisoning is to restrict or limit the amount of time records can stay in cache before they're updated. Which DNS record type allows you to set this restriction?

    A. NS

    B. PTR

    C. MX

    D. CNAME

    E. SOA

    ☑ **E.** The SOA record holds all sorts of information, and when it comes to DNS poisoning, the TTL is of primary interest. The shorter the TTL, the less time records are held in cache. While it won't prevent DNS poisoning altogether, it can limit the problems a successful cache poisoning attack causes.

    ☒ **A** is incorrect because an NS record shows the name servers found in the domain.

    ☒ **B** is incorrect because a PTR record provides for reverse lookup capability— an IP address to hostname mapping.

    ☒ **C** is incorrect because an MX record shows the mail exchange servers in the zone.

    ☒ **D** is incorrect because a CNAME record is used to provide alias entries for your zone (usually for multiple services or sites on one IP address).

17. Which of the following may be a security concern for an organization?

    A. The internal network uses private IP addresses registered to an Active Directory–integrated DNS server.

    B. An external DNS server is Active Directory integrated.

C. All external name resolution requests are accomplished by an ISP.

D. None of the above.

☑ **B.** If you have a Windows Active Directory (AD) network, having AD-integrated DNS servers has some great advantages. For example (and directly from Microsoft, I might add), "with directory-integrated storage, dynamic updates to DNS are conducted based upon a multimaster update model. In this model, any authoritative DNS server, such as a domain controller running a DNS server, is designated as a primary source for the zone. Because the master copy of the zone is maintained in the Active Directory database, which is fully replicated to all domain controllers, the zone can be updated by the DNS servers operating at any domain controller for the domain." Zones are also replicated and synchronized to new domain controllers automatically whenever a new one is added to an Active Directory domain, and directory replication is faster and more efficient than standard DNS replication. But having an Active Directory server facing externally is a horrible idea.

☒ **A** is incorrect because having AD-integrated DNS servers inside your network, with all private IP addresses, is just fine. Actually, it's a pretty good idea if you think about it for a bit.

☒ **C** is incorrect because having an external ISP answer all name resolution requests for your public-facing servers isn't a bad idea at all. Even if the ISP's DNS is subject to attack, nothing is there but the public-facing hosts anyway.

☒ **D** is incorrect because there is a correct answer provided.

18. Which of the following is a good footprinting tool for discovering information on a publicly traded company's founding, history, and financial status?

    A. SpiderFoot

    B. EDGAR Database

    C. Sam Spade

    D. Pipl.com

    ☑ **B.** The EDGAR Database—www.sec.gov/edgar.shtml—holds all sorts of competitive intelligence information on businesses and is an old favorite of EC-Council. From the website, "All companies, foreign and domestic, are required to file registration statements, periodic reports, and other forms electronically through EDGAR. Anyone can access and download this information for free. Here you'll find links to a complete list of filings available through EDGAR and instructions for searching the EDGAR database." Finally, one more note on EDGAR and the SEC: They have purview only over publicly traded companies. Privately held companies are not regulated or obligated to put information in EDGAR. Additionally, even publicly traded companies might not provide information about privately owned subsidiaries, so be careful and diligent.

☒ **A** is incorrect because SpiderFoot is a free, open source, domain footprinting tool. From the site, "it will scrape the websites on that domain, as well as search Google, Netcraft, Whois and DNS to build up information."

☒ **C** is incorrect because Sam Spade is a DNS footprinting tool.

☒ **D** is incorrect because pipl.com is a site used for "people search." When footprinting, pipl.com can use so-called deep web searching for loads of information you can use. From the site, "Also known as 'invisible web,' the term 'deep web' refers to a vast repository of underlying content, such as documents in online databases that general-purpose web crawlers cannot reach. The deep web content is estimated at 500 times that of the surface web, yet has remained mostly untapped due to the limitations of traditional search engines."

19. What method does traceroute use to map routes traveled by a packet?

   A. By carrying a hello packet in the payload, forcing the host to respond

   B. By using DNS queries at each hop

   C. By manipulating the time to live (TTL) parameter

   D. By using ICMP Type 5, code 0 packets

   ☑ **C.** Traceroute tracks a packet across the Internet by incrementing the TTL on each packet it sends by one after each hop is hit and returns, ensuring the response comes back explicitly from that hop and returns its name and IP address. This provides route path and transit times. It accomplishes this by using ICMP ECHO packets to report information on each "hop" (router) from the source to destination.

   ☒ **A** is incorrect because ICMP simply doesn't work that way. A hello packet is generally used between clients and servers as a check-in/health mechanism, not a route tracing method.

   ☒ **B** is incorrect because a DNS lookup at each hop is pointless and does you no good. DNS isn't for route tracing; it's for matching hostnames and IP addresses.

   ☒ **D** is incorrect because an ICMP Type 5, code 0 packet is all about message redirection and not about a ping request (Type 8).

20. Brad is auditing an organization and is asked to provide suggestions on improving DNS security. Which of the following would be valid options to recommend? (Choose all that apply.)

    A. Implementing split-horizon operation

    B. Restricting zone transfers

    C. Obfuscating DNS by using the same server for other applications and functions

    D. Blocking all access to the server on port 53

    ☑ **A and B.** Split-horizon DNS (also known as split-view or split DNS) is a method of providing different answers to DNS queries based on the source address of the DNS request. It can be accomplished with hardware or software solutions and provides one more step of separation between you and the bad guys. Restricting zone transfers to only those systems you desire to have them is always a good idea. If you leave it open for anyone to grab, you're just asking for trouble.

    ☒ **C** is incorrect because you generally should not put DNS services on a machine performing other tasks or applications. Does it happen in the real world? Sure, it does, and just like it's not too far-fetched to find a stray Windows 2000 machine in any given organization's network, it's probably more common than we'd like to guess.

    ☒ **D** is incorrect because restricting all port 53 access to the server means it's not acting as a DNS server anymore: No one can query for name lookups, and no zone transfers are going to happen. I guess in some weird way the DNS side of it is *really* secure, but its functionality has dropped to nothing.

21. A zone file consists of which records? (Choose all that apply.)

    A. PTR

    B. MX

    C. SN

    D. SOA

    E. DNS

    F. A

    G. AX

☑ **A, B, D,** and **F.** A zone file contains a list of all the resource records in the namespace zone. Valid resource records are as follows:

SRV	**Service** This record defines the hostname and port number of servers providing specific services, such as a Directory Services server.
SOA	**Start of Authority** This record identifies the primary name server for the zone. The SOA record contains the hostname of the server responsible for all DNS records within the namespace, as well as the basic properties of the domain.
PTR	**Pointer** This record maps an IP address to a hostname (providing for reverse DNS lookups). You don't absolutely need a PTR record for every entry in your DNS namespace, but PTR records are usually associated with e-mail server records.
NS	**Name Server** This record defines the name servers within your namespace. These servers are the ones that respond to your client's requests for name resolution.
MX	**Mail Exchange** This record identifies your e-mail servers within your domain.
CNAME	**Canonical Name** This record provides for domain name aliases within your zone. For example, you may have an FTP server and a web service running on the same IP address. CNAME records could be used to list both within DNS for you.
A	**Address** This record maps an IP address to a hostname and is used most often for DNS lookups.

☒ **C, E,** and **G** are incorrect because they are not valid DNS resource records.

22. Examine the following SOA record:

```
@  IN  SOARTDNSRV1.somebiz.com.  postmaster.somebiz.com. (
200408097    ; serial number
                          3600          ; refresh    [1h]
                          600           ; retry      [10m]
                          86400         ; expire     [1d]
7200 )       ; min TTL    [2h]
```

How long will the secondary server wait before asking for an update to the zone file?

A. 1 hour

B. 2 hours

C. 10 minutes

D. 1 day

☑ **A.** The refresh interval defines the amount of time a secondary will wait before checking in to see whether it needs a zone update.

☒ **B** is incorrect because the refresh interval is set to 3,600 seconds (1 hour). If you chose this because the TTL interval appealed to you, note that the TTL interval is the minimum time to live for all records in the zone (if it's not updated by a zone transfer, the records will perish).

☒ **C** is incorrect because the refresh interval is set to 3,600 seconds (1 hour). If you chose this because the retry interval appealed to you, note that the retry interval is the amount of time a secondary server will wait to retry *if the zone transfer fails*.

☒ **D** is incorrect because the refresh interval is set to 3,600 seconds (1 hour). If you chose this because the expire interval appealed to you, note the expire interval is the maximum amount of time a secondary server will spend trying to complete a zone transfer.

23. A colleague enters the following into a Google search string:

    ```
    intitle:intranet inurl:intranet +intext:"finance"
    ```

    Which of the following is most correct concerning this attempt?

    A. The search engine will not respond with any result because you cannot combine Google hacks in one line.

    B. The search engine will respond with all pages having the word *intranet* in their title and *finance* in the URL.

    C. The search engine will respond with all pages having the word *intranet* in the title and in the URL.

    D. The search engine will respond with only those pages having the word *intranet* in the title and URL and with *finance* in the text.

    ☑ **D.** This is a great Google hack that's listed on several websites providing Google hacking examples. Think about what you're looking for here—an internal page (*intranet* in title and URL) possibly containing finance data. Don't you think that would be valuable? This example shows the beauty of combining Google hacks to really burrow down to what you want to grab. Granted, an Intranet being available from the Internet, indexed by Google and open enough for you to touch it, is unlikely, but these are questions concerning syntax, not reality.

    ☒ **A** is incorrect because Google hack operators *can* be combined. In fact, once you get used to them, you'll spend more time combining them to narrow an attack than launching them one by one.

    ☒ **B** is incorrect because the operator does not say to look for *human resources* in the URL. It specifically states that should be looked for in the text of the page.

☒ **C** is incorrect because there is more to the operation string than just *intranet* in the URL and title. Don't just glaze over the *intext:"human resources"* operator—it makes Answer D more correct.

24. Amanda works as a senior security analyst and overhears a colleague discussing confidential corporate information being posted on an external website. When questioned on it, he claims about a month ago he tried random URLs on the company's website and found confidential information. Amanda visits the same URLs but finds nothing. Where can Amanda go to see past versions and pages of a website?

    A. Search.com

    B. Google cache

    C. Pasthash.com

    D. Archive.org

    ☑ **D.** The Internet Archive (http://archive.org) is a nonprofit organization "dedicated to build an Internet library. Its purposes include offering permanent access for researchers, historians, scholars, people with disabilities, and the general public to historical collections that exist in digital format." The good-old Wayback Machine has been used for a long time to pull up old copies of websites, for good and maybe not-so-good purposes. Archive.org includes "snapshots of the World Wide Web," which are archived copies of pages taken at various points in time dating back to 1996.

    ☒ **A** is incorrect because Search.com is simply another search engine at your disposal. It does not hold archived copies.

    ☒ **B** is incorrect because Google cache holds a copy of the site only from the latest "crawl"—usually nothing older than a couple to few days.

    ☒ **C** is incorrect because, as far as I know, Pasthash.com doesn't even exist.

25. Which of the following is a primary service of the U.S. Computer Security Incident Response Team (CSIRT)?

    A. CSIRT provides an incident response service to enable a reliable and trusted single point of contact for reporting computer security incidents worldwide.

    B. CSIRT provides computer security surveillance to governments, supplying important intelligence information on individuals traveling abroad.

    C. CSIRT provides pen testing services to individuals and multinational corporations.

    D. CSIRT provides vulnerability assessment services to law enforcement agencies.

☑ **A.** EC-Council *loves* CSIRT, and I promise you'll see it mentioned somewhere on the exam. The Computer Security Incident Response Team (CSIRT; www.csirt.org/) "provides 24x7 Computer Security Incident Response Services to any user, company, government agency or organization. CSIRT provides a reliable and trusted single point of contact for reporting computer security incidents worldwide. CSIRT provides the means for reporting incidents and for disseminating important incident-related information." A privately held company that started in 2001, CSIRT seeks "to raise awareness among its customers of computer security issues, and provides information for secure protection of critical computing infrastructure and equipment against potential organized computer attacks."

☒ **B, C,** and **D** are incorrect because these statements do not match CSIRT's purpose or actions.

26. Your client's business is headquartered in Japan. Which regional registry would be the best place to look for footprinting information?

    A. APNIC

    B. RIPE

    C. ASIANIC

    D. ARIN

    E. LACNIC

    ☑ **A.** This one is easy as pie and should be a free one if you see it on the test. There are five regional Internet registries that provide overall management of the public IP address space within a given geographic region. APNIC handles Asia and Pacific realms.

    ☒ **B** is incorrect because RIPE handles Europe, Middle East, and parts of Central Asia/Northern Africa. If you're wondering, the name is French and stands for Réseaux IP Européens.

    ☒ **C** is incorrect because ASIANIC is not a regional registry. It's purely a distractor here.

    ☒ **D** is incorrect because the ARIN service region includes Canada, many Caribbean and North Atlantic islands, and the United States. Caribbean islands falling under ARIN include Puerto Rico, the Bahamas, Antigua, American and British Virgin Islands, Turks and Caicos Islands, and the Cayman Islands (among others).

    ☒ **E** is incorrect because LACNIC handles Latin America and parts of the Caribbean. It stands for Latin America and Caribbean Network Information Center. LACNIC coverage includes most of South America, Guatemala, French Guiana, Dominican Republic, and Cuba (among others). This one and ARIN most often get confused.

Scanning and Enumeration

This chapter includes questions from the following topics:

- Describe EC-Council's scanning methodology
- Describe scan types and the objectives of scanning
- Understand the use of various scanning and enumeration tools
- Describe TCP communication (three-way handshake and flag types)
- Understand OS fingerprinting through banner grabbing
- Understand enumeration and its techniques
- Describe NULL sessions and their countermeasures
- Describe SNMP enumeration and its countermeasures
- Describe the steps involved in performing enumeration

I love fishing. Scratch that—a better statement is that I obsess over fishing. I dream about it. I think about it during my workday, and I plan my weekends around it. And, on days like today where the lake behind my house looks like a mirror that God is using to comb his hair in as He looks down from above, it's all I can do not to grab the rods and race out of the house. Instead, I'm sitting here in my little home office dedicating my morning to you and your needs, Dear Reader. You're welcome.

All fishing is good, and I've tried most of it. I'm not really wild about catching fish with your hands (those noodling guys don't have all the cheese on their crackers), and ice fishing isn't a favorite of mine because I hate the cold, but I love kayak fishing. Don't get me wrong—I still really enjoy going out on a deep-sea boat or riding along in someone's bass boat, flying across the top of the water—but being in a kayak just seems more *personal*. Sitting right on top of the water, sneaking up to fish, and watching them eat the bait is pure awesomeness.

Here on the flats of East-Central Florida, you can catch fish just by paddling around and casting blindly all around you. But if you want to catch good fish and catch them with more regularity, you have learned how to read the water. Look around in your mind's eye with me and scan the water around us. See that little ripple over there? Those are mullet swimming around in circles lazily. Nothing is after them, so there's no point in paddling that way. That heavy wake over there that kind of looks like a small submarine under water? That's a redfish, and we should definitely take a shot his way. And those tails poking out of the water over there? Yeah, that's a bunch of them.

Much like the signs we can see by scanning the surface of the water here on the flats, your scanning and enumeration efforts in the virtual world will point you in the right direction and, once you get some experience with what you're looking at, will improve your hook-up percentage. As stated in the companion book to this study guide, you know how to footprint your client; now it's time to learn how to dig around what you found for relevant, salient information. After footprinting, you'll need to scan for basics; then when you find a machine up and about, you'll need to get to know it really well, asking some rather personal questions.

 STUDY TIPS　There are certain things about each section that EC-Council just absolutely adores, and there are some sections it gets downright giddy about. This section is one of them, and there are definitely things to focus on. If you check EC-Council's website, you'll find that questions from scanning and enumeration can make up close to 70 percent of your exam (www.eccouncil.org/ Certification/exam-information/ceh-exam-312-50). I'm not saying they will; I'm just saying that 70 percent of the exam matches this section, so you'd better pay attention.

First and foremost, get your basic network knowledge down pat. Know your port numbers, protocols, and communications handshakes like the back of your hand, and learn how routing/switching basics can affect your efforts. EC-Council absolutely adores the IDLE scan, so know your IPID action well. And brush up on sequence numbering because you'll definitely see a couple questions about it.

Definitely get to know the scanning and enumeration tools very well, in particular, Nmap. You're going to be quizzed on use, output, and syntax, so prep by practicing—it's the absolute best way to prepare for this exam.

Windows and Linux architecture basics aren't going to make up the majority of your exam, but rest assured you will be tested on them. Know netstat especially well, as well as your security identifiers (SIDs) and relative identifiers (RIDs).

1. Which of the following is *not* part of the CEH scanning methodology?

    A. Check for live systems.

    B. Check for open ports.

    C. Perform banner grabbing.

    D. Prepare proxies.

    E. Check for social engineering attacks.

    F. Scan for vulnerabilities.

    G. Draw network diagrams.

2. What is the second step in the TCP three-way handshake?

    A. SYN

    B. ACK

    C. SYN/ACK

    D. ACK-SYN

    E. FIN

3. Which of the following tools are used for enumeration? (Choose three.)

    A. SolarWinds

    B. User2SID

    C. Snow

    D. SID2User

    E. DumpSec

4. You want to perform a ping sweep of a subnet within your target organization. Which of the following Nmap command lines is your best option?

    A. nmap 192.168.1.0/24

    B. nmap -sT 192.168.1.0/24

    C. nmap –sP 192.168.1.0/24

    D. nmap –P0 192.168.1.0/24

5. Which of the following TCP flags is used to reset a connection?

    A. SYN

    B. ACK

    C. PSH

    D. URG

    E. FIN

    F. RST

6. A pen test team member is attempting to enumerate a Windows machine and uses a tool called enum to enumerate user accounts on the device. Doubtful this can be done, a junior team member is shocked to see the local users enumerated. The output of his enum use is provided here:

```
C:\>enum -U 192.168.17.5
server 192.168.17.5
setting up session... success.
gettings user list (pass 1, index 0)... success, got 6
Admin  JfiedlerMsander Poop  Guest  Support123
cleaning up... success.
```

The junior team member asks what type of connection is used by this tool to accomplish its task and is told it requires a NULL session to be established first. If the machine allows null connections, which of the following command strings will successfully connect?

A. net use "" /u: \\192.169.5.12\share ""

B. net use \\192.168.5.12\c$ /u:""

C. net use \\192.168.5.12\share "" /u:""

D. net use \\192.168.5.12\c$ /u:""

7. A colleague enters the following command:

```
root@mybox: # hping3 -A 192.168.2.x -p 80
```

What is being attempted here?

A. An ACK scan using hping3 on port 80 for a single address

B. An ACK scan using hping3 on port 80 for a group of addresses

C. Address validation using hping3 on port 80 for a single address

D. Address validation using hping3 on port 80 for a group of addresses

8. You are examining traffic between hosts and note the following exchange:

```
Source              Prot   Port   Flag          Destination
192.168.5.12        TCP    4082   FIN/URG/PSH   192.168.5.50
192.168.5.12        TCP    4083   FIN/URG/PSH   192.168.5.50
192.168.5.12        TCP    4084   FIN/URG/PSH   192.168.5.50
192.168.5.50        TCP    4083   RST/ACK       192.168.5.12
192.168.5.12        TCP    4085   FIN/URG/PSH   192.168.5.50
```

Which of the following statements are true regarding this traffic? (Choose all that apply.)

A. It appears to be part of an ACK scan.

B. It appears to be part of an XMAS scan.

C. It appears port 4083 is open.

D. It appears port 4083 is closed.

9. You are examining traffic and notice an ICMP type 3, code 13, response. What does this normally indicate?

   A. The network is unreachable.

   B. The host is unknown.

   C. Congestion control is enacted for traffic to this host.

   D. A firewall is prohibiting connection.

10. You have a zombie system ready and begin an IDLE scan. As the scan moves along, you notice that fragment identification numbers gleaned from the zombie machine are incrementing randomly. What does this mean?

   A. Your IDLE scan results will not be useful to you.

   B. The zombie system is a honeypot.

   C. There is a misbehaving firewall between you and the zombie machine.

   D. This is an expected result during an IDLE scan.

11. As a pen test on a major international business moves along, a colleague discovers an IIS server and a mail exchange server on a DMZ subnet. You review a ping sweep accomplished earlier in the day on that subnet and note neither machine responded to the ping. What is the most likely reason for the lack of response?

   A. The hosts might be turned off or disconnected.

   B. ICMP is being filtered.

   C. The destination network might be down.

   D. The servers are Linux based and do not respond to ping requests.

12. Which of the following tools is not the best choice for determining possible vulnerabilities on live targets you have identified?

   A. SAINT

   B. Nmap

   C. Nessus

   D. Retina

13. Which of the following commands is the best choice to use on a Linux machine when attempting to list processes and the UIDs associated with them in a reliable manner?

   A. ls

   B. chmod

   C. pwd

   D. lsof

14. Which of the following tools can be used for operating system prediction from network and communication analysis? (Choose all that apply.)

    A. Nmap

    B. Whois

    C. Queso

    D. ToneLoc

    E. MBSA

15. You are in training for your new pen test assignment. Your trainer enters the following command:

    `telnet 192.168.12.5 80`

    After typing the command, he hits ENTER a few times. What is being attempted?

    A. A DoS attack against a web server

    B. A zone transfer

    C. Banner grabbing

    D. Configuring a port to "listening" state

16. What is being attempted with the following command?

    `nc -u -v -w2 192.168.1.100 1-1024`

    A. A full connect scan on ports 1–1024 for a single address

    B. A full connect scan on ports 1–1024 for a subnet

    C. A UDP port scan of ports 1–1024 on a single address

    D. A UDP scan of ports 1–1024 on a subnet

17. You are told to monitor a packet capture for any attempted DNS zone transfer. Which port should you focus your search on?

    A. TCP 22

    B. TCP 53

    C. UDP 22

    D. UDP 53

18. In the scanning and enumeration phase of your attack, you put tools such as ToneLoc, THC-Scan, and WarVox to use. What are you attempting to accomplish?

    A. War dialing

    B. War driving

    C. Proxy discovery

    D. Ping sweeping

19. Which of the following are SNMP enumeration tools? (Choose all that apply.)

    A. Nmap

    B. SNMPUtil

    C. ToneLoc

    D. OpUtils

    E. Solar Winds

    F. NSAuditor

20. The following results are from an Nmap scan:

```
Starting nmap V. 3.10A ( www.insecure.org/nmap/
<http://www.insecure.org/nmap/> )
Interesting ports on 192.168.15.12:
(The 1592 ports scanned but not shown below are in state: filtered)
Port State Service
21/tcp open ftp
25/tcp open smtp
53/tcp closed domain
80/tcp open http
443/tcp open https
Remote operating system guess: Too many signatures match to
    reliably guess the OS.
Nmap run completed   1 IP address (1 host up) scanned in 263.47 seconds
```

    Which of the following is the best option to assist in identifying the operating system?

    A. Attempt an ACK scan.

    B. Traceroute to the system.

    C. Run the same Nmap scan with the -vv option.

    D. Attempt banner grabbing.

21. You want to run a scan against a target network. You're concerned about it being a reliable scan, with legitimate results, but want to take steps to ensure it is as stealthy as possible. Which scan type is best in this situation?

    A. nmap –sN targetIPaddress

    B. nmap –sO targetIPaddress

    C. nmap –sS targetIPaddress

    D. nmap –sT targetIPaddress

22. Which of the following ports are not required for a NULL session connection? (Choose all that apply.)

    A. 135

    B. 137

    C. 139

    D. 161

    E. 443

    F. 445

23. You are enumerating a subnet. While examining message traffic, you discover SNMP is enabled on multiple targets. If you assume default settings in setting up enumeration tools to use SNMP, which community strings should you use?

    A. Public (read-only) and Private (read/write)

    B. Private (read-only) and Public (read/write)

    C. Read (read-only) and Write (read/write)

    D. Default (both read and read/write)

24. Nmap is a powerful scanning and enumeration tool. What does the following Nmap command attempt to accomplish?

    `nmap -sA -T4 192.168.15.0/24`

    A. A serial, slow operating system discovery scan of a Class C subnet

    B. A parallel, fast operating system discovery scan of a Class C subnet

    C. A serial, slow ACK scan of a Class C subnet

    D. A parallel, fast ACK scan of a Class C subnet

25. You are examining a packet capture of all traffic from a host on the subnet. The host sends a segment with the SYN flag set in order to set up a TCP communications channel. The destination port is 80, and the sequence number is set to 10. Which of the following statements are *not* true regarding this communications channel? (Choose all that apply.)

    A. The host will be attempting to retrieve an HTML file.

    B. The source port field on this packet can be any number between 1023 and 65535.

    C. The first packet from the destination in response to this host will have the SYN and ACK flags set.

    D. The packet returned in answer to this SYN request will acknowledge the sequence number by returning 10.

26. Which TCP flag instructs the recipient to ignore buffering constraints and immediately send all data?

    A. URG

    B. PSH

    C. RST

    D. BUF

27. You receive a RST-ACK from a port during a SYN scan. What is the state of the port?

    A. Open

    B. Closed

    C. Filtered

    D. Unknown

28. Which port-scanning method presents the most risk of discovery but provides the most reliable results?

    A. Full-connect

    B. Half-open

    C. Null scan

    D. XMAS scan

29. The following output appears on the screen after an attempted telnet session to a machine:

```
HTTP/1.0 200 OK
Date: Wed, 19 Feb 2014 10:16:22 GMT
Content-Length: 30344
Content-Type: text/html
Expires: Wed, 19 Feb 2014 10:22:22 GMT
Cache-Control: max-age=300
Server: Apache/1.3.33 <Darwin> PHP /4.3.10
Age: 120
```

    Which of the following best matches the output provided?

    A. An attacker has attempted a zone transfer successfully.

    B. An attacker has attempted a zone transfer unsuccessfully.

    C. An attacker has successfully grabbed a banner.

    D. An attacker has successfully uploaded a denial-of-service script.

1. E
2. C
3. B, D, E
4. C
5. F
6. C
7. B
8. B, C
9. D
10. A
11. B
12. B
13. D
14. A, C
15. C
16. C
17. B
18. A
19. B, D, E, F
20. D
21. C
22. A, B, C, F
23. A
24. D
25. A, D
26. B
27. B
28. A
29. C

1. Which of the following is *not* part of the CEH scanning methodology?

   A. Check for live systems.

   B. Check for open ports.

   C. Perform banner grabbing.

   D. Prepare proxies.

   E. Check for social engineering attacks.

   F. Scan for vulnerabilities.

   G. Draw network diagrams.

   ☑ **E.** OK, I'll admit it—methodology questions aren't my favorite either. But we're covering them here and throughout the study guide for a couple of reasons. First, you'll see these on the test, and you absolutely need to commit them to memory. Second, especially if you're new to the field, a methodology ensures you don't forget something. In this case, the scanning methodology defined by EC-Council includes the following:

   1. Check for live systems.

   2. Check for open ports.

   3. Perform scanning beyond IDS.

   4. Perform banner grabbing.

   5. Scan for vulnerabilities.

   6. Draw network diagrams.

   7. Prepare proxies.

   ☒ **A, B, C, D, F,** and **G** are incorrect because these are all parts of the scanning methodoloy.

2. What is the second step in the TCP three-way handshake?

   A. SYN

   B. ACK

   C. SYN/ACK

   D. ACK-SYN

   E. FIN

   ☑ **C.** Admittedly, this is an easy one, but I'd bet dollars to doughnuts you see it in some form on your exam. It's such an important part of scanning and enumeration because, without understanding this basic principle of communication channel setup, you're almost doomed to failure. A three-way

TCP handshake has the originator forward a SYN. The recipient, in step 2, sends a SYN and an ACK. In step 3, the originator responds with an ACK. The steps are referred to as SYN, SYN/ACK, ACK.

☒ **A** is incorrect because SYN is the first step (flag set) in the three-way handshake.

☒ **B** is incorrect because ACK is the last step (flag set) in the three-way handshake.

☒ **D** is incorrect because of the order listed. True, both these flags are the flags set in the three-way handshake. However, in the discussion of this step-by-step process, at least as far as your exam is concerned, it's SYN/ACK, not the other way around. And, yes, this distractor, in some form, will most likely be on your exam. You won't care about the order in the real world since flags are a mathematical property of the packet and not some ridiculous order, but for your exam you'll need to know it this way.

☒ **E** is incorrect because the FIN flag brings an orderly close to a communication session.

3. Which of the following tools are used for enumeration? (Choose three.)

   A. SolarWinds

   B. User2SID

   C. Snow

   D. SID2User

   E. DumpSec

   ☑ **B, D,** and **E** are correct. User2SID and SID2User are two of the old standbys in local enumeration tools. User2SID provides the SID for a given user, and the reverse is true for SID2User. DumpSec (from SomarSoft; www.system-tools.com/somarsoft/?somarsoft.com) "dumps the permissions (DACLs) and audit settings (SACLs) for the file system, registry, printers and shares in a concise, readable format, so that holes in system security are readily apparent. DumpSec also dumps user, group and replication information."

   ☒ **A** is incorrect because SolarWinds is used more for network monitoring. EC-Council does not recognize this as a pure enumeration tool.

   ☒ **C** is incorrect because Snow is a steganography tool.

4. You want to perform a ping sweep of a subnet within your target organization. Which of the following Nmap command lines is your best option?

   A. nmap 192.168.1.0/24

   B. nmap -sT 192.168.1.0/24

   C. nmap –sP 192.168.1.0/24

   D. nmap –P0 192.168.1.0/24

☑ **C.** The –sP switch within nmap is designed for a ping sweep. Nmap syntax is fairly straightforward: nmap<scan options><target>. If you don't define a switch, Nmap performs a basic enumeration scan of the targets. The switches, though, provide the real power with this tool.

☒ **A** is incorrect because this syntax will not perform a ping sweep. This syntax will run a basic scan against the entire subnet.

☒ **B** is incorrect because the –sT switch does not run a ping sweep. It stands for a TCP Connect scan, which is the slowest—but most productive and loud—scan option.

☒ **D** is incorrect because this syntax will not perform a ping sweep. The –P0 switch actually runs the scan without ping (ICMP). This is a good switch to use when you don't seem to be getting responses from your targets. It forces Nmap to start the scan even if it thinks that the target doesn't exist (which is useful if the computer is blocked by a firewall).

5. Which of the following TCP flags is used to reset a connection?

   A. SYN

   B. ACK

   C. PSH

   D. URG

   E. FIN

   F. RST

☑ **F.** The RST flag, when set, indicates to both parties that communications need to be closed and restarted. It forces a termination of communications in both directions and is used to reset a connection.

☒ **A** is incorrect because the SYN flag is used to initiate a connection between hosts. The synchronize flag is set during initial communication establishment and indicates negotiation of parameters and sequence numbers.

☒ **B** is incorrect because the ACK flag is used to acknowledge receipt of a packet. It is set as an acknowledgment to SYN flags and is set on all segments after the initial SYN flag.

☒ **C** is incorrect because the PSH flag is used to instruct the sender to immediately send all buffered data: It forces the delivery of data without concern for any buffering.

☒ **D** is incorrect because the URG flag is used to indicate a packet that needs to be processed immediately. When this flag is set, it indicates the data inside is being sent out of band.

☒ **E** is incorrect because the FIN flag is used to tell the recipient there will be no more traffic. It signifies an ordered close to communications.

6. A pen test team member is attempting to enumerate a Windows machine and uses a tool called enum to enumerate user accounts on the device. Doubtful this can be done, a junior team member is shocked to see the local users enumerated. The output of his enum use is provided here:

```
C:\>enum -U 192.168.17.5
server 192.168.17.5
setting up session... success.
gettings user list (pass 1, index 0)... success, got 6
Admin  JfiedlerMsander Poop  Guest  Support123
cleaning up... success.
```

The junior team member asks what type of connection is used by this tool to accomplish its task and is told it requires a NULL session to be established first. If the machine allows null connections, which of the following command strings will successfully connect?

A. net use "" /u: \\192.169.5.12\share ""

B. net use \\192.168.5.12\c$ /u:""

C. net use \\192.168.5.12\share "" /u:""

D. net use \\192.168.5.12\c$ /u:""

☑ **C.** You will definitely be asked about NULL sessions on the exam and will need to know the syntax well. A NULL session occurs when you log into a system with no user ID and password at all. This type of connection can't be made to a regular share, but it can be done to the Interprocess Communication (IPC) administrative share, which is used by Windows processes under the SYSTEM username to communicate with other processes across the network. Some tools that make use of the null session are enum, SuperScan, User2SID, and SID2User. The correct syntax for establishing a NULL session is as follows: net use \\IPAddress\share "" /u: "".

☒ **A** is incorrect because the correct syntax is not used.

☒ **B** is incorrect because the correct syntax is not used. Additionally, see the C$ entry there? That's a dead giveaway, and CEH test question writers love using it to confuse you, especially if the question has something about "a NULL session to exploit an administrative share." This, of course, is referencing the IPC$, but some candidates immediately see that term and go for C$ every time. Don't fall for it. Remember, NULL sessions = IPC$ share.

☒ **D** is incorrect because the correct syntax is not used.

7. A colleague enters the following command:

```
root@mybox: # hping3 -A 192.168.2.x -p 80
```

What is being attempted here?

A. An ACK scan using hping3 on port 80 for a single address

B. An ACK scan using hping3 on port 80 for a group of addresses

C. Address validation using hping3 on port 80 for a single address

D. Address validation using hping3 on port 80 for a group of addresses

☑ **B.** Hping is a great tool providing all sorts of options. You can craft packets with it, audit and test firewalls, and do all sorts of crazy man-in-the-middle stuff with it. In this example, you're simply performing a basic ACK scan (the –A switch) using port 80 (–p 80) on an entire Class C subnet (the *x* in the address runs through all 254 possibilities). Hping3, the latest version, is scriptable (TCL language) and implements an engine that allows a human-readable description of TCP/IP packets.

☒ **A** is incorrect because the syntax is for an entire subnet (or, I guess to be technically specific, all 254 addresses that start with 192.168.2). The *x* in the last octet tells hping to fire away at all those available addresses.

☒ **C** and **D** are both incorrect because "address validation" is not a scan type.

8. You are examining traffic between hosts and note the following exchange:

```
Source          Prot  Port  Flag         Destination
192.168.5.12    TCP   4082  FIN/URG/PSH  192.168.5.50
192.168.5.12    TCP   4083  FIN/URG/PSH  192.168.5.50
192.168.5.12    TCP   4084  FIN/URG/PSH  192.168.5.50
192.168.5.50    TCP   4083  RST/ACK      192.168.5.12
192.168.5.12    TCP   4085  FIN/URG/PSH  192.168.5.50
```

Which of the following statements are true regarding this traffic? (Choose all that apply.)

A. It appears to be part of an ACK scan.

B. It appears to be part of an XMAS scan.

C. It appears port 4083 is open.

D. It appears port 4083 is closed.

☑ **B** and **C.** The exam will ask you to define scan types in many, many ways. It may be a simple definition match; sometimes it'll be some crazy Wireshark or tcpdump listing. In this example, you see a cleaned-up traffic exchange showing packets from one host being sent one after another to the second host, indicating a scan attempt. The packets have the FIN, URG, and PSH flags all set, which tells you it's an XMAS scan. If the destination port is open, we should receive a RST/ACK response; if it's closed, we get nothing. This tells us port 4083 looks like it's open. As an addendum, did you know there are two reasons why it's called an XMAS scan? The first is because it lights up an IDS like a Christmas tree, and the second is because the flags themselves are all lit. As an aside, you probably won't see this much out in the real world because it just really doesn't have much applicability. But on your exam? Oh yes—it'll be there.

☒ **A** is incorrect because there is no indication this is an ACK scan. An ACK scan has only the ACK flag set and is generally used in firewall filter tests: No response means a firewall is present, and RST means the firewall is not there (or the port is not filtered).

☒ **D** is incorrect because you did receive an answer from the port (a RST/ACK was sent in the fourth line of the capture).

9. You are examining traffic and notice an ICMP type 3, code 13 response. What does this normally indicate?

   A. The network is unreachable.

   B. The host is unknown.

   C. Congestion control is enacted for traffic to this host.

   D. A firewall is prohibiting connection.

   ☑ **D.** ICMP types will be covered in depth on your exam, so know them well. Type 3 messages are all about "destination unreachable," and the code in each packet tells you why it's unreachable. A code 13 indicates "communication administratively prohibited," which indicates a firewall filtering traffic. Granted, this occurs only when a network designer is nice enough to configure the device to respond in such a way, and you'll probably never get that nicety in the real world, but the definitions of what the "type" and "code" mean are relevant here.

   ☒ **A** is incorrect because "network unreachable" is type 3, code 0. It's generated by a router to inform the source that the destination address is unreachable; that is, it does not have an entry in the route table to send the message to.

   ☒ **B** is incorrect because "host unknown" is type 3, code 7. There's a route to the network the router knows about, but that host is not there (this sometimes refers to a naming or DNS issue).

   ☒ **C** is incorrect because "congestion control" ICMP messaging is type 4.

10. You have a zombie system ready and begin an IDLE scan. As the scan moves along, you notice that fragment identification numbers gleaned from the zombie machine are incrementing randomly. What does this mean?

    A. Your IDLE scan results will not be useful to you.

    B. The zombie system is a honeypot.

    C. There is a misbehaving firewall between you and the zombie machine.

    D. This is an expected result during an IDLE scan.

☑ **A.** An IDLE scan makes use of a zombie machine and IP's knack for incrementing fragment identifiers (IPIDs). However, it is absolutely essential the zombie remain idle to all other traffic during the scan. The attacker will send packets to the target with the (spoofed) source address of the zombie. If the port is open, the target will respond to the SYN packet with a SYN/ACK, but this will be sent to the zombie. The zombie system will then craft a RST packet in answer to the unsolicited SYN/ACK, and the IPID will increase. If this occurs randomly, then it's probable your zombie is not, in fact, idle, and your results are moot. See, if it's not idle, it's going to increment haphazardly because communications from the device will be shooting hither and yon with wild abandon. You're banking on the fact the machine is quietly doing your bidding—and nothing else.

☒ **B** is incorrect because there is not enough information here to identify the zombie machine as anything at all—much less a machine set up as a "honeypot."

☒ **C** is incorrect because a firewall between you and the zombie won't have any effect at all on the zombie's IPIDs.

☒ **D** is incorrect because this is definitely *not* expected behavior during an IDLE scan. Expected behavior is for the IPID to increase regularly with each discovered open port, not randomly, as occurs with traffic on an active system.

11. As a pen test on a major international business moves along, a colleague discovers an IIS server and a mail exchange server on a DMZ subnet. You review a ping sweep accomplished earlier in the day on that subnet and note neither machine responded to the ping. What is the most likely reason for the lack of response?

A. The hosts might be turned off or disconnected.

B. ICMP is being filtered.

C. The destination network might be down.

D. The servers are Linux based and do not respond to ping requests.

☑ **B.** Admittedly, this one is a little tricky, and, yes, I purposefully wrote it this way (mainly because I've seen questions like this before). The key here is the "most likely" designator. It's entirely possible—dare I say, even *expected*—that the systems administrator on those two important machines would turn off ICMP. Of the choices provided, this one is the most likely explanation.

☒ **A** is incorrect, but only because there is a better answer. This is a major firm that undoubtedly does business at all times of day and with customers and employees around the world (the question did state it was an international business). Is it possible that both these servers are down? Sure, you might have timed your ping sweep so poorly that you happened to hit a maintenance window or something, but it's highly unlikely.

☒ **C** is incorrect because, frankly, the odds of an entire DMZ subnet being down while you're pen testing are very slim. And I can promise you if the subnet did drop while you were testing, your test is over.

☒ **D** is incorrect because this is simply not true.

12. Which of the following tools is not the best choice for determining possible vulnerabilities on live targets you have identified?

   A. SAINT

   B. Nmap

   C. Nessus

   D. Retina

☑ **B.** Nmap is a great scanning tool, providing all sorts of options for you. It can do a great job of identifying "live" machines and letting you know what ports a machine has open—not to mention helping you to identify the operating system in use on the machine. But when it comes to identifying actual vulnerabilities the machine may be open to, other tools are *designed* for that purpose. Some super-talented folks can turn Nmap into a basic vulnerability scanner, but it's not the best choice for the job (especially provided the other choices here).

☒ **A** is incorrect because SAINT (Security Administrator's Integrated Network Tool) is a vulnerability-scanning tool. It's now commercially available (it used to be free and open source, but no longer) and runs on Linux and Mac OS X. SAINT is one of the few scanners that doesn't provide a Windows version at all.

☒ **C** is incorrect because Nessus is a very well-known and popular vulnerability assessment scanner. Also once free and open source, Nessus can now be purchased commercially. It is continually updated and has thousands of plug-ins available for almost any usage you can think of.

☒ **D** is incorrect because Retina is a vulnerability-scanning application. Owned by eEye, Retina is a popular choice on Department of Defense (DoD) and government networks.

13. Which of the following commands is the best choice to use on a Linux machine when attempting to list processes and the UIDs associated with them in a reliable manner?

   A. ls

   B. chmod

   C. pwd

   D. lsof

☑ **D.** Supported in most Unix-like flavors, the "list open files" command (lsof) provides a list of all open files and the processes that opened them. The lsof command describes, among other things, the identification number of the process (PID) that has opened the file, the command the process is executing, and the owner of the process. With optional switches you can also receive all sorts of other information.

☒ **A** is incorrect because ls (list) simply displays all the files and folders in your current directory. Its counterpart in the PC world is dir.

☒ **B** is incorrect because chmod is used to set permissions on files and objects in Linux.

☒ **C** is incorrect because pwd (print working directory) is a command used to display the directory you are currently working in.

14. Which of the following tools can be used for operating system prediction from network and communication analysis? (Choose all that apply.)

    A. Nmap

    B. Whois

    C. Queso

    D. ToneLoc

    E. MBSA

    ☑ **A and C.** Operating system guessing—also known as *fingerprinting* or, if you're really trying to impress someone, *stack fingerprinting*—can be accomplished by either Nmap or Queso. Granted, Queso is an older tool, but it's still a staple of this certification.

    ☒ **B** is incorrect because whois is used to look up registrar information for a web registration.

    ☒ **D** is incorrect because ToneLoc is a war dialing tool used to look for open modems on an enterprise.

    ☒ **E** is incorrect because Microsoft Baseline Security Advisor (MBSA) is a tool for examining the security posture of a Windows machine. MBSA can provide vulnerability information on the host, locally or remotely.

15. You are in training for your new pen test assignment. Your trainer enters the following command:

    `telnet 192.168.12.5 80`

    After typing the command, he hits ENTER a few times. What is being attempted?

    A. A DoS attack against a web server

    B. A zone transfer

C. Banner grabbing

D. Configuring a port to "listening" state

☑ **C.** Banner grabbing is a great enumerating method. The tactic involves sending an unsolicited request to an open port to see what, if any, default message is returned. The returned banner can provide all sorts of details, depending on what application is actually on the port. Things such as error messages, HTTP headers, and login messages can indicate potential vulnerabilities. There are lots of ways to accomplish this. For example, with netcat you can use the following command:

```
nc -v -n 212.77.64.88 80
```

However, using Telnet (to a port other than 23) is one of the easiest methods for accomplishing the task.

☒ **A** is incorrect because the worse that can happen on this attempt is a closed session with no banner return. Nothing about this will create or bolster a DoS attack.

☒ **B** is incorrect because this attempt is clearly not a zone transfer (accomplished on the command line using nslookup or dig).

☒ **D** is incorrect because Telnet is not used in this fashion.

16. What is being attempted with the following command?

```
nc -u -v -w2 192.168.1.100 1-1024
```

A. A full connect scan on ports 1–1024 for a single address

B. A full connect scan on ports 1–1024 for a subnet

C. A UDP port scan of ports 1–1024 on a single address

D. A UDP scan of ports 1–1024 on a subnet

☑ **C.** In this example, netcat is being used to run a scan on UDP ports (the –u switch gives this away) from 1 to 1024. The address provided is a single address, not a subnet. Other switches in use here are –v (for verbose) and –w2 (defines the two-second timeout for connection, where netcat will wait for a response).

☒ **A** is incorrect because the –u switch shows this as a UDP scan. By default (that is, no switch in place), netcat runs in TCP.

☒ **B** is incorrect because the –u switch shows this as a UDP scan. Additionally, this is aimed at a single address, not a subnet.

☒ **D** is incorrect because this is aimed at a single address, not a subnet.

17. You are told to monitor a packet capture for any attempted DNS zone transfer. Which port should you focus your search on?

    A. TCP 22

    B. TCP 53

    C. UDP 22

    D. UDP 53

    ☑ **B.** DNS uses port 53 in both UDP and TCP. Port 53 over UDP is used for DNS lookups. Zone transfers are accomplished using port 53 over TCP. Considering the reliability and error correction available with TCP, this makes perfect sense.

    ☒ **A** is incorrect because TCP port 22 is for SSH, not DNS.

    ☒ **C** is incorrect because UDP port 22 simply doesn't exist (SSH is TCP based).

    ☒ **D** is incorrect because UDP port 53 is used for DNS lookups. Because lookups are generally a packet or two and we're concerned with speed on a lookup, UDP's fire-and-forget speed advantage is put to use here.

18. In the scanning and enumeration phase of your attack, you put tools such as ToneLoc, THC-Scan, and WarVox to use. What are you attempting to accomplish?

    A. War dialing

    B. War driving

    C. Proxy discovery

    D. Ping sweeping

    ☑ **A.** ToneLoc, THC-Scan, and WarVox are all war dialing applications. In war dialing, the attacker dials an entire set of phone numbers looking for an open modem. Modems are designed to answer the call, and despite that they are for the most part outdated, they can easily provide backdoor access to a system otherwise completely secured from attack.

    ☒ **B** is incorrect because war driving refers to a method of discovering wireless access points. Although you may not need a vehicle any longer to do so, war driving used to refer to, quite literally, driving around in a car looking for open access points. In the ethical hacking realm, it still indicates a search for open WAPs.

    ☒ **C** is incorrect because the tools listed here have nothing to do with locating and identifying proxies.

    ☒ **D** is incorrect because the tools listed here have nothing to do with ping sweeping. Tools such as Angry IP, Nmap, Solar Winds, and PingScannerPro are ping sweepers.

19. Which of the following are SNMP enumeration tools? (Choose all that apply.)

   A. Nmap

   B. SNMPUtil

   C. ToneLoc

   D. OpUtils

   E. SolarWinds

   F. NSAuditor

   ☑ **B, D, E,** and **F.** SNMP (in all its versions) is a great protocol designed to help network managers get the most out of their devices and nets. Unfortunately, it's so powerful and easy to use that hackers abuse it frequently, leading many administrators to simply turn it off. Enumerating a device using SNMP—crawling the Management Information Base (MIB) for the device—is relatively easy. SNMPUtil, SolarWinds, and OpUtils are probably the most well-known of this group. NSAuditor is probably better known for its vulnerability-scanning features, but it is listed by CEH as an SNMP enumerator.

   ☒ **A** is incorrect because Nmap is not an SNMP enumerator; it's a scanning tool.

   ☒ **C** is incorrect because ToneLoc is a war-dialing tool used for discovering open modems.

20. The following results are from an Nmap scan:

```
Starting nmap V. 3.10A ( www.insecure.org/nmap/
<http://www.insecure.org/nmap/> )
Interesting ports on 192.168.15.12:
(The 1592 ports scanned but not shown below are in state: filtered)
Port State Service
21/tcp open ftp
25/tcp open smtp
53/tcp closed domain
80/tcp open http
443/tcp open https
Remote operating system guess: Too many signatures match to reliably
guess the OS.
Nmap run completed -- 1 IP address (1 host up) scanned in 263.47 seconds
```

   Which of the following is the best option to assist in identifying the operating system?

   A. Attempt an ACK scan.

   B. Traceroute to the system.

   C. Run the same Nmap scan with the -vv option.

   D. Attempt banner grabbing.

☑ **D.** Of the options presented, banner grabbing is probably your best bet. In fact, it's a good *start* for operating system fingerprinting. You can telnet to any of these active ports or run an Nmap banner grab. Either way, the returning banner may help in identifying the OS.

☒ **A** is incorrect because an ACK scan isn't necessarily going to help here. For that matter, it may have already been run.

☒ **B** is incorrect because traceroute does not provide any information on fingerprinting. It will show you a network map, hop by hop, to the target, but it won't help tell you whether it's a Windows machine.

☒ **C** is incorrect because the –vv switch provides only more (verbose) information on what Nmap already has. Note that the original run presented this message on the OS fingerprinting effort: "Remote operating system guess: Too many signatures match to reliably guess the OS."

21. You want to run a scan against a target network. You're concerned about it being a reliable scan, with legitimate results, but want to take steps to ensure it is as stealthy as possible. Which scan type is best in this situation?

    A. nmap –sN targetIPaddress

    B. nmap –sO targetIPaddress

    C. nmap –sS targetIPaddress

    D. nmap –sT targetIPaddress

☑ **C.** A half-open scan, as defined by this Nmap command line, is the best option in this case. The SYN scan was created with stealth in mind because the full connect scan was simply too noisy (or created more entries in an application-level logging system, whichever your preference). Granted, most IDSs can pick it up; however, if you go slow enough, it is almost invisible: A connect scan is indistinguishable from a real connection where a SYN scan can be.

☒ **A** is incorrect because a null scan may not provide the reliability you're looking for. Remember, this scan won't work on a Windows host at all.

☒ **B** is incorrect because the –sO switch tells you this is a operating system scan. Fingerprinting scans are not stealthy by anyone's imagination, and they won't provide the full information you're looking for here.

☒ **D** is incorrect because the –sT option indicates a full connect scan. Although this is reliable, it is noisy, and you will most likely be discovered during the scan.

22. Which of the following ports are required for a NULL session connection? (Choose all that apply.)

   A. 135

   B. 137

   C. 139

   D. 161

   E. 443

   F. 445

   ☑ **A, B, C,** and **F.** NULL sessions have been virtually eliminated from the hacking arsenal since Windows XP was released; however, many machine are still vulnerable to this attack and—more importantly to you—the CEH test loves covering it. NULL session connections make use of TCP ports 135, 137, 139, and 445.

   ☒ **D** is incorrect because port 161 is used for SNMP, which has nothing to do with NULL session connections.

   ☒ **E** is incorrect because port 443 is used for SSL connections and has nothing to do with NULL sessions.

23. You are enumerating a subnet. While examining message traffic you discover SNMP is enabled on multiple targets. If you assume default settings in setting up enumeration tools to use SNMP, which community strings should you use?

   A. Public (read-only) and Private (read/write)

   B. Private (read-only) and Public (read/write)

   C. Read (read-only) and Write (read/write)

   D. Default (both read and read/write)

   ☑ **A.** SNMP uses a community string as a form of a password. The read-only version of the community string allows a requester to read virtually anything SNMP can drag out of the device, whereas the read/write version is used to control access for the SNMP SET requests. The read-only default community string is *public*, whereas the read/write string is *private*. If you happen upon a network segment using SNMPv3, though, keep in mind that SNMPv3 can use a hashed form of the password in transit versus the clear text.

   ☒ **B** is incorrect because the community strings are listed in reverse here.

   ☒ **C** is incorrect because Read and Write are not community strings.

   ☒ **D** is incorrect because Default is not a community string in SNMP.

24. Nmap is a powerful scanning and enumeration tool. What does this Nmap command attempt to accomplish?

```
nmap -sA -T4 192.168.15.0/24
```

A. A serial, slow operating system discovery scan of a Class C subnet

B. A parallel, fast operating system discovery scan of a Class C subnet

C. A serial, slow ACK scan of a Class C subnet

D. A parallel, fast ACK scan of a Class C subnet

☑ **D.** You are going to need to know Nmap switches well for your exam. In this example, the –A switch indicates an ACK scan (the only scan that returns no response on a closed port), and the –T4 switch indicates an "aggressive" scan, which runs fast and in parallel.

☒ **A** is incorrect because a slow, serial scan would use the –T, –T0, or –T! switch. Additionally, the OS detection switch is –O, not –A.

☒ **B** is incorrect because although this answer got the speed of the scan correct, the operating system detection portion is off.

☒ **C** is incorrect because although this answer correctly identified the ACK scan switch, the –T4 switch was incorrectly identified.

25. You are examining a packet capture of all traffic from a host on the subnet. The host sends a segment with the SYN flag set in order to set up a TCP communications channel. The destination port is 80, and the sequence number is set to 10. Which of the following statements are *not* true regarding this communications channel? (Choose all that apply.)

A. The host will be attempting to retrieve an HTML file.

B. The source port field on this packet can be any number between 1023 and 65535.

C. The first packet from the destination in response to this host will have the SYN and ACK flags set.

D. The packet returned in answer to this SYN request will acknowledge the sequence number by returning "10."

☑ **A and D.** Yes, it is true that port 80 traffic is generally HTTP; however, there are two problems with this statement. The first is all that is happening here is an arbitrary connection to something on port 80. For all we know, it's a listener, telnet connection, or anything at all. Second, assuming it's actually an HTTP server, the sequence described here would do nothing but make a connection—not necessarily transfer anything. Sure, this is picky, but it's the truth. Next, sequence numbers are acknowledged between systems during the three-way handshake by incrementing by 1. In this example, the source sent an opening sequence number of 10 to the recipient. The recipient, in crafting the SYN/ACK response, will first acknowledge the opening sequence number by incrementing it to 11. After this, it will add its own sequence number to the packet (a random number it will pick) and send both off.

☒ **B** is incorrect because it's a true statement. Source port fields are dynamically assigned using anything other than the "well-known" port range (0–1023). IANA has defined the following port number ranges: Ports 1024 to 49151 are the registered ports (assigned by IANA for specific service upon application by a requesting entity), and ports 49152 to 65535 are dynamic or private ports that cannot be registered with IANA.

☒ **C** incorrect because it's a true statement. The requesting machine has sent the first packet in the three-way handshake exchange—a SYN packet. The recipient will respond with a SYN/ACK and wait patiently for the last step—the ACK packet.

26. Which TCP flag instructs the recipient to ignore buffering constraints and immediately send all data?

    A. URG

    B. PSH

    C. RST

    D. BUF

    ☑ **B.** This answer normally gets mixed up with the URG flag because we all read it as urgent. However, just remember the key word with PSH is "buffering." In TCP, buffering is used to maintain a steady, harmonious flow of traffic. Every so often, though, the buffer itself becomes a problem, slowing things down. A PSH flag tells the recipient stack that the data should be pushed up to the receiving application immediately.

    ☒ **A** is incorrect because the URG flag is used to inform the receiving stack that certain data within a segment is urgent and should be prioritized. As an aside, URG isn't used much by modern protocols.

    ☒ **C** is incorrect because the RST flag forces a termination of communications (in both directions).

    ☒ **D** is incorrect because BUF isn't a TCP flag at all.

27. You receive a RST-ACK from a port during a SYN scan. What is the state of the port?

    A. Open

    B. Closed

    C. Filtered

    D. Unknown

☑ **B.** Remember, a SYN scan occurs when you send a SYN packet to all open ports. If the port is open, you'll obviously get a SYN/ACK back. However, if the port is closed, you'll get a RST-ACK.

☒ **A** is incorrect because an open port would respond differently (SYN/ACK).

☒ **C** is incorrect because a filtered port would likely not respond at all. (The firewall wouldn't allow the packet through, so no response would be generated.)

☒ **D** is incorrect because you know exactly what state the port is in because of the RST-ACK response.

28. Which port-scanning method presents the most risk of discovery but provides the most reliable results?

    A. Full-connect

    B. Half-open

    C. Null scan

    D. XMAS scan

    ☑ **A.** A full-connect scan runs through an entire TCP three-way handshake on all ports you aim at. It's loud and easy to see happening, but the results are indisputable. As an aside, the –sT switch in Nmap runs a full-connect scan (you should go ahead and memorize that one).

    ☒ **B** is incorrect because a half-open scan involves sending only the SYN packet and watching for responses. It is designed for stealth but may be picked up on IDS sensors (both network and most host-based IDSs).

    ☒ **C** is incorrect because a null scan sends packets with no flags set at all. Responses will vary, depending on the OS and version, so reliability is spotty. As an aside, null scans are designed for UNIX/Linux machines and don't work on Windows systems.

    ☒ **D** is incorrect because although an XMAS scan is easily detectable (as our celebrated technical editor put it, "a fairly well-trained monkey would see it"), the results are oftentimes sketchy. The XMAS scan is great for test questions but won't result in much more than a derisive snort and an immediate disconnection in the real world.

29. The following output appears onscreen after an attempted telnet session to a machine:

```
HTTP/1.0 200 OK
Date: Wed, 19 Feb 2014 10:16:22 GMT
Content-Length: 30344
Content-Type: text/html
Expires: Wed, 19 Feb 2014 10:22:22 GMT
Cache-Control: max-age=300
Server: Apache/1.3.33 <Darwin> PHP /4.3.10
Age: 120
```

Which of the following best matches the output provided?

A. An attacker has attempted a zone transfer successfully.

B. An attacker has attempted a zone transfer unsuccessfully.

C. An attacker has successfully grabbed a banner.

D. An attacker has successfully uploaded a denial of service script.

☑ **C.** Alright, I admit it—this was a ridiculously easy one. The command output appears after a typical banner grabbing effort: telnet attempt to the box and press ENTER twice after seeing the standard HEAD / HTTP/1.0 response. You've probably already seen it a hundred times in your testing and in all your practice exams, so be confident you'll see it on your exam too.

☒ **A** and **B** are incorrect because this output obviously has nothing to do with a DNS zone transfer, successful or not.

☒ **D** is incorrect because there is nothing here to indicate a script has been uploaded at all.

Sniffing and Evasion

This chapter includes questions from the following topics:

- Learn about sniffing and protocols that are susceptible to sniffing
- Describe active and passive sniffing
- Describe ethical hacking techniques for layer 2 traffic
- Learn about sniffing tools and displays
- Describe sniffing countermeasures
- Learn about intrusion detection system (IDS) types, use, and placement
- Describe signature analysis within Snort
- List IDS evasion techniques
- Learn about firewall types, use, and placement
- Describe firewall hacking tools and techniques

Overhearing a conversation, whether intentionally or via eavesdropping, is just part of our daily lives. Sometimes we sniff conversations without even meaning or trying to—it just happens. Anyone who's worked in a cube-farm office environment knows how easy it is to overhear conversations even when we don't want to. Or, if you have kids in your house who don't yet understand that sound travels, eavesdropping is a constant part of your day.

Sometimes our very nature makes it impossible not to listen in. A study in *Psychological Science* explored a "paradox of eavesdropping": It's harder to *not* listen to a conversation when someone is talking on the phone (we hear only one side of the dialogue) than when two physically present people are talking to each other. Although the phone conversation contains much less information, we're much more curious about what's being said. That means we're hardwired to want to listen in. We can't help it.

But come on, admit it—you enjoy it sometimes too. Overhearing a juicy piece of information just makes us happy and, for the gossip crowd, provides lots of ammunition for the next watercooler session. And we all really like secrets. In fact, I think the thrill of learning and knowing a secret is matched only by the overwhelming desire to share it. For those working in the classified arena, this paradox of human nature is something that has to be guarded against every single day of their working lives.

Eavesdropping in the virtual world is almost always not accidental—there's purpose involved. You don't necessarily need to put a whole lot of effort into it, but it almost never happens on its own without your purposeful manipulation of something. Sniffing provides all sorts of information to the ethical hacker and is a skill all should be intimately familiar with. Just know that the secrets you overhear on your job as a pen tester might be really exciting, and you might *really* want to tell *somebody* about them, but you may find yourself *really* in jail over it too.

 STUDY TIPS   Just as with the previous chapter, review your basic network knowledge thoroughly. You'll see lots of questions designed to test your knowledge on how networking devices handle traffic, how addressing affects packet flow, and which protocols are susceptible to sniffing. Additionally, learn Wireshark *very* well. Pay particular attention to filters within Wireshark—how to set them up and what syntax they follow—and how to read a capture (not to mention the "follow TCP stream" option). If you haven't already, download Wireshark and start playing with it— right now, before you even read the questions that follow.

IDS types and ways to get around them won't make up a gigantic portion of your test, but they'll definitely be there. Pay particular attention to fragmentation and tunneling.

Snort is another tool you'll need to know inside and out. Be well versed in configuring rules and reading output from a Snort capture/alert. And when it comes to those captures, oftentimes you can peruse an answer just by pulling out port numbers and such, so don't panic when you see them.

Lastly, don't forget your firewall types—you won't see many questions on identifying a definition, but you'll probably see a least a couple of scenario questions where this knowledge comes in handy, in particular how stateful firewalls work and what they do.

1. Given the following Wireshark filter, what is the attacker attempting to view?
   ```
   ((tcp.flags == 0x02) || (tcp.flags == 0x12) ) ||
   ((tcp.flags == 0x10) && (tcp.ack==1) && (tcp.len==0) )
   ```

   A. SYN, SYN/ACK, ACK

   B. SYN, FIN, URG, and PSH

   C. ACK, ACK, SYN, URG

   D. SYN/ACK only

2. A target machine (with a MAC of 12:34:56:AB:CD:EF) is connected to a switch port. An attacker (with a MAC of 78:91:00:ED:BC:A1) is attached to a separate port on the same switch with a packet capture running. There is no spanning of ports or port security in place. Two packets leave the target machine. Message 1 has a destination MAC of E1:22:BA:87:AC:12. Message 2 has a destination MAC of FF:FF:FF:FF:FF:FF. Which of the following statements is true regarding the messages being sent?

   A. The attacker will see message 1.

   B. The attacker will see message 2.

   C. The attacker will see both messages.

   D. The attacker will see neither message.

3. You have successfully tapped into a network subnet of your target organization. You begin an attack by learning all significant MAC addresses on the subnet. After some time, you decide to intercept messages between two hosts. You begin by sending broadcast messages to Host A showing your MAC address as belonging to Host B. Simultaneously, you send messages to Host B showing your MAC address as belonging to Host A. What is being accomplished here?

   A. ARP poisoning to allow you to see all messages from both sides without interrupting their communications process

   B. ARP poisoning to allow you to see messages from Host A to Host B, and vice versa

   C. ARP poisoning to allow you to see messages from Host A destined to any address

   D. ARP poisoning to allow you to see messages from Host B destined to any address

   E. Failed ARP poisoning—you will not be able to see any traffic

4. Which of the following represents the loopback address in IPv6?

A. fe80::/10

B. fc00::/7

C. fec0::/10

D. ::1

5. An attacker has successfully tapped into a network segment and has configured port spanning for his connection, which allows him to see all traffic passing through the switch. Which of the following protocols protects any sensitive data from being seen by this attacker?

A. FTP

B. IMAP

C. Telnet

D. POP

E. SMTP

F. SSH

6. You have a large packet capture file in Wireshark to review. You want to filter traffic to show all packets with an IP address of 192.168.22.5 that contain the string HR_admin. Which of the following filters would accomplish this task?

A. ip.addr==192.168.22.5 &&tcp contains HR_admin

B. ip.addr 192.168.22.5 && "HR_admin"

C. ip.addr 192.168.22.5 &&tcp string ==HR_admin

D. ip.addr==192.168.22.5 + tcp contains tide

7. Which of the following techniques can be used to gather information from a fully switched network or to disable some of the traffic isolation features of a switch? (Choose two.)

A. DHCP starvation

B. MAC flooding

C. Promiscuous mode

D. ARP spoofing

8. Which of the following is true regarding the discovery of sniffers on a network?

A. To discover the sniffer, ping all addresses and examine latency in responses.

B. To discover the sniffer, send ARP messages to all systems and watch for NOARP responses.

C. To discover the sniffer, configure the IDS to watch for NICs in promiscuous mode.

D. It is almost impossible to discover the sniffer on the network.

9. Which of the following could provide useful defense against ARP spoofing? (Choose all that apply.)

   A. Use ARPWALL.

   B. Set all NICs to promiscuous mode.

   C. Use private VLANS.

   D. Use static ARP entries.

10. Examine the following Snort rule:

    ```
    alerttcp !$HOME_NET any -> $HOME_NET 23 (content:
    "admin";msg:"Telnet attempt..admin access";)
    ```

    Which of the following are true regarding the rule? (Choose all that apply.)

    A. This rule will alert on packets coming from the designated home network.

    B. This rule will alert on packets coming from outside the designated home address.

    C. This rule will alert on packets designated for any port, from port 23, containing the "admin" string.

    D. This rule will alert on packets designated on port 23, from any port, containing the "admin" string.

11. You want to begin sniffing, and you have a Windows 7 laptop. You download and install Wireshark but quickly discover your NIC needs to be in "promiscuous mode." What allows you to put your NIC into promiscuous mode?

    A. Installing lmpcap

    B. Installing npcap

    C. Installing winPcap

    D. Installing libPcap

    E. Manipulating the NIC properties through Control Panel, Network and Internet, Change Adapter Settings

12. You are attempting to deliver a payload to a target inside the organization; however, it is behind an IDS. You are concerned about successfully accomplishing your task without alerting the IDS monitoring team. Which of the following methods are possible options? (Choose all that apply.)

    A. Flood the network with fake attacks.

    B. Encrypt the traffic between you and the host.

    C. Session hijacking.

    D. Session splicing.

13. A pen test member has gained access to an open switch port. He configures his NIC for promiscuous mode and sets up a sniffer, plugging his laptop directly into the switch port. He watches traffic as it arrives at the system, looking for specific information to possibly use later. What type of sniffing is being practiced?

    A. Active

    B. Promiscuous

    C. Blind

    D. Passive

    E. Session

14. Which of the following are the best preventive measures to take against DHCP starvation attacks? (Choose two.)

    A. Block all UDP port 67 and 68 traffic.

    B. Enable DHCP snooping on the switch.

    C. Use port security on the switch.

    D. Configure DHCP filters on the switch.

15. What does this line from the Snort configuration file indicate?

    ```
    var RULE_PATH c:\etc\snort\rules
    ```

    A. The configuration variable is not in the proper syntax.

    B. It instructs the Snort engine to write rule violations in this location.

    C. It instructs the Snort engine to compare packets to the rule set named "rules."

    D. It defines the location of the Snort rules.

16. Which of the following tools is the best choice to use in sniffing NFS traffic?

    A. Macof

    B. Snow

    C. Filesnarf

    D. Snort

17. Examine the Snort output shown here:

    ```
    08/28-12:23:13.014491 01:10:BB:17:E3:C5 ->A5:12:B7:55:57:AB type:0x800
    len:0x3C
    190.168.5.12:33541 ->213.132.44.56:23 TCP TTL:128 TOS:0x0 ID:12365

    IpLen:20 DgmLen:48 DF
    ***A**S* Seq: 0xA153BD Ack: 0xA01657 Win: 0x2000 TcpLen: 28
    TCP Options (4) => MSS: 1460 NOP NOPSackOK
    0x0000: 00 02 B3 87 84 25 00 10 5A 01 0D 5B 08 00 45 00  .%..Z..[..E.
    0x0010: 00 30 98 43 40 00 80 06 DE EC C0 A8 01 04 C0 A8  .0.C@...
    0x0020: 01 43 04 DC 01 BB 00 A1 8B BD 00 00 00 00 70 02  .C....p.
    0x0030: 20 00 4C 92 00 00 02 04 05 B4 01 01 04 02        .L.....
    ```

Which of the following is true regarding the packet capture?

A. The capture indicates a NOP sled attack.

B. The capture shows step 2 of a TCP handshake.

C. The packet source is 213.132.44.56.

D. The packet capture shows an SSH session attempt.

18. Your IDS sits on the network perimeter and has been analyzing traffic for a couple of weeks. On arrival one morning, you find the IDS has alerted on a spike in network traffic late the previous evening. Which type of IDS are you using?

A. Stateful

B. Snort

C. Passive

D. Signature based

E. Anomaly based

19. You are performing an ACK scan against a target subnet. You previously verified connectivity to several hosts within the subnet but want to verify all live hosts on the subnet. Your scan, however, is not receiving any replies. Which type of firewall is most likely in use at your location?

A. Packet filtering

B. IPS

C. Stateful

D. Active

20. You are separated from your target subnet by a firewall. The firewall is correctly configured and allows requests only to ports opened by the administrator. In firewalking the device, you find that port 80 is open. Which technique could you employ to send data and commands to or from the target system?

A. Encrypt the data to hide it from the firewall.

B. Use session splicing.

C. Use MAC flooding.

D. Use HTTP tunneling.

21. Which of the following tools can be used to extract application layer data from TCP connections captured in a log file into separate files?

A. Snort

B. Netcat

C. TCPflow

D. Tcpdump

22. Examine the Wireshark filter shown here:

    `ip.src == 192.168.1.1 &&tcp.srcport == 80`

    Which of the following correctly describes the capture filter?

    A. The results will display all traffic from 192.168.1.1 destined for port 80.

    B. The results will display all HTTP traffic to 192.168.1.1.

    C. The results will display all HTTP traffic from 192.168.1.1.

    D. No results will display because of invalid syntax.

23. You need to put the NIC into listening mode on your Linux box, capture packets, and write the results to a log file named my.log. How do you accomplish this with tcpdump?

    A. tcpdump -i eth0 -w my.log

    B. tcpdump -l eth0 -c my.log

    C. tcpdump /i eth0 /w my.log

    D. tcpdump /l eth0 /c my.log

24. Which of the following tools can assist with IDS evasion? (Choose all that apply.)

    A. Whisker

    B. Fragroute

    C. Capsa

    D. Wireshark

    E. ADMmutate

    F. Inundator

25. Which command puts Snort into packet logger mode?

    A. `./snort -dev -l ./log`

    B. `./snort -v`

    C. `./snort -dev -l ./log -h 192.168.1.0/24 -c snort.conf`

    D. None of the above

26. A security administrator is attempting to "lock down" her network and blocks access from internal to external on all external firewall ports except for TCP 80 and TCP 443. An internal user wants to make use of other protocols to access services on remote systems (FTP, as well as some nonstandard port numbers). Which of the following is the most likely choice the user could attempt to communicate with the remote systems over the protocol of her choice?

    A. Use HTTP tunneling.

    B. Send all traffic over UDP instead of TCP.

    C. Crack the firewall and open the ports required for communication.

    D. MAC flood the switch connected to the firewall.

1. A

2. B

3. B

4. D

5. F

6. A

7. B, D

8. D

9. A, C, D

10. B, D

11. C

12. B, D

13. D

14. B, C

15. D

16. C

17. B

18. E

19. C

20. D

21. C

22. C

23. A

24. A, B, E, F

25. A

26. A

1. Given the following Wireshark filter, what is the attacker attempting to view?

   ```
   ((tcp.flags == 0x02) || (tcp.flags == 0x18) ) ||
   ((tcp.flags == 0x16) && (tcp.ack==1) && (tcp.len==0) )
   ```

   A. SYN, SYN/ACK, ACK

   B. SYN, FIN, URG, and PSH

   C. ACK, ACK, SYN, URG

   D. SYN/ACK only

   ☑ **A.** You'll see bunches of Wireshark questions on your exam, and EC-Council just *loves* the "TCP flags = decimal numbers" side of it all. Wireshark also has the ability to filter based on a decimal numbering system assigned to TCP flags. The assigned flag decimal numbers are FIN = 1, SYN = 2, RST = 4, PSH = 8, ACK = 16, and URG = 32. Adding these numbers together (for example, SYN + ACK = 18) allows you to simplify a Wireshark filter. For example, tcp.flags == 0x2 looks for SYN packets, tcp.flags == 0x16 looks for ACK packets, and tcp.flags == 0x18 looks for both (the attacker here will see all SYN packets, all SYN/ACK packets, and all ACK packets). In this example, the decimal numbers were used, just not in a simplified manner.

   ☒ **B, C,** and **D** are incorrect because these do not match the decimals provided in the capture (2 for SYN, 18 for SYN/ACK, and 16 for ACK).

2. A target machine (with a MAC of 12:34:56:AB:CD:EF) is connected to a switch port. An attacker (with a MAC of 78:91:00:ED:BC:A1) is attached to a separate port on the same switch with a packet capture running. There is no spanning of ports or port security in place. Two packets leave the target machine. Message 1 has a destination MAC of E1:22:BA:87:AC:12. Message 2 has a destination MAC of FF:FF:FF:FF:FF:FF. Which of the following statements is true regarding the messages being sent?

   A. The attacker will see message 1.

   B. The attacker will see message 2.

   C. The attacker will see both messages.

   D. The attacker will see neither message.

   ☑ **B.** *This question is all about how a switch works,* with a little MAC knowledge thrown in. Remember that switches are designed to filter unicast messages but to flood multicast and broadcast messages (filtering goes to only one port, whereas flooding sends to all). Broadcast MAC addresses in the frame are easy to spot—they're always all *F*s, indicating all 48 bits turned on in the address. In this case, message 1 is a unicast address and went off to its destination, whereas message 2 is clearly a broadcast message, which the switch will gladly flood to all ports, including the attacker's.

☒ **A** is incorrect because the unicast destination MAC does not match the attacker's machine. When the frame is read by the switch and compared to the internal address list (CAM table), it will be filtered and sent to the appropriate destination port.

☒ **C** is incorrect because the switch will not flood both messages to the attacker's port—it floods only broadcast and multicast.

☒ **D** is incorrect because the broadcast address will definitely be seen by the attacker.

3. You have successfully tapped into a network subnet of your target organization. You begin an attack by learning all significant MAC addresses on the subnet. After some time, you decide to intercept messages between two hosts. You begin by sending broadcast messages to Host A showing your MAC address as belonging to Host B. Simultaneously, you send messages to Host B showing your MAC address as belonging to Host A. What is being accomplished here?

   A. ARP poisoning to allow you to see all messages from both sides without interrupting their communications process

   B. ARP poisoning to allow you to see messages from Host A to Host B, and vice versa

   C. ARP poisoning to allow you to see messages from Host A destined to any address

   D. ARP poisoning to allow you to see messages from Host B destined to any address

   E. Failed ARP poisoning—you will not be able to see any traffic

   ☑ **B.** ARP poisoning is a relatively simple way to place yourself as the "man in the middle" and spy on traffic. (By the way, be careful with the term *man in the middle* because it usually refers to a position where you are not interrupting traffic.) The ARP cache is updated whenever your machine does a name lookup or when ARP (a broadcast protocol) receives an unsolicited message advertising a MAC-to-IP match. In this example, you've told Host A and Host B that you hold the MAC address for Host B and Host A, respectively. Both machines will update their cache, and when a message is being crafted by the OS, it will happily put the spoofed address in its place. Just remember that ARP poisoning is oftentimes noisy and may be easy to discover if port security is enabled: The port will lock (or *amber* in nerd terminology) when an incorrect MAC tries to use it or when multiple broadcasts claiming different MACs are seen. Additionally, watch out for denial-of-service side effects of attempting ARP poisoning—you may well bring down a target without even trying to.

   ☒ **A** is incorrect for a couple reasons. First, you won't receive messages from each host addressed to anywhere in the world—you'll only receive messages addressed from one to the other, and vice versa. Second, the communications flow between the two hosts will be affected by this. As a matter of fact, neither machine can talk to the other, even if you wanted to: The ARP poisoning has all messages going to the hacker.

☒ **C** is incorrect for a couple reasons. First, it's referencing only one host when the ARP poisoning is in both directions. Second, you would not get messages from Host A to any destination—only those that are addressed to Host B.

☒ **D** is incorrect for a couple reasons. First, it's referencing only one host when the ARP poisoning is in both directions. Second, you would not get messages from Host B to everywhere—only those that are addressed to Host A.

☒ **E** is incorrect because the ARP poisoning should work fine here, and you will see traffic between the two hosts.

4. Which of the following represents the loopback address in IPv6?

   A. fe80::/10

   B. fc00::/7

   C. fec0::/10

   D. ::1

   ☑ **D.** You won't get a ton of IPv6 questions on the exam, but I can almost guarantee you'll see some variant of this on it. In IPv4, the loopback address was 127.0.0.1. In IPv6, addressing was changed and now uses a 128-bit address instead of the 32-bit IPv4 version. It's represented as eight groups of four hexadecimal digits separated by colons but can be shortened in display by removing leading zeroes (replaced by a double colon). The loopback address, in full, is 0000:0000:0000:0000:0000:0000:0000:0001, which can be reduced all the way down to ::1.

   ☒ **A** is incorrect because this represents the address block reserved for link-local addressing.

   ☒ **B** is incorrect because this represents the unique local address (the counterpart of IPv4 private addressing) block.

   ☒ **C** is incorrect because prefixes for site local addresses will always be fec0::/10.

5. An attacker has successfully tapped into a network segment and has configured port spanning for his connection, which allows him to see all traffic passing through the switch. Which of the following protocols protects any sensitive data from being seen by this attacker?

   A. FTP

   B. IMAP

C. Telnet

D. POP

E. SMTP

F. SSH

☑ **F.** The biggest deterrent you have to sniffing is encryption (as an aside, it's also the biggest threat to an IDS, but that's for a different question). All the protocols listed here are susceptible to sniffing in one way or another because they pass information in the clear—that is, with no encryption. SSH is the only one listed that provides secured transmission and is, therefore, the only correct answer. The CEH exam objective here is to ensure you know which protocols pass information in the clear—thus making them easy to sniff—and which do not.

☒ **A** is incorrect because FTP sends its passwords and all data in clear text. If you're sniffing the wire and someone logs in with FTP—*voilà!*—you've got it all.

☒ **B** is incorrect because IMAP also passes all information—including passwords—in the clear.

☒ **C** is incorrect because Telnet is another open protocol, passing everything in the clear.

☒ **D** is incorrect because POP sends all information in clear text.

☒ **E** is incorrect because SMTP also sends everything in clear text—just look at your e-mail headers if you doubt me.

6. You have a large packet capture file in Wireshark to review. You want to filter traffic to show all packets with an IP address of 192.168.22.5 that contain the string HR_admin. Which of the following filters would accomplish this task?

A. ip.addr==192.168.22.5 &&tcp contains HR_admin

B. ip.addr 192.168.22.5 && "HR_admin"

C. ip.addr 192.168.22.5 &&tcp string ==HR_admin

D. ip.addr==192.168.22.5 + tcp contains tide

☑ **A.** This is a perfect example of a typical Wireshark question on your exam (and you will see a couple). This is the only answer that sticks to Wireshark filter syntax. Definitely know the ip.addr, ip.src, and ip.dst filters; the "tcp contains" filter is another favorite of test question writers. When you combine filters in one search, use the && designator.

☒ **B, C,** and **D** are all incorrect because the syntax is wrong for Wireshark filters. As an aside, a great way to learn the syntax of these filters is to use the expression builder directly beside the filter entry box. It's self-explanatory and contains thousands of possible expression builds.

7. Which of the following techniques can be used to gather information from a fully switched network or to disable some of the traffic isolation features of a switch? (Choose two.)

   A. DHCP starvation

   B. MAC flooding

   C. Promiscuous mode

   D. ARP spoofing

   ☑ **B** and **D**. Switches filter all traffic—unless you tell them otherwise, make them behave differently, or the traffic is broadcast or multicast. If you can gain administrative access to the IOS, you can tell it to behave otherwise by configuring a span port (which sends copies of messages from all ports to yours). Legitimate span ports are designed for things such as network IDS. To make the switch behave differently (at least on older switches because newer ones don't allow this much anymore), send more MAC addresses to the switch than it can handle. This fills the CAM and turns the switch, effectively, into a hub (sometimes called a *fail open* state). Using a tool such as MacOF or Yersinia, you can send thousands and thousands of fake MAC addresses to the switch's CAM table. ARP spoofing doesn't really involve the switch much at all—it continues to act and filter traffic just as it was designed to do. The only difference is you've lied to it by faking a MAC address on a connected port. The poor switch, believing those happy little ARP messages, will forward all packets destined for that MAC address to you instead of the intended recipient. How fun!

   ☒ **A** is incorrect because DHCP starvation is a form of a DoS attack, where the attacker "steals" all the available IP addresses from the DHCP server, which prevents legitimate users from connecting.

   ☒ **C** is incorrect because the term *promiscuous* applies to the way a NIC processes messages. Instead of tossing aside all messages that are not addressed specifically for the machine (or broadcast/multicast), promiscuous mode says, "Bring 'em all in so we can take a look at them using our handy sniffing application."

8. Which of the following is true regarding the discovery of sniffers on a network?

   A. To discover the sniffer, ping all addresses and examine latency in responses.

   B. To discover the sniffer, send ARP messages to all systems and watch for NOARP responses.

   C. To discover the sniffer, configure the IDS to watch for NICs in promiscuous mode.

   D. It is almost impossible to discover the sniffer on the network.

☑ **D.** I'm not saying it's impossible, because almost nothing is, but discovering a sniffer on your network is difficult. When a NIC is set to promiscuous mode, it just blindly accepts any packet coming by and sends it up the layers for further processing (which is what allows Wireshark and other sniffers to analyze the traffic). Because they're sitting there pulling traffic and not sending anything in order to get it, they're difficult to detect. Certainly if a machine is ARP spoofing or MAC flooding in order to pull off sniffing, it's easy to spot them, but passive sniffing is difficult.

☒ **A** is incorrect because the premise is absolutely silly. Thousands of things can affect latency in response to a ping, but running a sniffer on the box isn't necessarily one of them, nor an indicator of one being present.

☒ **B** is incorrect because NOARP is a Linux kernel module that filters and drops unwanted ARP requests. It's not a response packet we can discover sniffers with.

☒ **C** is incorrect because it's impossible to watch for NICs in promiscuous mode. The NIC is simply doing the same job every other NIC is doing—it's sitting there pulling traffic. The network IDS wouldn't know, or care, about it.

9. Which of the following could provide useful defense against ARP spoofing? (Choose all that apply.)

   A. Use ARPWALL.

   B. Set all NICs to promiscuous mode.

   C. Use private VLANS.

   D. Use static ARP entries.

   ☑ **A, C, and D.** ARPWALL (http://sourceforge.net/projects/arpwall/) is an application available for download from SourceForge. It gives an early warning when an ARP attack occurs and simply blocks the connection. Virtual LANs (VLANS) provide a means to create multiple broadcast domains within a single network. Machines on the same switch are in different networks, and their traffic is isolated. Since ARP works on broadcast, this can help prevent large-scale ARP spoofing. Static ARP entries are a great idea and probably the only true way to fix it all, since no matter what is banging around out on the network, the system uses the static mapping you configured. An IDS may also be helpful in spotting ARP naughtiness starting but wouldn't necessarily do anything about it.

   ☒ **B** is incorrect because setting NICS to promiscuous mode wouldn't do a thing to prevent a broadcast message (ARP) from being received.

10. Examine the following Snort rule:

```
alerttcp !$HOME_NET any -> $HOME_NET 23 (content:
"admin";msg:"Telnet attempt..admin access";)
```

Which of the following are true regarding the rule? (Choose all that apply.)

A. This rule will alert on packets coming from the designated home network.

B. This rule will alert on packets coming from outside the designated home address.

C. This rule will alert on packets designated for any port, from port 23, containing the "admin" string.

D. This rule will alert on packets designated on port 23, from any port, containing the "admin" string.

☑ **B** and **D**. Snort rules, logs, entries, and configuration files will definitely be part of your exam. This particular rule takes into account a lot of things you'll see. First, note the exclamation mark (!) just before the HOME_NET variable. Any time you see this, it indicates the opposite of the following variable—in this case, any packet from an address *not* in the home network and using any source port number, intended for any address that is within the home network. Following that variable is a spot for a port number, and the word *any* indicates we don't care what the source port is. Next, we spell out the destination information: anything in the home network and destined for port 23. Lastly, we add one more little search before spelling out the message we want to receive: The "content" designator allows us to spell out strings we're looking for.

☒ **A** and **C** are incorrect because these statements are polar opposite to what the rule is stating.

11. You want to begin sniffing, and you have a Windows 7 laptop. You download and install Wireshark but quickly discover your NIC needs to be in "promiscuous mode." What allows you to put your NIC into promiscuous mode?

A. Installing lmpcap

B. Installing npcap

C. Installing winPcap

D. Installing libPcap

E. Manipulating the NIC properties through Control Panel, Network and Internet, Change Adapter Settings

☑ **C**. To understand this, you have to know how a NIC is designed to work. The NIC "sees" lots of traffic but pulls in only the traffic it knows belongs to you. It does this by comparing the MAC address of each frame against its own: If they match, it pulls the frame in and works on it; if they don't match, the frame is ignored. If you plug a sniffer into a NIC that looks only at traffic designated for the machine you're on, you've kind of missed the point, wouldn't you say? Promiscuous mode tells the NIC to pull in *everything*. This allows you to see all those packets moving to and fro inside your collision domain. WinPcap is a library that allows NICs on Windows machines to operate in promiscuous mode.

☒ **A** is incorrect because lmpcap does not exist.

☒ **B** is incorrect because npcap does not exist.

☒ **D** is incorrect because libPcap is used on Linux machines for the same purpose—putting cards into promiscuous mode.

☒ **E** is incorrect because accessing the Change Adapter Setting window does not allow you to put the card into promiscuous mode—you still need winPcap for this.

12. You are attempting to deliver a payload to a target inside the organization; however, it is behind an IDS. You are concerned about successfully accomplishing your task without alerting the IDS monitoring team. Which of the following methods are possible options? (Choose all that apply.)

   A. Flood the network with fake attacks.

   B. Encrypt the traffic between you and the host.

   C. Session hijacking.

   D. Session splicing.

☑ **B** and **D**. Encryption has always been the enemy of network IDS. After all, if the traffic is encrypted and we can't see it, what good does it do to have a monitoring system look at the garbled bits? Granted, it would seem difficult to set up encryption between the target host and yourself, but it is plausible and, therefore, a good answer. Session splicing is a great tool to use as well. In session splicing, you put a payload into packets the IDS usually ignores, such as SYN segments. The fragments can then be reassembled later on the target machine. (If you want to get really sneaky, send them out of order.)

☒ **A** is incorrect, but just barely so. Yes, flooding a network with fake attacks can definitely work. The cover fire from all the other attacks *should* allow you to sneak by. However, there is no way to accomplish this without alerting the monitoring team—after all, the objective is to keep them busy looking at all those fake attacks long enough for you to pull off a real one. Keep in mind that if you're going to attempt this method, you'll need a block of sacrificial IP addresses you won't mind losing. The security staff will, no doubt, see your initial attempts and start blocking those IPs from network access. If you're hoping to provide cover fire for a "real" attack, you'll need to have plenty of "pawn" IPs to sacrifice.

☒ **C** is incorrect because session hijacking has almost nothing to do with IDS evasion. It has a lot to do with guessing sequence numbers and leaping into the middle of an existing, already-authenticated communications channel, but we're not on that chapter yet. Granted, you may be able to make use of some firewall applications or web sessions to bypass some IDS filters, but that's not the intent of this question (nor is that how it will be phrased on your exam).

13. A pen test member has gained access to an open switch port. He configures his NIC for promiscuous mode and sets up a sniffer, plugging his laptop directly into the switch port. He watches traffic as it arrives at the system, looking for specific information to possibly use later. What type of sniffing is being practiced?

    A. Active

    B. Promiscuous

    C. Blind

    D. Passive

    E. Session

    ☑ **D.** This is one of those weird CEH definitions that drive us all crazy on the exam. Knowing the definition of *passive* versus *active* isn't really going to make you a better pen tester, but it may save you a question on the test. When it comes to sniffing, if you are not injecting packets into the stream, it's a passive exercise. Tools such as Wireshark are passive in nature. A tool such as Ettercap, though, has built-in features to trick switches into sending all traffic their way, and all sorts of other sniffing hilarity. This type of sniffing, where you use packet interjection to force a response, is active in nature. As a quick aside here for you real-world preppers out there, true passive sniffing with a laptop is pretty difficult to pull off. As soon as you attach a Windows machine, it'll start broadcasting all kinds of stuff (ARP, etc.) which is, technically, putting packets on the wire. The real point is that passive sniffing is a mind-set where you are not *intentionally* putting packets on a wire.

    ☒ **A** is incorrect because in the example given, no packet injection is being performed. The pen tester is simply hooking up a sniffer and watching what comes by. The only way this can be more passive is if he has a hammock nearby.

    ☒ **B** is incorrect because the term *promiscuous* is not a sniffing type. Instead, it refers to the NIC's ability to pull in frames that are not addressed specifically for it.

    ☒ **C** is incorrect because the term *blind* is not a sniffing type. This is included as a distractor.

    ☒ **E** is incorrect because the term *session* is not a sniffing type. This is included as a distractor.

14. Which of the following are the best preventive measures to take against DHCP starvation attacks? (Choose two.)

    A. Block all UDP port 67 and 68 traffic.

    B. Enable DHCP snooping on the switch.

C. Use port security on the switch.

D. Configure DHCP filters on the switch.

☑ **B and C.** DHCP starvation is a denial-of-service attack EC-Council somehow slipped into the sniffing section. The attack is pretty straightforward: The attacker requests all available DHCP addresses from the server, so legitimate users cannot pull an address and connect or communicate with the network subnet. DHCP snooping on a Cisco switch (using the ip dhcp snooping command) creates a whitelist of machines that are allowed to pull a DHCP address. Anything attempting otherwise can be filtered. Port security, while not necessarily directly related to the attack, can be a means of defense as well. By limiting the number of MACs associated with a port, as well as whitelisting which specific MACs can address it, you could certainly reduce an attacker's ability to drain all DHCP addresses.

☒ **A** is incorrect because blocking all UDP 67 and 68 traffic would render the entire DHCP system moot because no one could pull an address.

☒ **D** is incorrect because DHCP filtering is done on the server and not the switch. DHCP filtering is configuring the whitelist on the server itself.

15. What does this line from the Snort configuration file indicate?

```
var RULE_PATH c:\etc\snort\rules
```

A. The configuration variable is not in proper syntax.

B. It instructs the Snort engine to write rule violations in this location.

C. It instructs the Snort engine to compare packets to the rule set named "rules."

D. It defines the location of the Snort rules.

☑ **D.** The var RULE_PATH entry in the config file defines the path to the rules for the IDS—in this case, they will be located in C:\etc\snort\rules. The rules container will hold tons of rule sets, with each available for you to "turn on." If you were configuring Snort to watch for fantasy football traffic, for example, you would tell it to look for all the rules in this container and then turn on the rule set you defined for fantasy football connection attempts.

☒ **A** is incorrect because this configuration line is in proper syntax.

☒ **B** is incorrect because this variable is not designed for that purpose. The rule violations will be written to a log file that you designate when starting the Snort engine. For example, the command

```
snort -l c:\snort\log\ -c c:\snort\etc\snort.conf
```

starts Snort and has the log file located at c:\snort\log.

☒ **C** is incorrect because the "include" variable is the one used for this purpose. Within this same configuration file, for example, you may have a rule set named fantasy.rules. To get Snort to alert on them, you point the configuration files to where all the rules are (accomplished by the variable RULE_PATH), and then you tell it which of the rule sets to bring into play:

```
include $RULE_PATH/fantasy.rules
```

16. Which of the following tools is the best choice to use in sniffing NFS traffic?

    A. Macof

    B. Snow

    C. Filesnarf

    D. Snort

    ☑ **C.** In yet another specific tool knowledge question, EC-Council wants you to know that filesnarf (www.irongeek.com/i.php?page=backtrack-3-man/filesnarf) is designed specifically with NFS in mind. It saves files sniffed from NFS traffic into the current working directory.

    ☒ **A** is incorrect because macof is a MAC flooding tool.

    ☒ **B** is incorrect because snow is a steganography tool.

    ☒ **D** is incorrect because Snort, while a perfectly acceptable sniffer, isn't designed specifically for NFS and isn't the best choice available here.

17. Examine the Snort output shown here:

```
08/28-12:23:13.014491 01:10:BB:17:E3:C5 ->A5:12:B7:55:57:AB type:0x800
len:0x3C
190.168.5.12:33541 ->213.132.44.56:23 TCP TTL:128 TOS:0x0 ID:12365

IpLen:20 DgmLen:48 DF
***A**S* Seq: 0xA153BD Ack: 0xA01657 Win: 0x2000 TcpLen: 28
TCP Options (4) => MSS: 1460 NOP NOPSackOK
0x0000: 00 02 B3 87 84 25 00 10 5A 01 0D 5B 08 00 45 00 .%..Z..[..E.
0x0010: 00 30 98 43 40 00 80 06 DE EC C0 A8 01 04 C0 A8 .0.C@...
0x0020: 01 43 04 DC 01 BB 00 A1 8B BD 00 00 00 00 70 02 .C....p.
0x0030: 20 00 4C 92 00 00 02 04 05 B4 01 01 04 02 .L.....
```

    Which of the following is true regarding the packet capture?

    A. The capture indicates a NOP sled attack.

    B. The capture shows step 2 of a TCP handshake.

    C. The packet source is 213.132.44.56.

    D. The packet capture shows an SSH session attempt.

    ☑ **B.** You'll probably see at least one or two Snort capture logs on the exam, and most of them are just this easy. If you examine the capture log, it shows a TCP port 23 packet from 190.168.5.12 headed toward 213.132.44.56. The

TCP flags are clearly shown in line 5 as ***A**S*, indicating the SYN and ACK flags are set. Because the three-way handshake is SYN, SYN/ACK, and ACK—*voilà!*—we've solved another one!

☒ **A** is incorrect because this is a single packet that is not attempting a NOP sled in any shape or form.

☒ **C** is incorrect because this answer has it in reverse—the source is 190.168.5.12.

☒ **D** is incorrect because the port number shown in the capture is 23 (Telnet), not 22 (SSH).

18. Your IDS sits on the network perimeter and has been analyzing traffic for a couple of weeks. On arrival one morning, you find the IDS has alerted on a spike in network traffic late the previous evening. Which type of IDS are you using?

   A. Stateful

   B. Snort

   C. Passive

   D. Signature based

   E. Anomaly based

   ☑ **E.** The scenario described here is precisely what an anomaly- or behavior-based system is designed for. The system watches traffic and, over time, develops an idea of what "normal" traffic looks like—everything from source and destinations, ports in use, and times of higher data flows. In one sense, it's better than a plain signature-based system because it can find things heuristically based on behavior; however, anomaly-based systems are notorious for the number of false positives they spin off—especially early on.

   ☒ **A** is incorrect because *stateful* refers to a firewall type, not an IDS.

   ☒ **B** is incorrect because Snort is a signature-based IDS.

   ☒ **C** is incorrect because the term *passive* isn't associated with IDS. Now, an IDS *can* react to an alert by taking action to stop or prevent an attack, but this is referred to as an *intrusion prevention system (IPS)*, not active or passive.

   ☒ **D** is incorrect because a signature-based IDS isn't going to care about the amount of traffic going by, nor what time it decides to do so. A signature-based IDS simply compares each packet against a list (signature file) you configure it to look at. If it doesn't match anything in the signature file, then no action is taken.

19. You are performing an ACK scan against a target subnet. You previously verified connectivity to several hosts within the subnet but want to verify all live hosts on the subnet. Your scan, however, is not receiving any replies. Which type of firewall is most likely in use at your location?

A. Packet filtering

B. IPS

C. Stateful

D. Active

☑ **C.** Most people think of a firewall as a simple packet filter, examining packets as they are coming in against an access list—if the port is allowed, let the packet through. However, the stateful inspection firewall has the ability to examine all sorts of information about a packet—including the payload—and make a determination on the state of the packet. For a common (dare I say, textbook) example, if a stateful firewall receives an ACK packet, it's smart enough to know whether there is an associated SYN packet that originated from inside the network to go along with it. If there isn't not—that is, if communications did not start from inside the subnet—it'll drop the packet.

☒ **A** is incorrect because a packet-filtering firewall wouldn't bother with the flags. It would be concerned about what port the packet was headed to. If, for instance, you host a web page out of that subnet but not an FTP server, your firewall should be set up to allow port 80 in but not port 21.

☒ **B** is incorrect because an intrusion prevention system (IPS) isn't a firewall at all. It's a network-monitoring solution that has the capability of recognizing malicious traffic and taking action to prevent or stop the attack.

☒ **D** is incorrect because the term *active* is not associated with a firewall type. This is included as a distractor.

20. You are separated from your target subnet by a firewall. The firewall is correctly configured and allows requests only to ports opened by the administrator. In firewalking the device, you find that port 80 is open. Which technique could you employ to send data and commands to or from the target system?

A. Encrypt the data to hide it from the firewall.

B. Use session splicing.

C. Use MAC flooding.

D. Use HTTP tunneling.

☑ **D.** HTTP tunneling is a successful "hacking" technique, but it's hardly new. Microsoft makes use of HTTP tunneling for lots of things, and it has been doing so for years. The tactic is fairly simple: Because port 80 is almost never filtered by a firewall, you can craft port 80 segments to carry a payload for protocols the firewall may have otherwise blocked. Of course, you'll need something on the other end to pull the payload out of all those port 80 packets that IIS is desperately wanting to answer, but that's not altogether difficult.

☒ **A** is incorrect because encryption won't do a thing for you here. The firewall isn't looking necessarily at content/payload—it's looking at the packet/frame header and port information. Encryption is a good choice to get around an IDS, not a firewall.

☒ **B** is incorrect because session splicing is a technique for evading an IDS, not a firewall. Again, the firewall is interested in the packet and frame header, not what fragments of code you've hidden in the payload.

☒ **C** is incorrect because MAC flooding is a technique for sniffing switches. The idea is to fill the CAM table to the brim with thousands of useless MAC addresses. This effectively turns the switch into a hub, because it is too confused to filter and just begins flooding all traffic to all ports.

21. Which of the following tools can be used to extract application layer data from TCP connections captured in a log file into separate files?

    A. Snort

    B. Netcat

    C. TCPflow

    D. Tcpdump

    ☑ **C.** TCPflow (https://github.com/simsong/tcpflow/wiki/tcpflow-%E2%80%94-A-tcp-ip-session-reassembler) is "a program that captures data transmitted as part of TCP connections (flows), and stores the data in a way that is convenient for protocol analysis and debugging. Each TCP flow is stored in its own file. Thus, the typical TCP flow will be stored in two files, one for each direction. tcpflow can also process stored 'tcpdump' packet flows. tcpflow is similar to 'tcpdump', in that both process packets from the wire or from a stored file. But it's different in that it reconstructs the actual data streams and stores each flow in a separate file for later analysis."

    ☒ **A** is incorrect because Snort is a great IDS, sniffer, and packet logger, but it isn't so great about separating TCP streams for application layer analysis.

    ☒ **B** is incorrect because netcat (the Swiss Army knife of hacking, as it's called) isn't designed for sniffing and packet analysis.

    ☒ **D** is incorrect because tcpdump will certainly pull everything for you but does not reconstruct the actual data streams or store each flow in a separate file for later analysis.

22. Examine the Wireshark filter shown here:

    ```
    ip.src == 192.168.1.1 &&tcp.srcport == 80
    ```

Which of the following correctly describes the capture filter?

A. The results will display all traffic from 192.168.1.1 destined for port 80.

B. The results will display all HTTP traffic to 192.168.1.1.

C. The results will display all HTTP traffic from 192.168.1.1.

D. No results will display because of invalid syntax.

☑ **C.** Wireshark filters will be covered quite a bit on your exam, and, as stated earlier, these are easy questions for you. The preceding syntax designates the source IP and combines it with a source TCP port. This is effectively looking at all answers to port 80 requests by 192.168.1.1. As another important study tip, watch for the period (.) between "ip" and "src:" on the exam because they'll drop it or change it to a dash (-) to trick you. And lastly, for real-world application, it's important to note that Wireshark considers certain friendly terms such as HTTP as simple placeholders for the actual port. This means in Wireshark, HTTP and 80 are more or less identical. As a budding ethical hacker, you should know by now that even though something is traveling on port 80, it may or may not be HTTP traffic.

☒ **A** is incorrect because port 80 is defined as the *source* port, not the destination. 192.168.1.1 is answering a request for an HTML page.

☒ **B** is incorrect because 192.168.1.1 is defined as the *source* address, not the destination.

☒ **D** is incorrect because the syntax is indeed correct.

23. You need to put the NIC into listening mode on your Linux box, capture packets, and write the results to a log file named my.log. How do you accomplish this with tcpdump?

A. tcpdump -i eth0 -w my.log

B. tcpdump -l eth0 -c my.log

C. tcpdump/i eth0 /w my.log

D. tcpdump/l eth0 /c my.log

☑ **A.** Tcpdump syntax is simple: tcpdump *flag(s) interface*. The –i flag specifies the interface (in this example, eth0) for tcpdump to listen on, and the –w flag defines where you want your packet log to go. For your own study, be aware that many study references—including EC-Council's official reference books—state that the –i flag "puts the interface into listening mode." It doesn't actually modify the interface at all, so this is a little bit of a misnomer—it just identifies to tcpdump which interface to listen on for traffic. Lastly, be aware that the –w flag dumps traffic in binary format. If you want it readable, you'll need to have it display onscreen. Better yet, you can dump it to a file using the | designator and a filename.

☒ **B** is incorrect because the –l flag does not put the interface in listening mode; it actually has to do with line buffering.

☒ **C** and **D** are incorrect for the same reason; flags are designated with a dash (-) not a slash (/).

24. Which of the following tools can assist with IDS evasion? (Choose all that apply.)

    A. Whisker

    B. Fragroute

    C. Capsa

    D. Wireshark

    E. ADMmutate

    F. Inundator

    ☑ **A, B, E,** and **F.** IDS evasion comes down to a few methods: encryption, flooding, and fragmentation (session splicing). Whisker is an HTTP scanning tool but also has the ability to craft session-splicing fragments. Fragroute intercepts, modifies, and rewrites egress traffic destined for the specified host and can be used to fragment an attack payload over multiple packets. ADMmutate can create multiple scripts that won't be easily recognizable by signature files, and Inundator is a flooding tool that can help you hide in the cover fire.

    ☒ **C** and **D** are incorrect because both Capsa (Colasoft) and Wireshark are sniffers.

25. Which command puts Snort into packet logger mode?

    A. ./snort -dev -l ./log

    B. ./snort –v

    C. ./snort -dev -l ./log -h 192.168.1.0/24 -c snort.conf

    D. None of the above

    ☑ **A.** This is the proper syntax to start Snort in packet logger mode. Assuming you have the /log folder created, Snort will start happily logging packets as it captures them. Here are some other flags of note within this command:

    - –v puts Snort in verbose mode, to look at all packets.

    - –d includes the application layer information, when used with the –v argument.

    - –e includes the data link layer information with the packet.

    When put altogether, the –dev arguments tell Snort to display all packet data, including the headers.

☒ **B** is incorrect because this syntax starts Snort in sniffer mode, meaning packet headers will be displayed directly to the screen.

☒ **C** is incorrect because this syntax starts Snort in network intrusion detection mode. Yes, the –l switch logs files, but the bigger issue for you here is the addition of the –c switch, indicating the configuration file the NIDS needs.

☒ **D** is incorrect because the correct syntax is indeed displayed.

26. A security administrator is attempting to "lock down" her network and blocks access from internal to external on all external firewall ports except for TCP 80 and TCP 443. An internal user wants to make use of other protocols to access services on remote systems (FTP, as well as some nonstandard port numbers). Which of the following is the most likely choice the user could attempt to communicate with the remote systems over the protocol of her choice?

   A. HTTP tunneling.

   B. Send all traffic over UDP instead of TCP.

   C. Crack the firewall and open the ports required for communication.

   D. MAC flood the switch connected to the firewall.

   ☑ **A.** If you happen to own the companion book to this practice exams tome, you're undoubtedly aware by now we harp on protocols not necessarily being tied to a given port number in the real world. Sure, FTP is supposed to be on TCP port 21, SMTP is supposed to ride on 25, and Telnet is supposed to be on 23, but the dirty little truth is *they don't have to*. An HTTP tunnel is a brilliant example of this. To the firewall and everyone else watching, traffic from your machine is riding harmless little old port 80—nothing to see here folks, just plain old, regular HTTP traffic. But a peek inside that harmless little tunnel shows you can run *anything you want*. Typically you connect to an external server over port 80, and it will unwrap and forward your other protocol traffic for you, once you've gotten it past your pesky firewall.

   ☒ **B** is incorrect because, well, this is just a ridiculous answer. UDP ports are filtered by a firewall just like TCP ports, so sending only UDP would be useless.

   ☒ **C** is incorrect because while it would certainly allow the communication, it wouldn't be for very long. Every sensor on the network would be screaming, and the happy little security admin would lock it back down ASAP. Not to mention, you'd get fired.

   ☒ **D** is incorrect because MAC flooding refers to active sniffing on a switch, not bypassing a firewall.

Attacking a System

This chapter includes questions from the following topics:
- Describe password attacks
- Describe best-effort password complexity and protection
- Describe Microsoft authentication mechanisms
- Understand Windows architecture
- Identify various password-cracking tools, keyloggers, and spyware technologies
- Define privilege escalation
- Describe file-hiding methods, alternate data streams, and evidence erasure
- Define rootkit
- Understand basic Linux file structure, directories, and commands

I hope nobody reading this will ever find themselves in this situation, but have you ever given any thought at all to what you would do if challenged to a fight? I'm not talking about the free-for-all brawls in elementary and middle school, surrounded by a circle of cheering, but ignorant, children; I'm talking about an actual street confrontation you cannot get out of. In almost every situation, most people are taught to leave the situation and protect themselves, and that's absolutely the right way to go. But every once in a while, good law-abiding folks are put in a situation they can't get out of, and a physical confrontation is inevitable.

Did you know there's a science to hand-to-hand combat? Pugilism (*pygmachia* in Greek, made into an Olympic sport in 688 BC) is the hand-to-hand combat sport better known as boxing. Despite the circus it has become in the past 20 years or so, boxing was a well-respected and carefully studied art for thousands of years. It's not just simply putting two guys in a ring and having them beat on each other; it's about crafting a strategy to accentuate strengths and exploit weaknesses. Sound familiar?

And we're not talking about just boxing here—hand-to-hand combat takes on many forms. Professional boxers, for example, might tell you that light punches are faster, require less energy, and leave you less vulnerable. They might also advise you that deception and speed in combat are much more valuable than strength and the "knockout punch." Self-defense experts might point out areas of the human anatomy that disable an attacker, providing you a means of escape. They might also point out things like the value of a knife versus a gun in defense situations and that one cleverly executed strike, set up and thrown with quickness (sometimes not even with power), may be all it takes to frustrate and confuse an attacker. The science of carrying out a physical attack on an individual, and protecting yourself against such an attack, is founded on the principles of distance, leverage, and timing. It's fascinating stuff, even if you don't ever plan on being in a situation requiring the knowledge.

You may be sitting there having no idea what kind of virtual damage you can do with the knowledge you've gained so far. Who knows if, put in the right situation, you'd knock out virtual targets with ease? I can see you now, looking down at your keyboard in awe and answering the "How did you do that?" question with, "I don't know—the training just kicked in." Granted, we still have a lot of training to do, and I doubt you'll be punching any virtual targets outside an agreed-upon scope (after all, you are an ethical hacker, right?). However, this chapter will help hone your skills. Here, we'll talk all about system attacks and putting to use some of the training and knowledge you already have in place.

STUDY TIPS System attacks come in many forms, but EC-Council *really* likes the password attacks. Know your password rules, attacks, and tools well. You will definitely see loads of questions about passwords, and the use, storage, hashing of, and attacks against passwords will be covered *ad nauseam* on your exam. Pull some of these tools down and play with them because you'll need to know what they look like, how they operate, and what capabilities they have.

Next, when it comes to this chapter, you really need to get to know Linux better. Questions regarding Linux will most likely revolve around kernel modules, file structure, storage locations, and the command-line interface. Again, the easiest way to learn all this is to download a Linux distro and run it in a VM on your machine. Take advantage of the thousands of Linux how-to videos and articles you can find on the Internet: It's one thing to read it in a book, but you'll learn far more if you actually perform it yourself.

1. Examine the following password hashes obtained from a Windows XP machine using LM hashing:

   B757BF5C0D87772FAAD3B435B51404EE

   BA810DBA98995F1817306D272A9441BB

   E52CAC67419A9A224A3B108F3FA6CB6D

   0182BD0BD4444BF836077A718CCDF409

   CEC52EB9C8E3455DC2265B23734E0DAC

   Which of the following is true regarding the hashes listed?

   A. The hashes are protected using Syskey.

   B. The third hash listed is the local administrator's password.

   C. The first hash listed is from a password of seven characters or less.

   D. The hashes can be easily decrypted by reversing the hash algorithm.

2. Amanda works as a security administrator for a large organization. She discovers some remote tools installed on a server and has no record of a change request asking for them. After some investigation, she discovers an unknown IP address connection that was able to access the network through a high-level port that was not closed. The IP address is first traced to a proxy server in Mexico. Further investigation shows the connection bounced between several proxy servers in many locations. Which of the following is the most likely proxy tool used by the attacker to cover his tracks?

   A. ISA proxy

   B. IAS proxy

   C. TOR proxy

   D. Netcat

3. Which of the following correctly describes brute force password attacks?

   A. Feeding a list of words into a cracking program

   B. Comparing the hash values to lists of prehashed values for a match

   C. Attempting all possible combinations of letters, numbers, and special characters in succession

   D. Threatening the user with physical violence unless they reveal their password

4. Which password theft method is almost always successful, requires little technical knowledge, and is nearly impossible to detect?

   A. Installing a hardware keylogger

   B. Installing a software keylogger

    C. Sniffing the network segment with Ettercap

    D. Attempting a brute-force attack using Cain and Abel

5. Which of the following will extract an executable file from NTFS streaming?

    A. c:\> cat file1.txt:hidden.exe > visible.exe

    B. c:\> more file1.txt | hidden.exe > visible.exe

    C. c:\> type notepad.exe > file1.txt:hidden.exe

    D. c:\> list file1.txt$hidden.exe > visible.exe

6. Which command is used to allow all privileges to the user, read-only to the group, and read-only for all others to a particular file, on a Linux machine?

    A. chmod 411 file1

    B. chmod 114 file1

    C. chmod 117 file1

    D. chmod 711 file1

    E. chmod 744 file1

7. Examine the following passwd file:

```
root:x:0:0:root:/root:/bin/bash
mwalk:x:500:500:Matt Walker,Room 2238,email:/home/mwalk:/bin/sh
jboll:x:501:501:Jason Bollinger,Room 2239,email:/home/jboll:/bin/sh
rbell:x:502:502:Rick Bell,Room 1017,email:/home/rbell:/bin/sh
afrench:x:503:501:Alecia French,Room 1017,email:/home/afrench:/bin/sh
```

Which of the following statements are true regarding this passwd file? (Choose all that apply.)

    A. None of the user accounts has passwords assigned.

    B. The system makes use of the shadow file.

    C. The root account password is root.

    D. The root account has a shadowed password.

    E. Files created by Alecia will initially be viewable by Jason.

8. You are attempting to hack a Windows machine and want to gain a copy of the SAM file. Where can you find it? (Choose all that apply.)

    A. /etc/passwd

    B. /etc/shadow

    C. c:\windows\system32\config

    D. c:\winnt\config

    E. c:\windows\repair

9. Which of the following statements are true concerning Kerberos? (Choose all that apply.)

   A. Kerberos uses symmetric encryption.

   B. Kerberos uses asymmetric encryption.

   C. Clients ask for authentication tickets from the KDC in clear text.

   D. KDC responses to clients never include a password.

   E. Clients decrypt a TGT from the server.

10. What is the difference between a dictionary attack and a hybrid attack?

    A. Dictionary attacks are based solely on word lists, whereas hybrid attacks make use of both word lists and rainbow tables.

    B. Dictionary attacks are based solely on whole word lists, whereas hybrid attacks can use a variety of letters, numbers, and special characters.

    C. Dictionary attacks use predefined word lists, whereas hybrid attacks substitute numbers and symbols within those words.

    D. Hybrid and dictionary attacks are the same.

11. Which of the following contains a listing of port numbers for well-known services defined by IANA?

    A. %windir%\etc\lists

    B. %windir%\system32\drivers\etc\lmhosts

    C. %windir%\system32\drivers\etc\services

    D. %windir%\system32\drivers\etc\hosts

12. Which of the following SIDs indicates the true administrator account?

    A. S-1-5-21-1388762127-2960977290-773940301-1100

    B. S-1-5-21-1388762127-2960977290-773940301-1101

    C. S-1-5-21-1388762127-2960977290-773940301-500

    D. S-1-5-21-1388762127-2960977290-773940301-501

13. In which step of EC-Council's system hacking methodology would you find steganography?

    A. Cracking passwords

    B. Escalating privileges

    C. Executing applications

    D. Hiding files

    E. Covering tracks

14. Examine the following extract from a compromised system:

```
c:\> cmd /c type c:\winnt\repair\sam > c:\syskey.txt
```

Which of the following is the best description of what the attacker is attempting to accomplish?

A. Replacing the SAM file with a file of his choosing

B. Copying the SAM file for offline cracking attempts

C. Cracking any Syskey encryption on the SAM file

D. Uploading a virus

15. Which password would be considered the most secure?

A. CEH123TEST

B. CEHisaHARDTEST

C. 638154849675

D. C3HisH@rd

16. Which of the following are true statements? (Choose all that apply.)

A. John the Ripper does not display the case of cracked LM hash passwords.

B. NTLMV1 represents an effective countermeasure to password cracking.

C. Syskey provides additional protection against password cracking.

D. The hash value of a Windows LM password that is seven characters or less will always be passed as 00112233445566778899.

E. Enforcing complex passwords provides additional protection against password cracking.

17. Which of the following are considered offline password attacks? (Choose all that apply.)

A. Using a hardware keylogger

B. Brute-force cracking with Cain and Abel on a stolen SAM file

C. Using John the Ripper on a stolen passwd file

D. Shoulder surfing

18. If a rootkit is discovered on the system, which of the following is the *best* alternative for recovery?

A. Replacing all data files from a good backup

B. Installing Tripwire

C. Reloading the entire system from known good media

D. Deleting all data files and reboot

19. Examine the following portion of a log file, captured during a hacking attempt:

```
[matt@localhost]#rm -rf /tmp/mykit_headers
[matt@localhost]#rm -rf /var/log/messages
[matt@localhost]#rm -rf /root/.bash_history
```

What was the attacker attempting to do?

A. Copy files for later examination

B. Cover his tracks

C. Change the shell to lock out other users

D. Upload a rootkit

20. You suspect a hack has occurred against your Linux machine. Which command will display all running processes for you to review?

A. ls -d

B. ls -l

C. su

D. ps -ef

E. ifconfig

21. An organization wants to control network traffic and perform stateful inspection of traffic going into and out of their DMZ. Which built-in functionality of Linux can achieve this?

A. iptables

B. ipchains

C. ipsniffer

D. ipfirewall

22. Which of the following best describes Cygwin?

A. Cygwin is a UNIX subsystem running on top of Windows.

B. Cygwin is a Windows subsystem running on top of UNIX.

C. Cygwin is a C++ compiler.

D. Cygwin is a password cracking tool.

23. Which folder in Linux holds administrative commands and daemons?

A. /sbin

B. /bin

C. /dev

D. /mnt

E. /usr

24. Which of the following is the appropriate means to pivot within a Metasploit attack session?

   A. Use the pivot exploit outside meterpreter.

   B. Reconfigure network settings in meterpreter.

   C. Set the payload to propagate.

   D. Create a route statement in the meterpreter.

25. You are examining files on a Windows machine and note one file's attributes include "h." What does this indicate?

   A. The file is flagged for backup.

   B. The file is part of the help function.

   C. The file is fragmented because of size.

   D. The file has been quarantined by an antivirus program.

   E. The file is hidden.

26. You have gained access to a SAM file from an older Windows machine and are preparing to run a Syskey cracker against it. How many bits are used for Syskey encryption?

   A. 128

   B. 256

   C. 512

   D. 1024

27. Which of the following tools can assist in discovering the use of NTFS file streams? (Choose all that apply.)

   A. LADS

   B. ADS Spy

   C. Sfind

   D. Snow

28. Which of the following are true regarding Kerberos?

   A. Kerberos makes use of UDP as a transport protocol.

   B. Kerberos makes use of TCP as a transport protocol.

   C. Kerberos uses port 88 for the transmission of data.

   D. Kerberos makes use of both symmetric and asymmetric encryption techniques.

   E. All of the above.

29. Which authentication method uses DES for encryption and forces 14-character passwords for hash storage?

A. NTLMv1

B. NTLMv2

C. LAN Manager

D. Kerberos

1. C
2. C
3. C
4. A
5. A
6. D
7. B, D, E
8. C, E
9. A, B, C, D, E
10. C
11. C
12. C
13. D
14. B
15. D
16. A, C, E
17. A, B, C
18. C
19. B
20. D
21. A
22. A
23. A
24. D
25. E
26. A
27. A, B, C
28. E
29. C

1. Examine the following password hashes obtained from a Windows XP machine using LM hashing:

   B757BF5C0D87772FAAD3B435B51404EE

   BA810DBA98995F1817306D272A9441BB

   E52CAC67419A9A224A3B108F3FA6CB6D

   0182BD0BD4444BF836077A718CCDF409

   CEC52EB9C8E3455DC2265B23734E0DAC

   Which of the following is true regarding the hashes listed?

   A. The hashes are protected using Syskey.

   B. The third hash listed is the local administrator's password.

   C. The first hash listed is from a password of seven characters or less.

   D. The hashes can be easily decrypted by reversing the hash algorithm.

   ☑ **C.** Windows 2000 and NT-type machines used something called LAN Manager, and then NT LAN Manager, to hash passwords. LM hashing is an older, outdated, and easily crackable method. It worked by converting all password characters to uppercase and, if necessary, appending blank spaces to reach 14 characters. Next, the password was split directly in the middle, and both sides would then be encrypted separately. The problem with this is the LM "hash" value (which is actually not a one-way function but a compilation of an encryption function using two DES keys created from each side of the original password) of seven blank characters will always be the same (AAD3B435B51404EE). This greatly simplifies your cracking efforts because running through only 7 characters is much easier than 14.

   ☒ **A** is incorrect because Syskey is not in use here. Syskey is an older, optional utility added in Windows NT 4.0 SP3 that encrypted hashed password information in a SAM database using a 128-bit encryption key. It was meant to protect against offline password-cracking attacks; however, security problems were discovered that rendered it moot: Brute-force attacking worked even with Syskey in place.

   ☒ **B** is incorrect because there is no way to tell from a hash which password belongs with which user.

   ☒ **D** is incorrect because hashes cannot be reversed.

2. Amanda works as a security administrator for a large organization. She discovers some remote tools installed on a server and has no record of a change request asking for them. After some investigation, she discovers an unknown IP address connection that was able to access the network through a high-level port that was not closed. The IP address is first traced to a proxy server in Mexico. Further investigation shows the connection bounced between several proxy servers in

many locations. Which of the following is the most likely proxy tool used by the attacker to cover his tracks?

A. ISA proxy

B. IAS proxy

C. TOR proxy

D. Netcat

☑ **C.** I've mentioned it before, and I'll mention it again here: Sometimes the CEH exam and real life just don't match up. Yes, this question may be, admittedly, a little on the "hokey" side, but it's valid insofar as EC-Council is concerned. The point here is that TOR (The Onion Routing; https://www.torproject.org/) provides a quick, easy, and really groovy way to hide your true identity when performing almost anything online. From the site, "Tor protects you by bouncing your communications around a distributed network of relays run by volunteers all around the world: it prevents somebody watching your Internet connection from learning what sites you visit, and it prevents the sites you visit from learning your physical location." (For the real-world folks out there, just know that without law enforcement and some serious network visibility, you'd probably be successful in tracking to the first hop, but that'd be it.) TOR is, by nature, dynamic, and a hacker can simply use a different path for each attack. Just remember the question is really about identifying TOR as a means of covering tracks and not necessarily a treatise on how it *really* works.

☒ **A** is incorrect because an Internet Security and Acceleration (ISA) server isn't designed to bounce between multiple proxies to obscure the original source. From Microsoft, ISA "is the successor to Microsoft's Proxy Server 2.0 (see proxy server) and provides the two basic services of an enterprise firewall and a Web proxy/cache server. ISA Server's firewall screens all packet-level, circuit-level, and application-level traffic. The Web cache stores and serves all regularly accessed Web content in order to reduce network traffic and provide faster access to frequently-accessed Web pages. ISA Server also schedules downloads of Web page updates for non-peak times."

☒ **B** is incorrect because Internet Authentication Service (IAS) is a component of servers that allows you to provide a Remote Authentication Dial-In User Service (RADIUS) connection to clients. It's not designed as an obfuscating proxy—its purpose is in authentication.

☒ **D** is incorrect because while you can set up a single proxy using Netcat and it may even be possible to chain several together, it's simply not designed to work that way (and that's what this question was all about to begin with). You can set up a listening port with it, but it's not designed to act as a proxy, and setting one up as a chain of proxies would be insanely complicated and unnecessary with the myriad other options available.

3. Which of the following correctly describes brute-force password attacks?

   A. Feeding a list of words into a cracking program

   B. Comparing the hash values to lists of prehashed values for a match

   C. Attempting all possible combinations of letters, numbers, and special characters in succession

   D. Threatening the user with physical violence unless they reveal their password

   ☑ C. A brute-force attack uses every possible combination of letters, numbers, and special characters against an authentication effort—whether in succession or (more commonly) at random. The drawbacks to its use are substantial: It takes the longest amount of time and a tremendous amount of processing resources. However, it is your best option on complex passwords, and there is no arguing its effectiveness: Given enough time, *every* password can be cracked using brute force. It may take years to try every combination, but if you keep at it long enough, it is successful 100 percent of the time.

   ☒ A is incorrect because this describes a dictionary attack. It is much easier and faster than a brute-force attack, and it uses far fewer resources. The attack works by using a list of passwords in a text file, which is then hashed by the same algorithm/process the original password was put through. The hashes are compared, and if a match is found, the password is cracked. Although this attack is supposed to (technically speaking) use only words you'd find in a dictionary, you can create your own word list to feed into the cracker. Using this method, you can crack "complex" passwords too. However, the word list you use must have the exact match in it—you can't get it close; it must be *exact*. Although it may be fun for you to spend hours of your day creating your own dictionary file, it's a lot easier to simply download one of the thousands already on the Internet.

   ☒ B is incorrect because this describes the use of rainbow tables. A rainbow table crack effort can be faster than anything else, assuming you can pull the right one to look through. Rainbow tables are created when someone, with lots of time on their hands, feeds every conceivable password in creation through a hash. The hashes are then saved to a table, to which you can compare the password hashes off your target machine. It's simple and easy; however, keep in mind these tables are huge. Additionally, "salting" a password makes rainbow tables moot. One final note for the purists in the reading audience: The use of multi-GPU cracking systems (employing computing resources to cracking passwords that boggle the mind) may be faster than using rainbow tables. Just don't say that on your exam!

   ☒ D is incorrect because this refers to something defined by EC-Council and the CEH exam as a *rubber hose attack*. No, I'm not making this up. And I'm not encouraging you to use this in your own pen testing—just know it for your exam.

4. Which password theft method is almost always successful, requires little technical knowledge, and is nearly impossible to detect?

   A. Installing a hardware keylogger

   B. Installing a software keylogger

   C. Sniffing the network segment with Ettercap

   D. Attempting a brute-force attack using Cain and Abel

   ☑ **A.** Questions on hardware keyloggers will almost always reference the fact that they're nearly impossible to detect. Unless the user notices them or you have dedicated security staff watching for them, these are foolproof, easy to install, and great tools to use. They are usually small devices connected between the keyboard cable and the computer that simply capture all keystrokes going by. Install one day and just wait—when you pick it up, it will be filled with all the access information you need. Just remember that the hardest part of using a hardware keylogger is the physical access required to install it: They're not remote access, introvert-friendly, work-in-the-shadows tools, so you'll have to actually get next to a system to put it into action.

   ☒ **B** is incorrect because although a software keylogger does the same thing as a hardware keylogger and will provide excellent results (I've used one on my kids before—it's fantastic), it's fairly easy to spot and requires a little configuration to get things just the way you want them.

   ☒ **C** is incorrect because sniffing a network tap with Ettercap isn't going to provide you with anything other than an open text protocol password (FTP and so on). Sniffing isn't guaranteed to provide anything password-wise. Yes, Ettercap is powerful, but it does require a fairly substantial amount of technical know-how to get the most out of it.

   ☒ **D** is incorrect because a brute-force attack—with any tool—is exceedingly easy to detect. Additionally, it's not just a point-and-shoot endeavor: You do need some technical ability to pull it off. Lastly, I know some of you are thinking that taking the passwords offline and pounding away at them is as quiet as you can get. Trust me, that's not the intent of this question, and don't let that fact trip you up.

5. Which of the following will extract an executable file from NTFS streaming?

   A. c:\> cat file1.txt:hidden.exe > visible.exe

   B. c:\> more file1.txt | hidden.exe > visible.exe

   C. c:\> type notepad.exe > file1.txt:hidden.exe

   D. c:\> list file1.txt$hidden.exe > visible.exe

☑ **A.** This is the correct syntax. The cat command will extract the executable directly into the folder you execute the command from. NTFS file steaming allows you to hide virtually any file behind any other file, rendering it invisible to directory searches. The file can be a text file, to remind you of steps to take when you return to the target, or even an executable file you can run at your leisure later. Alternate Data Streams (ADS) in the form of NTFS file streaming is a feature of the Windows-native NTFS file systems to ensure compatibility with Apple file systems (called HFS). Be careful on the exam—you will see ADS and NTFS file streaming used interchangeably. As an aside, the cat command isn't available on Windows 7 machines; you'll need a Linux emulator or something like it to pull this off on a Windows 7 system.

☒ **B** is incorrect because this is not the correct syntax. There is no pipe (|) function in extracting a file, and the more command is used to display the contents of a text file, not extract an executable from ADS.

☒ **C** is incorrect because this is not the correct syntax. This option would display the contents of a hidden text file—maybe one you've stowed away instructions in for use later.

☒ **D** is incorrect because the syntax is not correct by any stretch of the imagination. This is included as a distractor.

6. Which command is used to allow all privileges to the user, read-only to the group, and read-only for all others to a particular file, on a Linux machine?

   A. chmod 411 file1

   B. chmod 114 file1

   C. chmod 117 file1

   D. chmod 711 file1

   E. chmod 744 file1

☑ **D.** You're going to need to know some basic Linux commands to survive this exam, and one command I can guarantee you'll see a question on is chmod. File permissions in Linux are assigned via the use of the binary equivalent for each rwx group: Read is equivalent to 4, write to 2, and execute to 1. To accumulate permissions, you add the number: 4 is read-only, 6 is read and write, and adding execute to the bunch means a 7. As an aside, if you think in binary, the numbers are just as easy to define: 111 equates to 7 in decimal, and each bit turned on gives read, write, and execute. Setting the bits to 101 turns on read, turns off write, and turns on execute; and its decimal equivalent is 5.

☒ **A, B, C,** and **E** are all incorrect syntax for what we're trying to accomplish here: 411 equates to read-only, execute, and execute (with 114 being the reverse of that), and 117 equates to execute, execute, full permissions, with 711 being the reverse.

7. Examine the following passwd file:

```
root:x:0:0:root:/root:/bin/bash
mwalk:x:500:500:Matt Walker,Room 2238,email:/home/mwalk:/bin/sh
jboll:x:501:501:Jason Bollinger,Room 2239,email:/home/jboll:/bin/sh
rbell:x:502:502:Rick Bell,Room 1017,email:/home/rbell:/bin/sh
afrench:x:503:501:Alecia French,Room 1017,email:/home/afrench:/bin/sh
```

Which of the following statements are true regarding this passwd file? (Choose all that apply.)

A. None of the user accounts has passwords assigned.

B. The system makes use of the shadow file.

C. The root account password is root.

D. The root account has a shadowed password.

E. Files created by Alecia will initially be viewable by Jason.

☑ **B, D, and E.** If there are not two to four questions on your exam regarding the Linux passwd file, I'll eat my hat. Every exam and practice exam I've ever taken references this file—a lot—and it's included here to ensure you pay attention. Fields in the passwd file, from left to right, are as follows:

- **User Name**   This is what the user types in as the login name. Each of these must be unique.

- **Password**   If a shadow file is being used, an *x* will be displayed here. If not, you'll see the password in clear text. As an aside, setting this to an asterisk (*) is a method to deactivate an account.

- **UID**   The user identifier is used by the operating system for internal purposes. It is typically incremented by 1 for each new user added.

- **GID**   The group identifier identifies the primary group of the user. All files that are created by this user will normally be accessible to this group, unless a chmod command prevents it (which is the reason for the "initial" portion of the question).

- **Gecos**   This is a descriptive field for the user, generally containing contact information separated by commas.

- **Home Directory**   This is the location of the user's home directory.

- **Startup Program**   This is the program that is started every time the user logs in. It's usually a shell for the user to interact with the system.

☒ **A** is incorrect because the *x* indicates a shadowed password, not the absence of one.

☒ **C** is incorrect because the *x* indicates that root does indeed have a password, but it is shadowed. Could it actually be root? Sure, but there's no way to tell that from this listing.

8. You are attempting to hack a Windows machine and want to gain a copy of the SAM file. Where can you find it? (Choose all that apply.)

A. /etc/passwd

B. /etc/shadow

C. c:\windows\system32\config

D. c:\winnt\config

E. c:\windows\repair

☑ **C and E.** From Microsoft's definition, the Security Account Manager (SAM) is a database that stores user accounts and security descriptors for users on the local computer. The SAM file can be found in c:\windows\system32\config. If you're having problems getting there, try pulling a copy from system restore (c:\windows\repair).

☒ **A and B** are both incorrect because /etc is a dead giveaway this is a Linux folder (note the forward slash instead of the Windows backward slash). The /etc folder contains all the administration files and passwords on a Linux system. Both the password and shadow files are found here.

☒ **D** is incorrect because this is not the correct location of the SAM. It's included as a distractor.

9. Which of the following statements are true concerning Kerberos? (Choose all that apply.)

A. Kerberos uses symmetric encryption.

B. Kerberos uses asymmetric encryption.

C. Clients ask for authentication tickets from the KDC in clear text.

D. KDC responses to clients never include a password.

E. Clients decrypt a TGT from the server.

☑ **A, B, C, D, and E.** All answers are correct. Kerberos makes use of both symmetric and asymmetric encryption technologies to securely transmit passwords and keys across a network. The entire process consists of a key distribution center (KDC), an authentication service (AS), a ticket granting service (TGS), and the Ticket Granting Ticket (TGT). A basic Kerberos exchange starts with a client asking the KDC, which holds the AS and TGS, for a ticket, which will be used to authenticate throughout the network. This request is in clear text. The server will respond with a secret key, which is hashed by the password copy kept on the server (passwords are never sent—only hashes and keys). This is known as the TGT. The client decrypts the message, since it knows the password, and the TGT is sent back to the server requesting a TGS service ticket. The server responds with the service ticket, and the client is allowed to log on and access network resources.

10. What is the difference between a dictionary attack and a hybrid attack?

   A. Dictionary attacks are based solely on word lists, whereas hybrid attacks make use of both word lists and rainbow tables.

   B. Dictionary attacks are based solely on whole word lists, whereas hybrid attacks can use a variety of letters, numbers, and special characters.

   C. Dictionary attacks use predefined word lists, whereas hybrid attacks substitute numbers and symbols within those words.

   D. Hybrid and dictionary attacks are the same.

   ☑ C. A hybrid attack is a variant on a dictionary attack. In this effort, you still have a word list; however, the cracker is smart enough to replace letters and characters within those words. For example, both attacks might use a list containing the word Password. To have multiple variants on it, the dictionary attack would need to have each variant added to the list individually (P@ssword, Pa$$word, and so on). A hybrid attack would require the word list only to include Password because it would swap out characters and letters to find different versions of the same word.

   ☒ A is incorrect because hybrid attacks don't use rainbow tables.

   ☒ B is incorrect because dictionary attacks can use all sorts of variants of a whole word; they just need to be listed separately in the list.

   ☒ D is incorrect because hybrid and dictionary attacks are most definitely different.

11. Which of the following contains a listing of port numbers for well-known services defined by IANA?

   A. %windir%\etc\lists

   B. %windir%\system32\drivers\etc\lmhosts

   C. %windir%\system32\drivers\etc\services

   D. %windir%\system32\drivers\etc\hosts

   ☑ C. I've sat back many times in writing these books struggling to determine why certain specific but not very useful things seem to be so near and dear to the test makers at EC-Council, but I can't find any particular rhyme or reason. Sometimes, Dear Reader, you just have to memorize and move on, and this example is no exception. If you happen to be out on your real job and completely forget every well-known port number, you'd probably just look up the list on an Internet search. If you're bored or really nerdy, though, you can pull up a list of them by visiting the services file. It's sitting right there beside the hosts and lmhosts files.

   ☒ A, B, and D are incorrect because these locations do not hold the services file.

12. Which of the following SIDs indicates the true administrator account?

    A. S-1-5-21-1388762127-2960977290-773940301-1100

    B. S-1-5-21-1388762127-2960977290-773940301-1101

    C. S-1-5-21-1388762127-2960977290-773940301-500

    D. S-1-5-21-1388762127-2960977290-773940301-501

    ☑ **C.** The security identifier (SID) in Windows is used to identify a "security principle." It's unique to each account and service and is good for the life of the principle. Everything else associated with the account is simply a property of the SID, allowing accounts to be renamed without affecting their security attributes. In a Windows system, the true administrator account always has an RID (relative identifier) of 500.

    ☒ **A** and **B** are incorrect because neither 1100 nor 1101 is the RID associated with the administrator account. RID values between 1000 and 1500 indicate a standard user account.

    ☒ **D** is incorrect because 501 is the RID for the guest account.

13. In which step of EC-Council's system hacking methodology would you find steganography?

    A. Cracking passwords

    B. Escalating privileges

    C. Executing applications

    D. Hiding files

    E. Covering tracks

    ☑ **D.** Yes, sometimes you get a question that's relatively easy, and this is a prime example. Hiding files is exactly what it sounds like—find a way to hide files on the system. There are innumerable ways to accomplish this, but steganography (which includes hiding all sorts of stuff inside images, video, and such) and NTFS file streaming are the two you'll most likely see referenced on the exam.

    ☒ **A, B, C,** and **E** are incorrect because you do not hide files in these steps. Cracking passwords is self-explanatory. Escalating privileges refers to the means taken to elevate access to administrator level. Executing applications is exactly what it sounds like, and you'll probably see remote execution tools referenced (and, for some bizarre reason, keyloggers and spyware). Covering tracks deals with proxies, log files, and such.

14. Examine the following extract from a compromised system:

```
c:\> cmd /c type c:\winnt\repair\sam > c:\syskey.txt
```

Which of the following is the best description of what the attacker is attempting to accomplish?

A. Replacing the SAM file with a file of his choosing

B. Copying the SAM file for offline cracking attempts

C. Cracking any Syskey encryption on the SAM file

D. Uploading a virus

☑ **B.** This one is actually pretty simple to decipher, yet I've seen versions of this on nearly every practice exam I used in prepping for the exam myself. If you see something like this, don't get all wrapped up in the name of the text file. The command sequence should read pretty clearly: "Type the contents of the file named sam, which is located in the c:\winnt\reair\ folder into a new file called syskey.txt, and put that new file in the root directory (C:)." As an aside, you'll likely see a question or two referencing the location of the repair copy for SAM, so this one's a two-fer. You're welcome.

☒ **A** is incorrect because this command is outputting, not inputting.

☒ **C** is incorrect because there is no cracking attempt being made here.

☒ **D** is incorrect because there is no uploading going on at all here, virus or otherwise.

15. Which password would be considered the most secure?

A. CEH123TEST

B. CEHisaHARDTEST

C. 638154849675

D. C3HisH@rd

☑ **D.** According to EC-Council and the CEH exam, D is the correct answer. On this exam, complexity trumps length no matter what. Sure, an argument can be made that a longer password is better than a shorter one (regardless of complexity and if used for a shorter amount of time), but just stick with complexity—using letters, numbers, and special characters—and you'll be fine. However, obviously, a longer complex password is more secure than a shorter one.

☒ **A** is incorrect because it uses only letters and numbers.

☒ **B** is incorrect for the same reason. It is much longer than the correct answer, but there's no complexity.

☒ **C** is incorrect because it uses only numbers. It has no complexity, and it's a fairly short length.

16. Which of the following are true statements? (Choose all that apply.)

   A. John the Ripper does not display the case of cracked LM hash passwords.

   B. NTLMv1 represents an effective countermeasure to password cracking.

   C. Syskey provides additional protection against password cracking.

   D. The hash value of a Windows LM password that is seven characters or less will always be passed as 00112233445566778899.

   E. Enforcing complex passwords provides additional protection against password cracking.

   ☑ **A, C, and E.** John the Ripper is one of the more well-known password crackers, it's been around seemingly forever, and you'll definitely see it on your exam. On LM-hashed passwords, it displays the passwords in all caps. Syskey definitely isn't foolproof, but it does provide additional protection against password cracking. And, last but not least, complex passwords are harder to crack than simple ones, so this should've been an easy choice.

   ☒ **B is incorrect** because NTLMv1 is about as secure as sticky notes pasted to computer screens. It's old and easily cracked.

   ☒ **D is incorrect** because even a seven-character password will generate a unique first half of the hash. It's the second part that always remains the same on seven-character (or less) passwords: AAD3B435B51404EE.

17. Which of the following are considered offline password attacks? (Choose all that apply.)

   A. Using a hardware keylogger

   B. Brute-force cracking with Cain and Abel on a stolen SAM file

   C. Using John the Ripper on a stolen passwd file

   D. Shoulder surfing

   ☑ **A, B, and C.** An offline password attack occurs when you take the password file (or the passwords themselves) offline for work. Common methods are stealing the SAM or passwd (shadow) files and then running dictionary, hybrid, or brute-force attacks against them (using a password-cracking tool such as Cain and Abel or John the Ripper). Keyloggers are also considered offline attacks because you examine the contents off network.

   ☒ **D is incorrect** because shoulder surfing is considered another form of attack altogether—a nonelectronic attack. No, I'm not making this up; it's actually a term in CEH lingo and refers to social engineering methods of obtaining a password. Shoulder surfing is basically standing behind someone and watching their keystrokes.

18. If a rootkit is discovered on the system, which of the following is the best alternative for recovery?

   A. Replacing all data files from a good backup

   B. Installing Tripwire

   C. Reloading the entire system from known good media

   D. Deleting all data files and reboot

   ☑ **C.** Sometimes a good old wipe and reload is not only faster than a clean effort but is just flat out better. When it comes to rootkits, it's really your only option. If it's an off-the-shelf rootkit that has been documented, it's likely that good instructions on how to fully remove it are available somewhere. However, just remember that while you *think* you may have it removed by following removal instructions, you *know* it's gone if you blow the system away and reload it.

   ☒ **A** and **D** are incorrect because nearly anything you're doing with the data files themselves isn't going to help in getting rid of a rootkit. The device has been rooted, so all data should be treated as suspect.

   ☒ **B** is incorrect because while Tripwire is a great tool, it isn't really useful to you once the machine has been infected.

19. Examine the following portion of a log file, captured during a hacking attempt:

    ```
    [matt@localhost]#rm -rf /tmp/mykit_headers
    [matt@localhost]#rm -rf /var/log/messages
    [matt@localhost]#rm -rf /root/.bash_history
    ```

    What was the attacker attempting to do?

    A. Copy files for later examination

    B. Cover his tracks

    C. Change the shell to lock out other users

    D. Upload a rootkit

    ☑ **B.** You'll definitely see basic Linux commands on your test, and this is one example of how you'll be asked about them. In this example, the rm command is used to remove (delete) files on a Linux system. Looking at what the hacker is attempting to remove, it seems logical to assume—even without seeing the rest of the log—that the hacker is covering his tracks.

    ☒ **A** is incorrect because the command for copy in Linux is cp.

    ☒ **C** is incorrect because the shell is not being tampered with. This answer is included as a distractor.

☒ **D** is incorrect because there is no evidence in this capture that anything is being uploaded; all commands are for removal of files (using the rm command). Granted, it's highly likely something was uploaded before this portion, but we're not privy to that information here.

20. You suspect a hack has occurred against your Linux machine. Which command will display all running processes for you to review?

    A. ls -d

    B. ls -l

    C. su

    D. ps -ef

    E. ifconfig

    ☑ **D**. The ps command is used in Linux to display processes. The –e switch selects all processes, running or not, and the –f switch provides a full listing. A couple of other options you might see include –r (restrict output to running processes), –u (select by effective user ID; supports names), and –p (select by process ID).

    ☒ **A and B** are incorrect because the ls command in Linux lists files inside a storage directory. A couple switches of note include –d (list directory entries instead of contents), –h (print sizes in human readable format), –l (use a long listing format), and –p (file type).

    ☒ **C** is incorrect because the su command in Linux is for "switch user." Assuming you have permission/authentication to do so, this allows you to change the effective user ID and group ID to whatever you want.

    ☒ **E** is incorrect because ifconfig is used to configure a network interface in Linux. It looks, and works, very much like the ipconfig command in Windows, which makes it an easy target for test question writers, so pay close attention to the OS when asked about configuring your NIC.

21. An organization requires an option to control network traffic and perform stateful inspection of traffic going into and out of the DMZ. Which built-in functionality of Linux can achieve this?

    A. iptables

    B. ipchains

    C. ipsniffer

    D. ipfirewall

☑ **A.** iptables is a built-in "user space" application in Linux that allows you to configure the tables used by the Linux kernel firewall. It must be executed with root privileges and allows for stateful inspection. On most Linux systems, iptables is installed as /usr/sbin/iptables.

☒ **B** is incorrect because ipchains won't allow for stateful inspection.

☒ **C** and **D** are incorrect because as far as I know there's no such thing as ipsniffer or ipfirewall.

22. Which of the following best describes Cygwin?

    A. Cygwin is a UNIX subsystem running on Windows.

    B. Cygwin is a Windows subsystem running on top of UNIX.

    C. Cygwin is a C++ compiler.

    D. Cygwin is a password cracking tool.

☑ **A.** Cygwin (www.cygwin.com/) provides a Linux-like environment for Windows. It's a large collection of GNU and open source tools that provide functionality similar to a Linux distribution on Windows, as well as a DLL (cygwin1.dll) that provides substantial POSIX API functionality, according to the website. The Cygwin DLL currently works with all recent, commercially released x86 32-bit and 64-bit versions of Windows, starting with Windows XP SP3.

☒ **B, C,** and **D** are incorrect descriptions of Cygwin.

23. Which folder in Linux holds administrative commands and daemons?

    A. /sbin

    B. /bin

    C. /dev

    D. /mnt

    E. /usr

☑ **A.** The system binaries folder holds most administrative commands (/etc holds others) and is the repository for most of the routines Linux runs (known as *daemons*).

☒ **B** is incorrect because this folder holds all sorts of basic Linux commands (a lot like the C:\Windows\System32 folder in Windows).

☒ **C** is incorrect because this folder contains the pointer locations to the various storage and input/output systems you will need to mount if you want to use them, such as optical drives and additional hard drives or partitions. By the way, everything in Linux is a file. Everything.

☒ **D** is incorrect because this folder holds the access locations you've actually mounted.

☒ **E** is incorrect because this folder holds most of the information, commands, and files unique to the users.

24. Which of the following is the appropriate means to pivot within a Metasploit attack session?

A. Use the pivot exploit outside meterpreter.

B. Reconfigure network settings in meterpreter.

C. Set the payload to propagate.

D. Create a route statement in the meterpreter.

☑ **D.** To answer this, you have to know what *pivot* means and what the meterpreter is, and the best explanation for both are found right on the Offensive Security website (www.offensive-security.com/): "Pivoting is the unique technique of using an instance (also referred to as a *plant* or *foothold*) to be able to 'move' around inside a network. Basically using the first compromise to allow and even aid in the compromise of other otherwise inaccessible systems. Metasploit has an autoroute meterpreter script that allows an attack into a secondary network through a first compromised machine. Meterpreter is an advanced, dynamically extensible payload that uses in-memory DLL injection stagers and is extended over the network at runtime. Meterpreter resides entirely in memory and writes nothing to disk." Adding a route statement inside the dynamic meterpreter environment allows the attack to "pivot" to a new target. Neat, eh?

☒ **A, B,** and **C** are incorrect because they are neither legitimate nor accurate statements regarding a pivot attack.

25. You are examining files on a Windows machine and note one file's attributes include "h." What does this indicate?

A. The file is flagged for backup.

B. The file is part of the help function.

C. The file is fragmented because of size.

D. The file has been quarantined by an antivirus program.

E. The file is hidden.

☑ **E.** The hidden attribute can be set on any file to hide it from standard directory searches. You can accomplish this with the following command line:

```
attrib +h filename
```

or by right-clicking, choosing Properties, and checking the Hidden attribute check box at the bottom of the dialog.

☒ **A, B, C,** and **D** are all incorrect definitions of the hidden attribute.

26. You have gained access to a SAM file from an older Windows machine and are preparing to run a Syskey cracker against it. How many bits are used for Syskey encryption?

   A. 128

   B. 256

   C. 512

   D. 1024

   ☑ **A.** I know, Syskey is outdated, and you'll probably never see it again. However, it's still in your exam pool, so you have to know it. I could rehash the definition, but it appears in an earlier question, and you should have it memorized by now anyway. Just know it provides additional security on older Windows NT boxes and uses 128 bits for encryption.

   ☒ **B, C,** and **D** are incorrect because Syskey uses only 128 bits for encryption.

27. Which of the following tools can assist in discovering the use of NTFS file streams? (Choose all that apply.)

   A. LADS

   B. ADS Spy

   C. Sfind

   D. Snow

   ☑ **A, B,** and **C.** NTFS streaming (alternate data streaming) isn't a huge security problem, but it is something many security administrators concern themselves with. If you want to know where it's going on, you can use any of these tools: LADS and ADS Spy are freeware tools that list all alternate data streams of an NTFS directory. ADS Spy can also remove Alternate Data Streams (ADS) from NTFS file systems. Sfind, probably the oldest one here, is a Foundstone forensic tool you can use for finding ADS.

   ☒ **D** is incorrect because Snow is a steganography tool used to conceal messages in ASCII text by appending whitespace to the end of lines.

28. Which of the following are true regarding Kerberos?

   A. Kerberos makes use of UDP as a transport protocol.

   B. Kerberos makes use of TCP as a transport protocol.

   C. Kerberos uses port 88 for the transmission of data.

   D. Kerberos makes use of both symmetric and asymmetric encryption techniques.

   E. All of the above.

☑ **E.** Kerberos uses both symmetric and asymmetric encryption technologies to securely transmit passwords and keys across a network. The entire process consists of a key distribution center (KDC), an authentication service (AS), a ticket granting service (TGS), and the ticket granting ticket (TGT). It can make use of both TCP and UDP and runs over port 88.

☒ **A, B, C,** and **D** are incorrect because they're all true regarding Kerberos, which makes them correct but wrong choices.

29. Which authentication method uses DES for encryption and forces 14-character passwords for hash storage?

   A. NTLMv1

   B. NTLMv2

   C. LAN Manager

   D. Kerberos

☑ **C.** LAN Manager is an older authentication model that burst onto the scene around the Windows 95 launch. It uses DES as an encryption standard (a 56-bit key DES, to be technical) and, as covered before, has a quirky habit of capitalizing passwords and splitting them into two seven-character halves. Believe it or not, this is still in use in the field. It's most often found in places where backward compatibility was needed for something and, eventually, it was just forgotten or overlooked.

☒ **A** is incorrect because NTLMv1 (NT LAN Manager) improved upon LM methods. It stopped crazy practices such as padding passwords to 14 characters, and so on, and it supported stronger encryption.

☒ **B** is incorrect because NTLMv2 also did not follow the encryption methods used by LM. In addition to the improvements from version 1, NTLMv2 made use of 128-bit MD5 hashing.

☒ **D** is incorrect because Kerberos is a strong and secure authentication method that does not work like LM. Kerberos makes use of a key distribution center (KDC) and grants tickets to properly authenticated clients to access resources on the network.

Web-Based Hacking: Servers and Applications

This chapter includes questions from the following topics:

- Identify features of common web server architecture
- Identify web application function and architecture points
- Describe web server and web application attacks
- Identify web server and application vulnerabilities
- Identify web application hacking tools
- Describe SQL injection techniques, attacks, and tools
- Describe buffer overflow attacks

One of the easiest ways to get nerds all up in a bother, outside of comparing Jean-Luc Picard versus James T. Kirk as Captain of the Enterprise, is to mention Linux is "more secure" than Windows. Linux zealots (a touchy group that band together in the defense of their beloved open source OS) point to the general lack of cases involving Linux servers versus their Microsoft counterparts. Windows supporters fire back that there are simply more Microsoft boxes on the Internet and, therefore, it's only logical that there would be more attacks and more vulnerabilities discovered because of the extra scrutiny. So, what's the real truth?

If you're bored someday, a little Google searching on the subject is enlightening. A study done by the SANS Institute seems to suggest that the Linux guys might be on the right side of the argument—at least from a web server perspective—although maybe not for the reason you might initially think. Their research showed that while attackers may not specifically target Microsoft web servers, they actually try to *avoid* attacking a Linux one—or at least one they think may be on a Linux system. To pull this off, they set up a fake bank with Apache (on a Linux box) and IIS servers supplying access. They found that when the OS was obscured, attackers spent relatively the same amount of effort on both sides; however, when the OS was easily discernable, the IIS attacks outnumbered Apache by almost 2 to 1.

Does this mean IIS is inherently less secure than an Apache install on Linux, or is it a treatise on the availability of more attack information on Microsoft machines than Linux "how-tos"? There's plenty of evidence that Microsoft's discovered security flaws and its respective critical patches for those flaws far outweigh those of its Apache peers. And there's also plenty of evidence that the numbers argument no longer applies, since Microsoft IIS could be on its way down to third in the web server dominance race (Netcraft's April numbers show Apache with 51 percent and IIS with 20 percent, with nginx at 19 percent). If there are, in fact, so many more Apache servers than IIS, by almost two to one, then logic would seem to dictate attackers would focus more on that offering. However, the facts just don't show that.

I think the real answer to all this is, it depends on your perspective. No matter what OS/web server combination you use, there are steps to take in securing them that will frustrate an attacker's ability to do you harm. With IIS, it may simply be that the ease of use leads to a lot more default vulnerabilities and attackers are counting on that. Or it may be that there are so many potential security flaws discovered with IIS, the return on investment in time of the attack means Windows is a better target. In any case, hackers have shown an aversion to attacking Apache and a preference for Windows. I'll leave the "mine is more secure" argument to the nerd legions out there, although we may all soon be arguing nginx anyway.

These questions surround the web server and web application attacks you'll need to be aware of. Businesses and corporations have many defenses arrayed against an attacker but oftentimes overlook the web server and applications they have sitting there, facing the public. Many attackers would argue that the customized, internal web applications are your best attack point to begin with, and it's not a hard argument to make. After all, if the target organization is going to trust the public-facing stuff, why not have a look?

 STUDY TIPS Thankfully, most questions you'll see about these topics are of the straightforward, definition-based variety. Be careful with the wording in these questions, though, because they'll sometimes try to trick you up with petty minutiae instead of actually testing your knowledge. SQL injection and buffer overflow topics will more than likely make up the majority of your questions. Oh, you'll see plenty of XSS and directory traversal stuff, and you'll need to at least have an idea what Unicode and HTML entities are, but most of it is pretty easy. Lastly, you won't be bothered with too many actual architecture questions (in regard to the web server type itself), but don't give away an easy one.

1. Which of the following is used to disable file extensions in Apache servers?

    A. disable_FS

    B. mod_negotiation

    C. stop_files

    D. httpd.conf

2. You are examining connection logs from a client machine and come across this entry:

    http://www.business123.com/../../../../../Windows/system.ini

    Which attack does this most likely indicate?

    A. Parameter manipulation

    B. XSS

    C. SQL injection

    D. Directory traversal

3. A hacker is looking at a publicly facing web front end. One of the pages provides an entry box with the heading "Forgot password? Enter your e-mail address." In the entry, he types **anything' OR '1'='1**.

    A message appears stating "Your login information has been sent to a_user-name@emailaddress.target.com."

    Which of the following is true?

    A. The cross-site scripting attempt has succeeded.

    B. The SQL injection attempt has succeeded.

    C. The parameter tampering has succeeded.

    D. The buffer overflow attempt has succeeded.

4. Which of the following uses HTML entities properly to represent <script>?

    A. <script>

    B. (script)

    C. &script&

    D. "script"

5. A pen tester is examining a web front end on a target network. The page displays a Search text box form entry, allowing the user to search for items on the site. Instead of entering a search text string, the tester enters the following:

    <script> function myFunction() { alert("It worked!"); } </script>

Chapter 6: Web-Based Hacking: Servers and Applications

145

After the tester clicks the Search button beside the entry box, a pop-up appears stating "It Worked." Which of the following is true regarding this attempt?

    A. The site is vulnerable to XSS.

    B. Coding on the site is poor, and a buffer overflow attack may result in a DoS.

    C. The attacker's next entry in the Search box should be ' OR '1'='1.

    D. This is expected behavior on properly configured sites.

6. Which of the following is used by SOAP services to format information?

    A. Unicode

    B. HTML entities

    C. NTFS

    D. XML

7. A security administrator is called for advice. The sales staff has noticed a large number of orders being filled at prices far below those posted on the site. After some research, it does not appear that the web server or the underlying SQL database has been directly compromised. Next, the security administrator reviews the IDS logs and finds nothing unusual. Additionally, the local logs on the server itself do not show anything indicating a problem. Which of the following is the most likely explanation for the false orders?

    A. The website uses hidden fields for price values, which have been altered by the attacker.

    B. SQL injection has been used to update pricing in the database. After the order was placed, pricing was reset to normal, to cover tracks.

    C. Server-side scripting was used to alter the price.

    D. A tool such as Metasploit was used to carry out the attack.

8. Which of the following is a common SOA vulnerability?

    A. SQL injection

    B. XSS

    C. XML denial of service

    D. CGI manipulation

9. The source code of software used by your client seems to have a large number of gets() alongside sparsely used fgets(). What kind of attack is this software potentially susceptible to?

    A. SQL injection

    B. Buffer overflow

    C. Parameter tampering

    D. Cookie manipulation

10. Which code entry will stop input at 100 characters?

    A. if (I > 100) then exit (1)

    B. if (I >= 100) then exit (1)

    C. if (I <= 100) then exit (1)

    D. if (I < 100) then exit (1)

11. You are examining log files and come across this URL:

http://www.example.com/script.ext?template%2e%2e%2e%2e%2e%2f%2e%2f%65%74%63%2f%70%61%73%73%77%64

    Which of the following best describes this potential attack?

    A. This is not an attack but a return of SSL handshakes.

    B. An attacker appears to be using Unicode.

    C. This appears to be a buffer overflow attempt.

    D. This appears to be an XSS attempt.

12. Which of the following tools can be used to clone a copy of a website to your machine, to be scrutinized later?

    A. BurpSuite

    B. NetCraft

    C. HttpRecon

    D. BlackWidow

13. Which character is your best option in testing for SQL injection vulnerability?

    A. The @ symbol

    B. A double dash

    C. The + sign

    D. A single quote

14. An angry former employee of the organization discovers a web form vulnerable to SQL injection. Using the injection string SELECT * FROM Orders_Pend WHERE Location_City = 'Orlando', he is able to see all pending orders from Orlando. If he wanted to delete the Orders_Pend table altogether, which SQL injection string should be used?

    A. SELECT * FROM Orders_Pend WHERE Location_City = Orlando';DROP TABLE Orders_Pend --

    B. SELECT * FROM Orders_Pend WHERE 'Orlando';DROP_TABLE --

    C. DROP TABLE Orders_Pend WHERE 'Orlando = 1' --

    D. WHERE Location_City = Orlando'1 = 1': DROP_TABLE --

15. Efforts to gain information from a target website have produced the following error message:

```
Microsoft OLE DB Provider for ODBC Drivers error '80040e08'
[Microsoft]{OBDC SQL Server Driver}
```

Which of the following best describes the error message?

A. The site may be vulnerable to XSS.

B. The site may be vulnerable to buffer overflow.

C. The site may be vulnerable to SQL injection.

D. The site may be vulnerable to a malware injection.

16. Which buffer overflow attack is designed to make use of memory that remains in use while a program is running?

A. Stack

B. Heap

C. Active

D. Permanent

17. Which of the following is a standard method for web servers to pass a user's request to an application and receive data back to forward to the user?

A. SSI

B. SSL

C. CGI

D. CSI

18. An attacker performs a SQL injection attack but receives nothing in return. She then proceeds to send multiple SQL queries, soliciting TRUE or FALSE responses. Which attack is being carried out?

A. Blind SQL injection

B. SQL denial of service

C. SQL code manipulation

D. SQL replay

19. Which of the following can be used for remote password cracking of web servers? (Choose all that apply.)

A. Brutus

B. Nikto

C. THC-Hydra

D. Nessus

20. An attacker is attempting to elevate privileges on a machine by using Java or other functions, through nonvalidated input, to cause the server to execute a malicious piece of code and provide command-line access. Which of the following best describes this action?

A. Shell injection

B. File injection

C. SQL injection

D. URL injection

21. An attacker is successful in replaying a secure cookie, stolen during an XSS attack, even during an invalid session on the server. How is this possible?

A. A cookie can be replayed at any time, no matter the circumstances.

B. Encryption was accomplished at the application layer, using a single key.

C. Authentication was accomplished using XML.

D. Encryption was accomplished at the network layer.

22. HTML forms include several methods for transferring data back and forth. Inside a form, which of the following encodes the input into the Uniform Resource Identifier (URI)?

A. HEAD

B. PUT

C. GET

D. POST

23. An attacker is looking at a target website and is viewing an account from the store on URL http://www.anybiz.com/store.php?id=2. He next enters the following URL:

http://www.anybiz.com/store.php?id=2 and 1=1

The web page loads normally. He then enters the following URL.

http://www.anybiz.com/store.php?id=2 and 1=2

A generic page noting "An error has occurred" appears.

Which of the following is a correct statement concerning these actions?

A. The site is vulnerable to cross-site scripting.

B. The site is vulnerable to blind SQL injection.

C. The site is vulnerable to buffer overflows.

D. The site is not vulnerable to SQL injection.

24. Which of the following is the hexadecimal value of a NOP instruction?

   A. 0x60

   B. 0x70

   C. 0x80

   D. 0x90

25. An attacker is viewing a blog entry showing a news story and asking for comments. In the comment field, the attacker enters the following:

```
Nice post and a fun read
<script>onload=window.location='http://www.badsite.com'</script>
```

   What is the attacker attempting to perform?

   A. A SQL injection attack against the blog's underlying database

   B. A cross-site scripting attack

   C. A buffer overflow DoS attack

   D. A file injection DoS attack

26. An attacker attempts to manipulate an application by advancing the instruction pointer with a long run of instructions containing no action. What is this attack called?

   A. File injection

   B. Stack flipping

   C. NOP-sled

   D. Heap based

27. You are examining website files and find the following text file:

```
# robots.txt for http://www.anybiz.com/
User-agent: Googlebot
Disallow: /tmp/
User-agent: *
Disallow: /
Disallow: /private.php
Disallow: /listing.html
```

   Which of the following is a true statement concerning this file?

   A. All web crawlers are prevented from indexing the listing.html page.

   B. All web crawlers are prevented from indexing all pages on the site.

   C. The Googlebot crawler is allowed to index pages starting with /tmp/.

   D. The Googlebot crawler can access and index everything on the site except for pages starting with /tmp/.

1. B

2. D

3. B

4. A

5. A

6. D

7. A

8. C

9. B

10. B

11. B

12. D

13. D

14. A

15. C

16. B

17. C

18. A

19. A, C

20. A

21. B

22. C

23. B

24. D

25. B

26. C

27. D

1. Which of the following is used to disable file extensions in Apache servers?

   A. disable_FS

   B. mod_negotiation

   C. stop_files

   D. httpd.conf

   ☑ **B.** mod_negotiation allows you to set items such as disabling file extensions. See, in HTTP, Accept headers are used to specify certain media types that are acceptable for the response. Accept headers can be used to indicate that the request is limited to a specific type of response, such as in a request for an in-line image. mod_negotiation is an Apache module that selects the document, from many available, that best matches the client's capabilities. If the Accept header on the client side happens to be invalid, the server will respond with a 406 Not Acceptable error containing a pseudodirectory listing. If you're a bad guy, this can be useful in learning more about the target system (for instance, an attacker might generate a list of base names or a list of interesting extensions or might look for backup files).

   ☒ **A and C** are incorrect because so far as I know they do not exist.

   ☒ **D** is incorrect because httpd.conf is a configuration file used in Apache to control what modules do and do not get loaded.

2. You are examining connection logs from a client machine and come across this entry:

   http://www.business123.com/../../../../../Windows/system.ini.

   Which attack does this most likely indicate?

   A. Parameter manipulation

   B. XSS

   C. SQL injection

   D. Directory traversal

   ☑ **D.** Sure, directory traversal is an older attack (working mainly on now-outdated servers), but it's still worth a shot and, more importantly to you, Dear Reader, it's going to be on your test. In this attack, the hacker attempts to access restricted directories and execute commands outside intended web server directories. Also known as the *dot-dot-slash* attack, *directory climbing*, and *backtracking*, this attack basically sends HTTP requests asking the server to drop back to the root directory and give access to other folders. Assuming you know the folder directory structure, the location where you want to run commands, and so on, this one is easy enough to pull off.

☒ **A** is incorrect because parameter manipulation (also known as *parameter tampering*) deals with changing portions of the URL string in hopes of modifying data or eliciting a response. An example might be changing the orderID portion of a URL string to see whether you can peruse other users' information.

☒ **B** is incorrect because cross-site scripting (XSS) isn't being discussed in this question. XSS is all about website design and dynamic content, passing client-side scripts into a web page viewed by a different person. In addition to simply bringing a machine down in a good old DoS attack, XSS can also be used to steal users' cookies, upload malicious code to users connected to the server, and send pop-up messages to users.

☒ **C** is incorrect because SQL injection is not being performed here. SQL injection involves passing SQL queries through a web front end to manipulate, display, replace, or destroy records in the underlying database.

3. A hacker is looking at a publicly facing web front end. One of the pages provides an entry box with the heading "Forgot password? Enter your email address." In the entry, he types **anything' OR '1'='1**.

A message appears stating "Your login information has been sent to a_username @emailaddress.target.com."

Which of the following is true?

A. The cross-site scripting attempt has succeeded.

B. The SQL injection attempt has succeeded.

C. The parameter tampering has succeeded.

D. The buffer overflow attempt has succeeded.

☑ **B.** Any time you see *' or 1=1*, I can promise you it's a SQL injection question. Because the hacker got a response, this site is susceptible to SQL injection. As an aside, it's just as likely an attempt like this may fail to return an actual record, but if it does, you may wind up getting valuable information anyway in the form of an error message from the underlying SQL database. Remember, with SQL you're simply trying to pass SQL queries through an entry point never made to take them (at least, not *designed* or *thought of* to do so anyway). What's going on here, as much as we can tell from the question, is a result has been returned from the site from input designed as a SQL query and not the designed user input (username or e-mail address).

☒ **A** is incorrect because this is not an XSS attempt. Cross-site scripting would involve something like JavaScript inserting data into the page—usually to manipulate web content.

☒ **C** is incorrect because parameter tampering is not in use here. Parameter tampering is inside the URL itself, manipulating parameters to change the response to something you're looking for (changing *order=13752+user=500* to *order =13752+user=1* inside the URL, or something like that).

☒ **D** is incorrect because buffer overflow is not in play here. Buffer overflow is an attempt to write more data into an application's prebuilt buffer area in order to overwrite adjacent memory, execute code, or crash a system (application).

4. Which of the following uses HTML entities properly to represent <script>?

   A. <script>

   B. (script)

   C. &script&

   D. "script"

   ☑ **A.** Cross-site scripting generally relies on web pages not properly validating user input, and HTML entities can be used to take the place of certain characters. In this case, the less-than sign (<) and the greater-than sign (>) surround the word script. The appropriate HTML entity for each is < and > (the *lt* and *gt* should give that one away).

   ☒ **B** is incorrect because (and) stand for the open and close parentheses, respectively. For example, *(hello)* would read (*hello*) using HTML entities.

   ☒ **C** is incorrect because & stands for the ampersand character (&).

   ☒ **D** is incorrect because " stands for the quote character (").

5. A pen tester is examining a web front end on a target network. The page displays a Search text box form entry, allowing the user to search for items on the site. Instead of entering a search text string, the tester enters the following:

   <script> function myFunction() { alert("It worked!"); } </script>

   After the tester clicks the Search button beside the entry box, a pop-up appears stating "It Worked." Which of the following is true regarding this attempt?

   A. The site is vulnerable to XSS.

   B. Coding on the site is poor, and a buffer overflow attack may result in a DoS.

   C. The attacker's next entry in the Search box should be ' OR '1'='1.

   D. This is expected behavior on properly configured sites.

   ☑ **A.** This is a somewhat simplistic but undeniably classic example of cross-site scripting. A common cross-site scripting attempt is to insert malicious script into an input field on a site. If the site is not configured properly, it'll become confused and execute the script instead of erroring out and telling you you're naughty. By manipulating input fields, you can accomplish all sorts of things, such as redirecting users to an alternate site, stealing cookies or other data from users, and performing a plain-old DoS against the site/server.

☒ **B** is incorrect because although the site is undeniably configured poorly, there is no indication here a buffer overflow will work at all. It might, later, but we just can't tell from this.

☒ **C** is incorrect because there is no indication here of a SQL injection vulnerability. As before, it may very well be vulnerable, but this question doesn't provide that information.

☒ **D** is incorrect because the site is configured poorly to even allow XSS in the first place.

6. Which of the following is used by SOAP services to format information?

   A. Unicode

   B. HTML entities

   C. NTFS

   D. XML

   ☑ **D.** Simple Object Access Protocol (SOAP) is a protocol designing for exchanging structured information within web services across multiple variant systems. In other words, it's a way for a program running in one kind of operating system (let's say Windows Server 2008) to communicate with a program on another (such as Linux). It uses HTTP and XML to exchange information and specifies how to encode HTTP headers and XML files so that applications can talk to each other. One great advantage to this is also a great detriment, security-wise: Since HTTP is generally allowed through most firewalls, applications using SOAP can generally communicate at will throughout networks. Hmmmm.

   ☒ **A** is incorrect because Unicode is not used by SOAP in this manner. It's a standard for representing text in computing.

   ☒ **B** is incorrect because HTML entities are not used by SOAP in this manner. They're used to represent characters in HTML code.

   ☒ **C** is incorrect because NTFS is a file system and has nothing to do with SOAP.

7. A security administrator is called for advice. The sales staff has noticed a large number of orders being filled at prices far below those posted on the site. After some research, it does not appear that the web server or the underlying SQL database has been directly compromised. Next, the security administrator reviews the IDS logs and finds nothing unusual. Additionally, the local logs on the server itself do not show anything indicating a problem. Which of the following is the most likely explanation for the false orders?

   A. The website uses hidden fields for price values, which have been altered by the attacker.

   B. SQL injection has been used to update pricing in the database. After the order was placed, pricing was reset to normal, to cover tracks.

C. Server-side scripting was used to alter the price.

D. A tool such as Metasploit was used to carry out the attack.

☑ **A.** This is actually more common than you might think. No, I'm not advising you to go do your Christmas shopping early—that could get you in serious trouble—I'm just stating an outright fact that many websites simply don't have their collective stuff together. If you view the source code for a site offering products for sale, many times you can find the pricing secreted away in a "hidden" field (just do a search for "hidden" on the form). If you copy that source to your computer, alter the value in the hidden field, save, and launch the page in the browser, you can order at whatever price you set. The real point is, if anything is moving back and forth between client and server, it can be manipulated.

☒ **B and C** are both incorrect for the same reason. This level of interaction would most certainly be easy to spot between the IDS and server logs. SQL injection involves passing SQL queries and commands through the interface and would be evident in the logs. Server-side includes (SSIs) are directives placed in HTML pages and evaluated on the server while the pages are being served.

☒ **D** is incorrect because there is simply no evidence any tool has been used here. Of course, this might have been a super-talented, ace hacker who jumped in and out of the site leaving absolutely no crumbs to track him down with, but it's *very* unlikely.

8. Which of the following is a common SOA vulnerability?

A. SQL injection

B. XSS

C. XML denial of service

D. CGI manipulation

☑ **C.** Service-oriented architecture (SOA) is a software design idea that is based on specific pieces of software providing functionality as services between applications. The idea is to define how two applications can interact so that one can perform a piece of work for the other (better said, on behalf of the other). Each interaction is independent of any other and is self-contained. SOA programmers make extensive use of XML to carry all this out, and that leaves it vulnerable to crafty XML tampering. If an attacker can somehow pass an XML message with a large payload, or any of a number of other bad content, they can DoS an SOA application. This isn't to imply it's the only DoS available or that SOA is uniquely vulnerable (for instance, the only thing a specifically crafted XML attack can affect): It's just a question, so don't read too much into it.

☒ **A, B**, and **D** are incorrect because these attacks don't necessarily apply here with SOA in this context.

9. The source code of software used by your client seems to have a large number of gets() alongside sparsely used fgets(). What kind of attack is this software potentially susceptible to?

A. SQL injection

B. Buffer overflow

C. Parameter tampering

D. Cookie manipulation

☑ **B.** A buffer overflow is an attempt to write more data into an application's prebuilt buffer area in order to overwrite adjacent memory, execute code, or crash a system (application). By inputting more data than the buffer is allocated to hold, you may be able to crash the application or machine or alter the application's data pointers. gets() is a common source of buffer overflow vulnerabilities because it reads a line from standard input into a buffer until a terminating EOF is found. It performs no check for buffer overrun and is largely replaced by fgets().

☒ **A** is incorrect because SQL injection has nothing to do with this scenario. No evidence is presented that this software even interacts with a database.

☒ **C** is incorrect because parameter tampering deals with manipulating a URL.

☒ **D** is incorrect because cookie manipulation has nothing to do with this software. As covered earlier, a cookie is a small file used to provide a more consistent web experience for a web visitor. Because it holds all sorts of information, though, it can be manipulated for nefarious purposes (using the Firefox add-on Cookie Editor, for instance).

10. Which code entry will stop input at 100 characters?

A. if (I > 100) then exit (1)

B. if (I >= 100) then exit (1)

C. if (I <= 100) then exit (1)

D. if (I < 100) then exit (1)

☑ **B.** There won't be very many pure coding type questions on the exam, and when they do appear, they're pretty clear cut. Because 0 (zero) is used in counting in computer programming code (many indeed start at 1, like FORTRAN, COBOL, and LUA, but the examples in your exam don't), any value from 0 to 99 would suffice. Thus, an entry of 100 would represent the 101st character. Therefore, you can accept anything less than 100 as a character count: "I" must be less than 100 to be accepted, and if it's 100 or above, exit and quit. So, if the character value count is equal to 100, or greater, exit the program (I >= 100).

☒ **A, C, and D** are all incorrect expressions. (I > 100) indicates any entry greater than 100, which *does* work; however, it leaves the extra 101st entry (that is, 100) as acceptable. (I < 100) would exit on any character entry less than 100 (meaning the only acceptable entries would be 101 characters or more—the exact opposite of what we're trying to accomplish). Finally, (I <= 100) is just as bad, for obvious reasons.

11. You are examining log files and come across this URL:

    http://www.example.com/script.ext?template%2e%2e%2e%2e%2e%2f%2e%2f%65%74%63%2f%70%61%73%73%77%64

    Which of the following best describes this potential attack?

    A. This is not an attack but a return of SSL handshakes.

    B. An attacker appears to be using Unicode.

    C. This appears to be a buffer overflow attempt.

    D. This appears to be an XSS attempt.

    ☑ **B.** Unicode is just another way to represent text, so why not use it to try to get past an IDS? Of course, in the real world every IDS would probably be looking for weird Unicode requests anyway (it isn't ciphered or encrypted and really does nothing more than provide a cursory obfuscation), but let's just stick with EC-Council and the CEH exam here for now. This request appears to be attempting a grab of some passwords:

    %2e%2e%2f%2e%2e%2f%2e%2f% = ../../../

    %65%74%63 = etc

    %2f = /

    %70%61%73%73%77%64 = passwd

    ☒ **A, C, and D** are all incorrect because this URL does not necessarily indicate any of these attacks and is quite clearly a Unicode attempt.

12. Which of the following tools can be used to clone a copy of a website to your machine, to be scrutinized later?

    A. BurpSuite

    B. NetCraft

    C. HttpRecon

    D. BlackWidow

    ☑ **D.** BlackWidow is an easy-to-use application that can perform all sorts of things—mainly, to this question, downloading a clone of a website for scanning and vulnerability discovery at your leisure. The following is from the developer's website (sbl.net): "Black Widow is a state-of-the-art website scanner for both experts and beginners. It can download an entire website, or download portions of a site, and can build a site structure first, then download later; you select what to download. The integrated scripting engine is an easy to learn and use programing language to facilitate scanning 'hard to scan' sites. It allows you to control the scan by trapping the scanner event so you can process the request yourself." Of course, there are plenty of other ways to do this—wget comes to mind as one—but, as I mentioned before, EC-Council will test specific tools on your exam, and this is an example.

☒ **A** is incorrect because BurpSuite isn't designed to pull an entire copy of a website externally and run through tests. The following is from the website (www.portswigger.net/burp/): "BurpSuite is an integrated platform for performing security testing of web applications. Its various tools work seamlessly together to support the entire testing process, from initial mapping and analysis of an application's attack surface, through to finding and exploiting security vulnerabilities."

☒ **B** is incorrect because NetCraft isn't a tool to be used for this purpose. NetCraft is actually a security corporation in England that provides all sorts of security tools aimed at the web sector. It's currently well known for its anti-phishing toolbar, which was hailed by Microsoft as being "among the most effective tools to combat phishing on the Internet." This probably explains why Microsoft purchased licensing for NetCraft and added that functionality in Internet Explorer 7 as Microsoft Phishing Filter (also known as SmartScreen Filter in IE8).

☒ **C** is incorrect because HttpRecon isn't used in this manner. HttpRecon is known as a web server fingerprinting tool, providing "highly accurate identification of given httpd implementations" (www.computec.ch/projekte/httprecon/). HttpRecon uses traditional approaches, such as banner-grabbing, status code enumeration, and header ordering analysis, but also adds other analytical techniques to increase accuracy.

13. Which character is your best option in testing for SQL injection vulnerability?

   A. The @ symbol

   B. A double dash

   C. The + sign

   D. A single quote

☑ **D.** SQL injection is all about entering queries and commands into a form field (or URL) to elicit a response, gain information, or manipulate data. On a web page, many times entries into a form field are inserted into a SQL command: When you enter your username and information into the fields and click the button, the SQL command in the background might read something like this:

```
SELECT OrderID, FirstName, Lastname FROM Orders
```

In SQL, a single quote is used to indicate an upcoming character string. Once SQL sees that open quote, it starts parsing everything behind it as string input. If there's no close quote, an error occurs because SQL doesn't know what to do with it. If the web page is configured poorly, that error will return to you and let you know it's time to start injecting SQL commands.

☒ **A, B,** and **C** are incorrect characters to use as part of a SQL injection test. The @ symbol is used to designate a variable in SQL (you'll need to define the variable, of course). The + sign is used to combine strings (as in Matt+Walker). A double dash indicates an upcoming comment in the line.

14. An angry former employee of the organization discovers a web form vulnerable to SQL injection. Using the injection string SELECT * FROM Orders_Pend WHERE Location_City = 'Orlando', he is able to see all pending orders from Orlando. If he wanted to delete the Orders_Pend table altogether, which SQL injection string should be used?

A. SELECT * FROM Orders_Pend WHERE Location_City = 'Orlando';DROP TABLE Orders_Pend --

B. SELECT * FROM Orders_Pend WHERE 'Orlando';DROP_TABLE --

C. DROP TABLE Orders_Pend WHERE 'Orlando = 1' --

D. WHERE Location_City = Orlando'1 = 1': DROP_TABLE --

☑ **A.** SQL queries usually read pretty straightforward, although they can get complicated pretty quickly. In this case you're telling the database, "Can you check the table Orders_Pend and see whether there's a city called Orlando? Oh, by the way, since you're executing any command I send anyway, just go ahead and drop the table called Orders_Pend while you're at it." The only thing missing from SQL queries is a thank-you at the end.

☒ **B, C,** and **D** are incorrect because these are not proper syntax.

15. Efforts to gain information from a target website have produced the following error message:

```
Microsoft OLE DB Provider for ODBC Drivers error '80040e08'
[Microsoft]{OBDC SQL Server Driver}
```

Which of the following best describes the error message?

A. The site may be vulnerable to XSS.

B. The site may be vulnerable to buffer overflow.

C. The site may be vulnerable to SQL injection.

D. The site may be vulnerable to a malware injection.

☑ **C.** Once again, you will get a few "gimme" questions on the exam. The error message clearly displays a SQL error, telling us there's an underlying SQL database to contend with and it's most likely not configured correctly (or we wouldn't be getting an error message like this—through a web interface and telling us exactly what's there—in the first place).

☒ **A, B,** and **D** are all incorrect for the same reason: The error message simply doesn't provide enough information to make those leaps. There is nothing here indicating cross-site scripting or buffer overflow on either side of the ledger. Although it's true the error may indicate which kinds of malware may increase your odds of success, there's nothing there to indicate, by itself, that the site is vulnerable.

16. Which buffer overflow attack is designed to make use of memory that remains in use while a program is running?

   A. Stack

   B. Heap

   C. Active

   D. Permanent

   ☑ **B.** Granted, this is a little bit of a picky question, but you'll definitely see something like this on your exam. Buffer overflows are all about the same thing: inputting more information into a buffer area that was designed for one action in order to write code to a different area of memory so it can be executed. At best, the code will execute, and you can do all sorts of good things. At worse, the program will reject the code and crash. A heap buffer attack takes advantage of the memory space set aside for the program itself. Heap is the memory area immediately "on top" of the program and is not temporary (it's supposed to remain in use as long as the application is running). Pages in the heap can be read from and written to, which is what the attacker will be trying to exploit.

   ☒ **A** is incorrect only because of the actual buffer area being exploited. Whereas heap is memory set aside in the application and is not "temporary," the stack is *designed* that way: Each task is added on top of the previous tasks and is executed in order. Overflow the buffer, and you can affect which area executes.

   ☒ **C** and **D** are incorrect because neither is a buffer overflow attack type. These are added as distractors.

17. Which of the following is a standard method for web servers to pass a user's request to an application and receive data back to forward to the user?

   A. SSI

   B. SSL

   C. CGI

   D. CSI

☑ **C.** Common Gateway Interface (CGI) is a standardized method for transferring information between a web server and an executable (a CGI script is designed to perform some task with the data). CGI is considered a server-side solution because processing is done on the web server and not the client. Because CGI scripts can run essentially arbitrary commands on your system with the permissions of the web server user and because they are almost always wrapped so that a script will execute as the owner of the script, they can be extremely dangerous if not carefully checked. Additionally, all CGI scripts on the server will run as the same user, so they have the potential to conflict (accidentally or deliberately) with other scripts (an attacker could, for example, write a CGI script to destroy all other CGI databases).

☒ **A** is incorrect because server-side includes (SSIs) are directives placed in HTML pages and evaluated on the server while the pages are being served. They let you add dynamically generated content to an existing HTML page, without having to serve the entire page via a CGI program or other dynamic technology.

☒ **B** and **D** are incorrect because both are included as distractors. By now you're certainly familiar with Secure Sockets Layer (SSL) and its value as an encryption method. CSI? Well, that's just good television. Or it used to be, anyway.

18. An attacker performs a SQL injection attack but receives nothing in return. She then proceeds to send multiple SQL queries, soliciting TRUE or FALSE responses. Which attack is being carried out?

    A. Blind SQL injection

    B. SQL denial of service

    C. SQL code manipulation

    D. SQL replay

    ☑ **A.** Blind SQL injection is really kinda neat, even if you're not a nerd. Sometimes a security admin does just enough to frustrate efforts, and you don't receive the error messages or returned information you originally counted on. So, to pull out the info you want, you start asking it (the SQL database) a lot of true and false questions. For example, you could ask the database, "True or false—you have a table called USERS?" If you get a TRUE, then you know the table name and can start asking questions about it. For example, "Hey, database, got an entry in your USERS table named admin?" (SELECT * from USERS where name='admin' and 1=1;#';). Blind SQL is a long, laborious effort, but it can be done.

☒ **B, C,** and **D** are all incorrect because, so far as I know, none of them is a recognized attack by EC-Council. I'm sure you can find ways to perform a DoS on a SQL database, and we're manipulating SQL all over the place in these injection attacks, but these terms just aren't recognized on your exam and are here solely as distractors.

19. Which of the following can be used for remote password cracking of web servers? (Choose all that apply.)

    A. Brutus

    B. Nikto

    C. THC-Hydra

    D. Nessus

    ☑ **A** and **C.** Brutus is a fast, flexible remote password cracker. According to the tool's website (www.hoobie.net/brutus/), it was originally invented to help its creator check routers and network devices for default and common passwords. It has since grown and evolved to much more and is among the more popular security tools available for remote password cracking. THC-Hydra (www.thc.org/thc-hydra/) is another remote password cracker. It's a "parallelized login cracker" that provides the ability to attack over multiple protocols.

    ☒ **B** is incorrect because Nikto is not a remote password cracker. It's an open source web-server-centric vulnerability scanner that performs comprehensive tests against web servers for multiple items.

    ☒ **D** is incorrect because Nessus is not a remote password cracker; it's a vulnerability assessment tool.

20. An attacker is attempting to elevate privileges on a machine by using Java or other functions, through nonvalidated input, to cause the server to execute a malicious piece of code and provide command-line access. Which of the following best describes this action?

    A. Shell injection

    B. File injection

    C. SQL injection

    D. URL injection

    ☑ **A.** When it comes to web application attacks, there are many vectors and avenues to take. One of the more common is injecting something into an input string to exploit poor code. EC-Council defines these attacks in many ways. Also known as *command injection*, shell injection is defined as an attempt to gain shell access using Java or other functions. In short, the attacker will pass commands through a form input (or other avenue) in order to elevate privileges and open a shell for further naughtiness. It occurs when commands are entered into form fields instead of the expected entry.

☒ **B** is incorrect because the EC-Council defines a file injection attack as one where the attacker injects a pointer in the web form input to an exploit hosted on a remote site. Sure, this may accomplish the same thing, but it's not the best choice in this case.

☒ **C** is incorrect because SQL injection attacks involve using SQL queries and commands to elicit a response or action.

☒ **D** is incorrect because URL injection is not an attack type and is included here as a distractor.

21. An attacker is successful in replaying a secure cookie, stolen during an XSS attack, during an invalid session on the server by forcing a web application to act on the cookie's contents. How is this possible?

   A. A cookie can be replayed at any time, no matter the circumstances.

   B. Encryption was accomplished using a single key.

   C. Authentication was accomplished using XML.

   D. Encryption was accomplished at the network layer.

   ☑ **B.** Cookies can be used for all sorts of things, and in this scenario it's being replayed by an attacker to gain access to goodies. If a single key is used in encryption, a replay attack is possible, and cookie authentication is carried out at the application layer.

   ☒ **A** is incorrect because a replay attack of anything—cookie, stolen authentication stream, and so on—can't necessarily be carried out at any time. Replay attacks require planning and proper setup.

   ☒ **C** is incorrect because XML has nothing to do with this.

   ☒ **D** is incorrect because encryption is not carried out at the network layer here.

22. HTML forms include several methods for transferring data back and forth. Inside a form, which of the following encodes the input into the Uniform Resource Identifier (URI)?

   A. HEAD

   B. PUT

   C. GET

   D. POST

   ☑ **C.** An HTTP GET is a method for returning data from a form that "encodes" the form data to the end of the URI (a character string that identifies a resource on the Web, such as a page of text, a video clip, an image, or an application). For example, if you were to enter a credit card number in a form using GET, the resulting URL might look something like https://somesite.com/creditcard.asp?c#=4013229567852219, where the long number is obviously a credit card number just sitting there waiting for anyone to use.

Generally speaking, a POST is "more secure" than a GET, although they both have their uses. If you're wondering when a GET should be used as opposed to a POST, the answer has to do with a vocabulary lesson: defining the term *idempotent*. Thrown about with HTTP GET, idempotent is a mathematical concept about an operation property: If the operation can be performed without changing results, even if it is run multiple times, it's considered idempotent. So, if the input return is assured of having no lasting effect on the state of the form in total, then using a GET is perfectly reasonable. Also, a GET can usually transfer only up to 8KB, whereas a POST can usually handle up to 2GB. However, keep in mind it may wind up including sensitive information in that URI. Suppose your form returns a credit card number and a bad guy is logging URIs: If HTTP GET is in place, the attacker may be able to derive the information. In short, users can manipulate both GET and POST, but GET is simply more visible because of its reliance on something that browsers render to the screen in an editable field. A POST is meant for pushing data directly, and a GET is used when the server is expected to pull something from the data submitted in the URL.

☒ **A** is incorrect because although HEAD and GET are similar, HEAD is not used in forms. It's usually used to pull header information from a web server (remember your banner grabbing from earlier?) and to test links.

☒ **B** is incorrect because HTTP PUT is not used in forms. It's used to transfer files to a web server.

☒ **D** is incorrect because POST does not include the form data in the URI request. According to the World Wide Web Consortium (www.w3.org/), HTML specifications define the difference between GET and POST so that GET means that form data will be encoded by a browser into a URL, whereas POST means the form data is to appear within the message body. In short, a GET can be used for basic, simple retrieval of data, and a POST should be used for most everything else (such as sending an e-mail, updating data on a database, and ordering an item).

23. An attacker is looking at a target website and is viewing an account from the store on URL http://www.anybiz.com/store.php?id=2. He next enters the following URL:

http://www.anybiz.com/store.php?id=2 and 1=1

The web page loads normally. He then enters the following URL:

http://www.anybiz.com/store.php?id=2 and 1=2

A generic page noting "An error has occurred" appears.

Which of the following is a correct statement concerning these actions?

A. The site is vulnerable to cross-site scripting.

B. The site is vulnerable to blind SQL injection.

C. The site is vulnerable to buffer overflows.

D. The site is not vulnerable to SQL injection.

☑ **B**. The URLs shown here are attempting to pass a SQL query through to see what may be going on in the background. Notice the first URL entered added **and 1=1**. Because this was a true statement, the page loaded without problem. However, changing that to a false statement—**and 1=2**—caused the database to return an error. This would now be considered "blind" SQL injection because the actual error was not returned to the attacker (instead, he got a generic page most likely configured by the database administrator). As an aside, sometimes the attacker won't receive the error message or error page at all, but the site will be displayed differently—images out of place, text messed up, and so on—which also indicates blind SQL may be in order.

☒ **A** and **C** are incorrect because neither this attack nor the results have anything to do with cross-site scripting or buffer overflows.

☒ **D** is incorrect because the results indicate SQL injection is possible. Granted, it will take longer, because we can't see error messaging, and will require lots of guesswork and trial and error, but it is susceptible.

24. Which of the following is the hexadecimal value of a NOP instruction?

A. 0x60

B. 0x70

C. 0x80

D. 0x90

☑ **D**. EC-Council just adores the NOP instruction. The no-operation instruction effectively does nothing at all: It's used to take up a few cycles doing absolutely nothing for the purpose of timing and lining up clock cycles. Bad guys can use it in scripting, though, to create a so-called *NOP-sled*, which slides the CPU instruction to a specific memory point (or just the end of the script). If you were to see something with a ton of 0x90 instructions in it, it may very well be a NOP-sled attempt.

☒ **A**, **B**, and **C** are incorrect because they do not represent the hex value of a NOP instruction.

25. An attacker is viewing a blog entry showing a news story and asking for comments. In the comment field, the attacker enters the following:

```
Nice post and a fun read
<script>onload=window.location='http://www.badsite.com'</script>
```

What is the attacker attempting to perform?

A. A SQL injection attack against the blog's underlying database

B. A cross-site scripting attack

C. A buffer overflow DoS attack

D. A file injection DoS attack

☑ **B.** This is a classic (an overly simplified but classic nonetheless) example of cross-site scripting. In a blog, the post entry field is intended to take text entry from a visitor and copy it to a database in the background. What's being attempted here is to have more than just the text copied—the <script> indicator is adding a nice little pointer to a naughty website. If it works, the next visitor to the site who clicks that news story will be redirected to the bad site location.

☒ **A, C,** and **D** are all incorrect because this example contains nothing to indicate a SQL injection or a buffer overflow. Additionally, the idea here is not to perform a denial of service. Actually, it's quite the opposite: The attacker wants the site up and operational so more and more users can be sent to badsite.com.

26. An attacker attempts to manipulate an application by advancing the instruction pointer with a long run of instructions containing no action. What is this attack called?

A. File injection

B. Stack flipping

C. NOP-sled

D. Heap based

☑ **C.** Computer languages usually contain a command most CPUs will recognize as "do nothing." This no-operation (NOP) instruction serves to advance an instruction pointer to a known memory area. The idea behind it is to provide time for unknown activities to occur until it's time to execute the main code (avoiding an exception code and a halt to the system or application). For a ridiculously over-simplified example, if you were "coding" a human's morning routine and wanted them to brush their teeth, you might provide a whole bunch of "do nothings" in front and behind the "pick up toothbrush, put toothpaste on brush, and so on" steps—to provide space for things you may not be aware of.

When it comes to attacks, hackers will send tons of NOP instructions in an effort to move the pointer to an area they control—and to execute the naughty payload there. This NOP-sled is relatively easy to see in action, and all IDSs will pick it up.

☒ **A** is incorrect because file injection occurs when the attacker injects a pointer in a web form input to an exploit hosted on a remote site. There is no file injection occurring in this example.

☒ **B** is incorrect because the term *stack flipping* is not a recognized term on the CEH exam and is included here as a distractor.

☒ **D** is incorrect because a heap-based buffer overflow deals with a buffer overflow specifically aimed at the lower part of the heap, to overwrite dynamic content there.

27. You are examining website files and find the following text file:

```
# robots.txt for http://www.anybiz.com/
User-agent: Googlebot
Disallow: /tmp/
User-agent: *
Disallow: /
Disallow: /private.php
Disallow: /listing.html
```

Which of the following is a true statement concerning this file?

A. All web crawlers are prevented from indexing the listing.html page.

B. All web crawlers are prevented from indexing all pages on the site.

C. The Googlebot crawler is allowed to index pages starting with /tmp/.

D. The Googlebot crawler can access and index everything on the site except for pages starting with /tmp/.

☑ **D.** The robots.txt file was created to allow web designers to control index access to their sites. There are a couple of things you need to know about this file—for your exam and the real world. The first is, no matter what the robots.txt file says, attackers using a crawler to index your site are going to ignore it anyway: It's valid only for "good-guy" crawlers. After that, the rest is easy: robots.txt is stored on the root, is available to anyone (by design), and is read in order from top to bottom, much like an ACL on a router. The format is simple: Define the crawler (User-agent :*name_of_crawler*) and then define what it does not have access to. Most robot.txt files will make use of the * variable to signify all crawlers, but you can certainly get specific with who is allowed in and what they can see.

In this example, from top to bottom, the Googlebot crawler is defined and restricted from seeing /tmp/ pages—no other restrictions are listed. After that, all other crawlers (User-agent: *) are restricted from seeing any page (Disallow: /). The last two lines are truly irrelevant because the condition to ignore all pages has been read.

For additional information here, if you think about what a robots.txt file does, you could consider it a pointer to pages you, as an attacker, really want to see. After all, if the security person on the site didn't want Google indexing it, useful information probably resides there. On the flip side, a security-minded person may get a little snippy with it and have a little fun, sending you to some truly terrible Internet locations should you try to access one of the pages listed there.

☒ A and B are incorrect because the Googlebot crawler is allowed to crawl the site.

☒ C is incorrect because Googlebot is instructed to ignore all /tmp/ pages.

Wireless Network Hacking

This chapter includes questions from the following topics:

- Identify wireless network architecture and terminology
- Identify wireless network types and forms of authentication
- Describe WEP, WPA, and WPA2 wireless encryption
- Identify wireless hacking methods and tools
- Define Bluetooth hacking methods

I grew up in a time when television had only three channels, the music industry was all up in arms because of the new technology allowing anyone to tape their own music (cassette tapes), and if you needed to talk to someone about something, you had to either meet them face to face or call their one and only home phone (and hope they were there). Oh, sure, the ultra-rich had phones (not really much more than glorified CB radio devices actually) built into their limos, but the idea of a cell phone didn't really hit the public consciousness until sometime in the early 1980s. In fact, the first real foray into the technology came in 1973, when a Motorola researcher created a mobile phone. The handset came in at a stealthy 8 by 5 inches, weighing approximately 2½ pounds, and offered a whopping 30 minutes of talk time.

After a decade or so of further research and attempts at bringing the technology to market, the first analog cellular network (Advanced Mobile Phone Service [AMPS]) hit the United States, and a company called DynaTAC released a device that has been ridiculed in technology circles for decades now—the bag phone. Despite the weight and bulkiness of the system and that it provided only a half hour of talk time and took nearly 10 hours to charge, demand for the thing was incredible, and people signed up on waiting lists by the thousands.

I remember quite clearly how jealous I felt seeing people driving around with those ultra-cool giant-battery phones that they could use anywhere. I even looked into buying one and can remember the first time I slung that big old bag over my head to rest the strap on my shoulder so I could heft the cord-connected handset and dial home. Looking back, it seems really silly, but that strong desire by the consumer population fueled an explosion in mobile device technology that has changed the world.

The wireless revolution touched everything in life—not just the humble phone. We looked at making everything wireless and just knew we could do it (*Star Trek* had been showing wireless communication for decades, so why not?). Computer networks were an obvious branch to follow, and seemingly everything else followed. Our wireless technologies are now as much part of life as the light switch on the wall—we wouldn't know what to do without them, and we all just *expect* it all to work. Hence the problem.

I've said repeatedly that almost every technological implementation designed to make our lives easier and better can be, and usually has already been, corrupted by the bad guys, and wireless tech is no exception. Wireless networks are everywhere, and they're broadcasting information across the air that anyone can pick up. Cellular devices are called smartphones, even though the users of the devices aren't, and mobile malware is as common and ubiquitous as teenagers texting during family dinner. And the opportunity for co-opting wireless signals that control everything else—like your car's built-in computer functions, your refrigerator, and maybe the turbine control at the local power plant? Let's just say that while all this wireless technology is really cool and offers us a whole lot of benefits, we better all pay attention to the security side of the whole thing. Who knows what kind of societal uproar could take place if cellular devices and computer networking were taken down and nobody could play Angry Birds?

 STUDY TIPS   Depending on the pool of test questions the system pulls for your exam, you'll either grow to love the test you're taking or hate it with a fiery passion. Questions on wireless are fairly easy and shouldn't bother you too much, except for the ones that aren't. Questions on war chalking, for instance, can sometimes be maddeningly obtuse (although these should be finding their way out of the exam system soon). Others that will drive you bonkers will be on the encoding methods used, channel interference, and things of that nature.

The vast majority of the questions, as you can read in this chapter, shouldn't pose much of a problem for you, though, and not a lot has changed or been updated since version 7. Most of it is pure memorization, and unfortunately, you won't really be asked much about actually hacking a wireless network. You'll get peppered on what the underlying technology is (network standard, encryption used, antenna in place, and what encoding method used), but the questions on actually how to pull it off are few and far between.

1. Which of the following is *not* true regarding SSIDs?

   A. The SSID is broadcast by APs in the network, unless otherwise configured.

   B. If the SSID changes, all clients must update to the new SSID to communicate.

   C. Turning off the SSID broadcast ensures only authorized clients, who know the SSID, can connect.

   D. The SSID serves to identify wireless networks.

   E. SSIDs are case sensitive.

2. Amanda is war driving and plans to use PrismStumbler. She wants to use the information gathered in a GPS mapping software application. Which of the following is the best choice to interface with PrismStumbler?

   A. GPSDrive

   B. GPSMap

   C. WinPcap

   D. Microsoft Mappoint

3. Which of the following tools would be used in a blackjacking attack?

   A. Aircrack

   B. BBCrack

   C. BBProxy

   D. Paros Proxy

4. Which of the following uses a 48-bit initialization vector? (Choose all that apply.)

   A. WEP

   B. WPA

   C. WPA2

   D. WEP2

5. Which of the following are true statements? (Choose all that apply.)

   A. WEP uses shared key encryption with TKIP.

   B. WEP uses shared key encryption with RC4.

   C. WPA2 uses shared key encryption with RC4.

   D. WPA2 uses TKIP and AES encryption.

6. Which of the following best describes the "evil twin" wireless hacking attack?

   A. An attacker sets up a client machine using the same MAC as an authorized user.

   B. An attacker connects using the same username and password as an authorized user.

C. An attacker sets up an access point inside the network range for clients to connect to.

D. An attacker sets up an authentication server on the wireless network.

7. Brad is responsible for wireless security in his organization. He has turned off SSID broadcasting, enabled MAC filtering, and instituted wireless encryption. While strolling around the area, he notices an employee using an HP laptop, and the organization purchases only Dell systems for employees. After reviewing access logs and site survey information, Brad determines there appears to be no rogue access points in the area, and all connection attempts in wireless appear to be valid. There are no obvious signs of an attack. Which of the following best describes the successful connection attempt by the employee on the HP laptop?

A. The employee has brute-forced the encryption.

B. The employee has spoofed a legitimate MAC address.

C. The laptop choice is irrelevant, as long as the OUI is the same.

D. An evil twin attack is in place.

8. During an outbrief of a pen test, you share successes your team has had against the target's wireless network. The client asks for an explanation of the results, stating directional antennas for the access points were strategically placed to provide coverage for the building instead of omnidirectional antennas. Which of the following statements provides the correct response?

A. Positioning and types of antennas are irrelevant.

B. Directional antennas provide only for weak encryption of signal.

C. Positioning of the antennas is irrelevant unless 802.11n is the standard chosen.

D. Wireless signals can be detected from miles away; therefore, this step alone will not secure the network.

9. An attacker is attempting to crack a WEP code to gain access to the network. After enabling monitor mode on wlan0 and creating a monitoring interface (mon 0), she types this command:

```
aireplay -ng -0 0 -a 0A:00:2B:40:70:80 -c mon0
```

What is she trying to accomplish?

A. Gain access to the WEP access code by examining the response to deauthentication packets, which contain the WEP code

B. Use deauthentication packets to generate lots of network traffic

C. Determine the BSSID of the access point

D. Discover the cloaked SSID of the network

10. Which wireless standard works at 54Mbps on a frequency range of 2.4GHz?

   A. 802.11a

   B. 802.11b

   C. 802.11g

   D. 802.11n

11. The team has discovered an access point configured with WEP encryption. What is needed to perform a fake authentication to the AP in an effort to crack WEP? Choose all that apply.

   A. A captured authentication packet

   B. The IP address of the AP

   C. The MAC address of the AP

   D. The SSID

12. Which of the tools listed here is a passive discovery tool?

   A. Aircrack

   B. Kismet

   C. NetStumbler

   D. Netsniff

13. You have discovered an access point using WEP for encryption purposes. Which of the following is the best choice for uncovering the network key?

   A. NetStumbler

   B. Aircrack

   C. John the Ripper

   D. Kismet

14. Which of the following statements are true regarding TKIP? (Choose all that apply.)

   A. Temporal Key Integrity Protocol forces a key change every 10,000 packets.

   B. Temporal Key Integrity Protocol ensures keys do not change during a session.

   C. Temporal Key Integrity Protocol is an integral part of WEP.

   D. Temporal Key Integrity Protocol is an integral part of WPA.

15. Regarding SSIDs, which of the following are true statements? (Choose all that apply.)

   A. SSIDs are always 32 characters in length.

   B. SSIDs can be up to 32 characters in length.

   C. Turning off broadcasting prevents discovery of the SSID.

D. SSIDs are part of every packet header from the AP.

E. SSIDs provide important security for the network.

F. Multiple SSIDs are needed to move between APs within an ESS.

16. You are discussing WEP cracking with a junior pen test team member. Which of the following are true statements regarding the initialization vectors? (Choose all that apply.)

A. IVs are 32 bits in length.

B. IVs are 24 bits in length.

C. IVs get reused frequently.

D. IVs are sent in clear text.

E. IVs are encrypted during transmission.

F. IVs are used once per encryption session.

17. A pen test member has configured a wireless access point with the same SSID as the target organization's SSID and has set it up inside a closet in the building. After some time, clients begin connecting to his access point. Which of the following statements are true regarding this attack? (Choose all that apply.)

A. The rogue access point may be discovered by security personnel using NetStumbler.

B. The rogue access point may be discovered by security personnel using NetSurveyor.

C. The rogue access point may be discovered by security personnel using Kismet.

D. The rogue access point may be discovered by security personnel using Aircrack.

E. The rogue access point may be discovered by security personnel using ToneLoc.

18. A pen test member is running the airsnarf tool from a Linux laptop. What is she attempting to do?

A. MAC flooding against an AP on the network

B. Denial-of-service attacks against APs on the network

C. Cracking network encryption codes from the WEP AP

D. Stealing usernames and passwords from an AP

19. What frequency does Bluetooth operate in?

A. 2.4–2.48GHz

B. 2.5GHz

C. 2.5–5GHz

D. 5GHz

20. Which of the following is true regarding wireless network architecture?

    A. The service area provided by a single AP is known as an ESS.

    B. The service area provided by a single AP is known as a BSSID.

    C. The service area provided by multiple APs acting within the same network is known as an ESS.

    D. The service area provided by multiple APs acting within the same network is known as an ESSID.

21. A pen tester boosts the signal reception capabilities of a laptop. She then drives from building to building in the target organization's campus searching for wireless access points. What attack is she performing?

    A. War chalking

    B. War walking

    C. War driving

    D. War moving

22. You are examining the physical configuration of a target's wireless network. You notice on the site survey that omnidirectional antenna access points are located in the corners of the building. Which of the following statements are true regarding this configuration? (Choose all that apply.)

    A. The site may be vulnerable to sniffing from locations outside the building.

    B. The site is not vulnerable to sniffing from locations outside the building.

    C. The use of dipole antennas may improve the security of the site.

    D. The use of directional antennas may improve the security of the site.

23. Which of the following is a true statement regarding wireless security?

    A. WPA2 is a better encryption choice than WEP.

    B. WEP is a better encryption choice than WPA2.

    C. Cloaking the SSID and implementing MAC filtering eliminate the need for encryption.

    D. Increasing the length of the SSID to its maximum increases security for the system.

24. A pen test colleague is attempting to use a wireless connection inside the target's building. On his Linux laptop he types the following commands:

```
ifconfig wlan0 down
ifconfig wlan0 hw ether 0A:0B:0C:1A:1B:1C
ifconfig wlan0 up
```

What is the most likely reason for this action?

A. Port security is enabled on the access point.

B. The SSID is cloaked from the access point.

C. MAC filtering is enabled on the access point.

D. Weak signaling is frustrating connectivity to the access point.

25. An individual attempts to make a call using his cell phone; however, it seems unresponsive. After a few minutes' effort, he turns it off and turns it on again. During his next phone call, the phone disconnects and becomes unresponsive again. Which Bluetooth attack is underway?

A. Bluesmacking

B. Bluejacking

C. Bluesniffing

D. Bluesnarfing

26. Which wireless standard achieves high data rate speeds by implementing MIMO antenna technology?

A. 802.11b

B. 802.11g

C. 802.11n

D. 802.16

1. C
2. A
3. C
4. B, C
5. B, D
6. C
7. B
8. D
9. B
10. C
11. C, D
12. B
13. B
14. A, D
15. B, D
16. B, C, D
17. A, B, C
18. D
19. A
20. C
21. C
22. A, D
23. A
24. C
25. A
26. A

1. Which of the following is *not* true regarding SSIDs?

   A. The SSID is broadcast by APs in the network, unless otherwise configured.

   B. If the SSID changes, all clients must update to the new SSID to communicate.

   C. Turning off the SSID broadcast ensures only authorized clients, who know the SSID, can connect.

   D. The SSID serves to identify wireless networks.

   E. SSIDs are case sensitive.

   ☑ **C.** The intent of a service set identifier (SSID) is solely to identify one wireless network from another. It is not designed, nor should it be relied on, as a security feature. Although you can turn off broadcasting of the SSID, just remember that it is sent in the header of every single packet the AP sends anyway—not to mention by every single device on the network as well. So, while you did make it a little harder to find (using a packet sniffer instead of just looking at "available networks" in wireless properties) and will frustrate the most lazy among us pen testers (or your pesky neighbors looking for free Internet access), it doesn't really keep anyone out.

   ☒ **A, B, D,** and **E** are incorrect choices because these are true statements. SSIDs are case-sensitive, 32-character strings that are *designed* to be broadcast. They're identifiers for networks, with their entire purpose on the planet being to provide a means for clients to differentiate between wireless networks they are capable of connecting to. So, unless you tell the access point (AP) not to, it will gladly broadcast the SSID for easy network discovery by potential clients. The SSID will also need to be updated on all clients if you change it on the AP, which should make perfect sense: If you change it on an AP and don't tell your clients, they will consistently send packets out with bad headers, pointing to a network that no longer exists.

2. Amanda is war driving and plans to use PrismStumbler. She wants to use the information gathered in a GPS mapping software application. Which of the following is the best choice to interface with PrismStumbler?

   A. GPSDrive

   B. GPSMap

   C. WinPcap

   D. Microsoft Mappoint

   ☑ **A.** Tool-specific questions sometimes enrage and confuse me because I don't know if EC-Council is trying to promote their use or just checking to see whether I know what's out there. In this case, PrismStumbler is a wireless network identifier application that is Linux-based. The information

PrismStumbler pulls can be ported into mapping software to build a neat-o map of what network is where, and the best location to set up your external antenna. GPSDrive (www.gpsdrive.de) is a free, Linux-based GPS map system that PrismStumbler can interface with. I've personally never used either but saw this mentioned on several study references and thought we should include it here.

As an aside, other wireless discovery applications include, but are not limited to, insider, NetSurveyor, NetStumbler, VisStumbler, and WirelessMon. Other GPS mapping tools include, but are not limited to, WIGLE and Skyhook. If you want to skip the whole effort, you can use jiWire or WeFi to display a map of thousands of free wireless access points around you.

🗵 **B** is incorrect because, as far as I know, there is no tool called GPSMap.

🗵 **C** is incorrect because winPcap is the Windows driver you'd use to allow a NIC to be in promiscuous mode.

🗵 **D** is incorrect because, while Mappoint is a GPS mapping application, it is Microsoft Windows based and won't interface with the Linux-based PrismStumbler.

3. Which of the following tools would be used in a blackjacking attack?

    A. Aircrack

    B. BBCrack

    C. BBProxy

    D. Paros Proxy

    ☑ **C.** This is another tool-specific question, but one that should be relatively easy. Blackjacking and BBProxy were exposed at DefCon several years ago, so this isn't anything new in terms of an attack. In short, a Blackberry device is, in effect, part of the internal network, and configuring an attack properly on the handset may provide access to resources on the internal network. BBProxy is used in part of this attack, and you can see the whole thing pulled off at this link from the original presentation in 2006: http://www .praetoriang.net/presentations/blackjack.html.

    🗵 **A, B,** and **D** are incorrect because these tools aren't used in blackjacking attempts. Aircrack is used in wireless network encryption cracking, and Paros is a proxy service, but neither is used in blackjacking. BBCrack doesn't exist.

4. Which of the following uses a 48-bit initialization vector? (Choose all that apply.)

    A. WEP

    B. WPA

    C. WPA2

    D. WEP2

☑ **B** and **C**. One of the improvements from WEP to WPA involved extending the initialization vector (IV) to 48 bits from 24 bits. An initialization vector (IV) provides for confidentiality and integrity. Wireless encryption algorithms use it to calculate an integrity check value (ICV), appending it to the end of the data payload. The IV is then combined with a key to be input into an algorithm (RC4 for WEP, AES for WPA2). Therefore, because the length of an IV determines the total number of potential random values that can possibly be created for encryption purposes, doubling to 48 bits increased overall security. By itself, this didn't answer *all* security problems— it only meant it took a little longer to capture enough IV packets to crack the code—however, combined with other steps it did provide for better security.

☒ **A** is incorrect because WEP uses a 24-bit IV. In WEP, this meant there were approximately 16 million unique IV values. Although this may seem like a large number, it's really not—a determined hacker can capture enough IVs in a brute-force attack in a matter of hours to crack the key.

☒ **D** is incorrect because there is no such thing as WEP2.

5. Which of the following are true statements? (Choose all that apply.)

   A. WEP uses shared key encryption with TKIP.

   B. WEP uses shared key encryption with RC4.

   C. WPA2 uses shared key encryption with RC4.

   D. WPA2 uses TKIP and AES encryption.

   ☑ **B** and **D**. WEP uses a 24-bit initialization vector and RC4 to "encrypt" data transmissions, although saying that makes me shake in disgust because it's really a misnomer. WEP was designed as *basic* encryption merely to simulate the "security" of being on a wired network—hence, the "equivalent" part in Wired Equivalent Privacy. It was never intended as true encryption protection. WPA was an improvement on two fronts. First, the shared key portion of encryption was greatly enhanced by the use of Temporal Key Integrity Protocol (TKIP). In short, the key used to encrypt data was made temporary in nature and is swapped out every 10,000 packets or so. Additionally, WPA2 uses NIST-approved encryption with AES as the algorithm of choice.

   ☒ **A** is incorrect because WEP does not use TKIP. Along with the same key being used to encrypt and decrypt (shared key), it's not changed and remains throughout the communication process—which is part of the reason it's so easy to crack.

   ☒ **C** is incorrect because WPA2 does not use RC4 as an encryption algorithm.

6. Which of the following best describes the "evil twin" wireless hacking attack?

   A. An attacker sets up a client machine using the same MAC as an authorized user.

   B. An attacker connects using the same username and password as an authorized user.

C. An attacker sets up an access point inside the network range for clients to connect to.

D. An attacker sets up an authentication server on the wireless network.

☑ **C.** The "evil twin" attack is one involving a rogue access point. The idea is pretty simple: Set up your own access point (AP) somewhere—even outside the building if you want, so long as it's within range for clients—and have users connect to your AP instead of the legitimate target's network. If a user looks at available wireless networks and connects to yours (because the signal strength is better, yours is free whereas the other is not, and so on), you effectively have control over all their network traffic. For example, you could configure completely new DNS servers and have your AP configure those addresses within the DHCP address offering, routing users to fake websites you've created to steal authentication information. Not to mention you could funnel everything through a packet capture or shut off access to anyone you felt like virtually neutering for the day. In real-world use, these are set up mostly for sniffing purposes—waiting for some juicy bit of authentication traffic to steal.

Keep in mind, though, the real drawback in this attack is it's fairly easy to spot, and you may run a substantial risk of discovery if the security staff is doing its job. Tools such as NetStumbler, NetSurveyor, Kismet, and a host of others can help ferret out these rogue APs.

☒ **A, B,** and **D** are all incorrect because they do not reflect an evil twin attack. MAC spoofing is not defined as evil twin (it may work as a way into APs that are using MAC filtering, but it's not called evil twin). User accounts and authentication, although definitely important throughout the network, even on the wireless side, have nothing to do with evil twin.

7. Brad is responsible for wireless security in his organization. He has turned off SSID broadcasting, enabled MAC filtering, and instituted wireless encryption. While strolling around the area, he notices an employee using an HP laptop, and the organization purchases only Dell systems for employees. After reviewing access logs and site survey information, Brad determines there appears to be no rogue access points in the area, and all connection attempts in wireless appear to be valid. There are no obvious signs of an attack. Which of the following best describes the successful connection attempt by the employee on the HP laptop?

A. The employee has brute-forced the encryption.

B. The employee has spoofed a legitimate MAC address.

C. The laptop choice is irrelevant, as long as the OUI is the same.

D. An evil twin attack is in place.

☑ **B.** This question is obviously aimed at the Mac-spoofing side of things. Are there other possible explanations for this "rogue" employee connections? Perhaps, but of the answers provided Mac spoofing is the most logical choice. When Brad saw an HP laptop in his Dell-only environment, he knew something was amiss. Having turned on MAC filtering, he was confident that only the MAC addresses he knew about—the ones from his Dell laptop machines in the environment—could connect to the AP. And he was absolutely correct. In this case, the employee simply spoofed the MAC address of his Dell system on the HP laptop he wanted to use. The AP couldn't care less, so he went about merrily doing his work on a different laptop.

☒ **A** is incorrect because a brute-force attempt would most likely have shown *something* in security logs and monitoring.

☒ **C** is incorrect because the organizational unique identifier (OUI) makes up only the first half of the MAC address; the second half is what makes each address singularly unique. As an aside, this one's doubly wrong, as HP and Dell both would have *different* OUIs in the first place.

☒ **D** is incorrect because the evil twin attack—a rogue access point set up in the environment—would've definitely shown up in the site survey.

8. During an outbrief of a pen test, you share successes your team has had against the target's wireless network. The client asks for an explanation of the results, stating directional antennas for the access points were strategically placed to provide coverage for the building instead of omnidirectional antennas. Which of the following statements provides the correct response?

   A. Positioning and types of antennas are irrelevant.

   B. Directional antennas provide only for weak encryption of signal.

   C. Positioning of the antennas is irrelevant unless 802.11n is the standard chosen.

   D. Wireless signals can be detected from miles away; therefore, this step alone will not secure the network.

   ☑ **D.** Also sometimes called a *yagi antenna* (all yagi antennas are directional, but not all directional antennas are yagi, so don't get confused), a directional antenna focuses the signal in a specific direction, which greatly increases signal strength *and* distance. The benefit in using them should be fairly obvious (controlling the signal's direction as opposed to using an omnidirectional antenna); however, it interjects its own problems. Because the signal is now greatly increased in strength and distance, you may find attackers actually have an easier time gaining network access. Sure, they will need a way to boost their own sending strength, but they'll be able to pick up your signal for *miles*. Wireless network design needs to take into account not only the type of antenna used but where it is placed and what is set up to contain or corral the signal. Additionally, don't forget that the narrower the beam, the less space is available for clients to connect. Show me a highly directional parabolic antenna, and I'll show you a lot of users who can't connect to the network.

☒ **A** is incorrect because antenna positioning is of great importance to your overall network security. The placement of antennas will dictate signal strength and direction for your clients. Not paying attention to signal spill—into parking lots or across to buildings you don't own—is a recipe for disaster because you're providing an easy means for an attacker to access your network.

☒ **B** is incorrect because antennas don't provide encryption by themselves. They are connected to devices that implement security, but the type of antenna used doesn't dictate your encryption method (WEP or WAP2).

☒ **C** is incorrect because the encoding method used—whether 802.11n or otherwise (for example, 802.11a)—has relatively nothing to do with keeping attackers out of your network.

9. An attacker is attempting to crack a WEP code to gain access to the network. After enabling monitor mode on wlan0 and creating a monitoring interface (mon 0), she types this command:

```
aireplay -ng -0 0 -a 0A:00:2B:40:70:80 -c mon0
```

What is she trying to accomplish?

A. Gain access to the WEP access code by examining the response to deauthentication packets, which contain the WEP code

B. Use deauthentication packets to generate lots of network traffic

C. Determine the BSSID of the access point

D. Discover the cloaked SSID of the network

☑ **B.** Within 802.11 standards, there are several different management-type frames in use, everything from a beacon and association request to something called (and I'm not making this up) a *probe request*. One of these management frames is a deauthentication packet, which basically shuts off a client from the network. The client then has to reconnect—and will do so quickly. The idea behind this kind of activity is to generate lots of traffic to capture in order to discern the WEP access code (from clients trying to reassociate to all the new ARP packets that will come flying around, since many machines will dump their ARP cache after being shut off the network). Remember the initialization vectors within WEP are relatively short (24 bits) and are reused frequently, so any attempt to crack the code requires, in general, around 15,000 or so packets. You can certainly gather these over time, but generating traffic can accomplish it much faster. One final note on this must be brought up: This type of attack can just as easily result in a denial-of-service attack against hosts and the AP in question, so be careful.

☒ **A** is incorrect because the response to a deauth packet does not contain the WEP access code in the clear. If it did, we wouldn't need to bother with all this traffic generation in the first place—one simple packet would be enough to crack all security.

☒ **C** is incorrect because the basic service set identifier (BSSID) is the MAC address of the AP. It's usually easy enough to gain from any number of methods (using airodump, for instance) and isn't a reason for sending multiple deauth packets. There are networks where the BSSID is hidden (referred to as *cloaking*), but other tools (airmon and airodump) can help with that.

☒ **D** is incorrect because even if an SSID is "cloaked," that doesn't mean it's actually hidden; all it means is that it is not *broadcast*. The SSID is still contained in every single packet sent from the AP, and discovering it is easy enough.

10. Which wireless standard is designed to work at 54Mbps on a frequency range of 2.4GHz?

    A. 802.11a

    B. 802.11b

    C. 802.11g

    D. 802.11n

    ☑ **C.** The 802.11 series of standards identifies all sorts of wireless goodies, such as the order imposed on how clients communicate, rules for authentication, data transfer, size of packets, how the messages are encoded into the signal, and so on. 802.11g combines the advantages of both the "a" and "b" standards without as many of the drawbacks. It's fast (at 54Mbps), is backward compatible with 802.11b clients, and doesn't suffer from the coverage area restrictions 802.11a has to contend with. Considering it operates in the 2.4GHz range, however, there may be some interference issues to deal with. Not only are a plethora of competing networks blasting their signals (sometimes on the same channel) near and around your network, but you also have to consider Bluetooth devices, cordless phones, and even baby monitors that may cause disruption (due to interference) of wireless signals. And microwave ovens happen to run at 2.45GHz—right smack dab in the middle of the range.

    ☒ **A** is incorrect because 802.11a operates at 54Mbps but uses the 5GHz frequency range. The big drawback to 802.11a was the frequency range itself—because of the higher frequency, network range was limited. Whereas 802.11b clients could be spread across a relative large distance, 802.11a clients could communicate much faster but had to be closer together. Combined with the increased cost of equipment, this contributed to 802.11a not being fully accepted as a de facto standard. That said, for security purposes, it may not be a bad choice. Not as many people use it, or even look for it, and its smaller range may work to assist you in preventing spillage outside your building.

☒ **B** is incorrect because 802.11b operates at 11Mbps on the 2.4GHz frequency range. It's slower than "a" or "g," but soon after its release it became the de facto standard for wireless. Price and network range contributed to this.

☒ **D** is incorrect because 802.11n works at 100 Mbps (+) in frequency ranges from 2.4GHz to 5GHz. It achieves this rate using multiple in, multiple out (MIMO) antennas.

11. The team has discovered an access point configured with WEP encryption. What is needed to perform a fake authentication to the AP in an effort to crack WEP? (Choose all that apply.)

A. A replay of a captured authentication packet

B. The IP address of the AP

C. The MAC address of the AP

D. The SSID

☑ **C and D.** Cracking WEP generally comes down to capturing a whole bunch of packets and running a little math magic to crack the key. If you want to generate traffic by sending fake authentication packets to the AP, you need the AP's MAC address and the SSID to make the attempt.

☒ **A and B** are incorrect because this information is not needed for a fake authentication packet. Sure, you can capture and replay an entire authentication packet, but it won't do much good, and the IP is not needed at all.

12. Which of the tools listed here is a passive discovery tool?

A. Aircrack

B. Kismet

C. NetStumbler

D. Netsniff

☑ **B.** A question like this one can be a little tricky, depending on its wording; however, per the EC-Council, Kismet works as a true passive network discovery tool, with no packet interjection whatsoever. The following is from www.kismetwireless.net: "Kismet is an 802.11 layer 2 wireless network detector, sniffer, and intrusion detection system. Kismet will work with any wireless card which supports raw monitoring (rfmon) mode, and (with appropriate hardware) can sniff 802.11b, 802.11a, 802.11g, and 802.11n traffic. Kismet also supports plugins which allow sniffing other media." You might also see two other interesting notables about Kismet on your exam: First, it works by *channel hopping*, which means to discover as many networks as possible. Second, it has the ability to sniff packets and save them to a log file, readable by Wireshark or TCPDump.

☒ **A** is incorrect because Aircrack is "an 802.11 WEP and WPA-PSK keys cracking program that can recover keys once enough data packets have been captured. It implements the standard FMS attack along with some optimizations like KoreK attacks, as well as the all-new PTW attack" (www.aircrack-ng.org).

☒ **C** is incorrect because NetStumbler is considered an active network discovery application. NetStumbler is among the most popular wireless tools you might see in anyone's arsenal.

☒ **D** is incorrect because Netsniff is included as a distractor and is not a valid tool.

13. You have discovered an access point using WEP for encryption purposes. Which of the following is the best choice for uncovering the network key?

   A. NetStumbler

   B. Aircrack

   C. John the Ripper

   D. Kismet

   ☑ **B.** Aircrack is a fast tool for cracking WEP. You'll need to gather a lot of packets (assuming you've collected at least 50,000 packets or so, it'll work swimmingly fast) using another toolset, but once you have them together, Aircrack does a wonderful job cracking the key. One method Aircrack uses that you may see referenced on the exam is *KoreK implementation*, which basically involves slicing bits out of packets and replacing them with guesses—the more this is done, the better the guessing and, eventually, the faster the key is recovered. Other tools for cracking WEP include Cain (which can also use KoreK), KisMac, WEPCrack, and Elcomsoft's Wireless Security Auditor tool.

   ☒ **A** is incorrect because NetStumbler is a network discovery tool. It can also be used to identify rogue access points and interference and is also useful in measuring signal strength (for aiming antennas and such).

   ☒ **C** is incorrect because John the Ripper is a Linux-based password-cracking tool, not a wireless key discovery one.

   ☒ **D** is incorrect because Kismet is a passive network discovery (and other auditing) tool but does not perform key cracking.

14. Which of the following statements are true regarding TKIP? (Choose all that apply.)

   A. Temporal Key Integrity Protocol forces a key change every 10,000 packets.

   B. Temporal Key Integrity Protocol ensures keys do not change during a session.

   C. Temporal Key Integrity Protocol is an integral part of WEP.

   D. Temporal Key Integrity Protocol is an integral part of WPA.

☑ **A and D.** TKIP is a significant step forward in wireless security. Instead of sticking with one key throughout a session with a client and reusing it, as occurred in WEP, *Temporal* Key Integrity Protocol changes the key out every 10,000 packets or so. Additionally, the keys are transferred back and forth during an Extensible Authentication Protocol (EAP) authentication session, which makes use of a four-step handshake process in proving the client belongs to the AP, and vice versa. TKIP came about in WPA.

☒ **B and C** are simply incorrect statements. TKIP does not maintain a single key, it changes the key frequently, and it is part of WPA (and WPA2), not WEP.

15. Regarding SSIDs, which of the following are true statements? (Choose all that apply.)

   A. SSIDs are always 32 characters in length.

   B. SSIDs can be up to 32 characters in length.

   C. Turning off broadcasting prevents discovery of the SSID.

   D. SSIDs are part of every packet header from the AP.

   E. SSIDs provide important security for the network.

   F. Multiple SSIDs are needed to move between APs within an ESS.

   ☑ **B and D.** Service set identifiers have only one real function in life, so far as you're concerned on this exam: identification. They are not a security feature in any way, shape, or form, and they are designed solely to identify one access point's network from another's. SSIDs can be up to 32 characters in length but don't have to be that long (in fact, you'll probably discover most of them are not).

   ☒ **A** is incorrect because SSIDs do not *have* to be 32 characters in length. They *can* be, but they do not have to fill 32 characters of space.

   ☒ **C** is incorrect because "cloaking" the SSID really doesn't do much at all. It's still part of every packet header, so discovery is relatively easy.

   ☒ **E** is incorrect because SSIDs are not considered a security feature for wireless networks.

   ☒ **F** is incorrect because an extended service set (ESS, an enterprise-wide wireless network consisting of multiple APs) requires only a single SSID that all APs work with.

16. You are discussing WEP cracking with a junior pen test team member. Which of the following are true statements regarding the initialization vectors? (Choose all that apply.)

   A. IVs are 32 bits in length.

   B. IVs are 24 bits in length.

C. IVs get reused frequently.

D. IVs are sent in clear text.

E. IVs are encrypted during transmission.

F. IVs are used once per encryption session.

☑ **B**, **C**, and **D**. Weak initialization vectors and poor encryption are part of the reason WEP implementation is not encouraged as a true security measure on wireless networks. And, let's be fair here, it was never truly designed to be, which is why it's named Wired Equivalent Privacy instead of Wireless Encryption Protocol (as some have erroneously tried to name it). IVs are 24 bits in length, are sent in clear text, and are reused a lot. Capture enough packets, and you can easily crack the code.

☒ **A**, **E**, and **F** are incorrect statements. IVs are not 32 bits in length, are not encrypted themselves, and are definitely not used once per session (that would be even worse than being reused).

17. A pen test member has configured a wireless access point with the same SSID as the target organization's SSID and has set it up inside a closet in the building. After some time, clients begin connecting to his access point. Which of the following statements are true regarding this attack? (Choose all that apply.)

A. The rogue access point may be discovered by security personnel using NetStumbler.

B. The rogue access point may be discovered by security personnel using NetSurveyor.

C. The rogue access point may be discovered by security personnel using Kismet.

D. The rogue access point may be discovered by security personnel using Aircrack.

E. The rogue access point may be discovered by security personnel using ToneLoc.

☑ **A**, **B**, and **C**. Rogue access points (sometimes called *evil twin attacks*) can provide an easy way to gain useful information from clueless users on a target network. However, be forewarned, security personnel can use multiple tools and techniques to discover rogue APs. NetStumbler is one of the more popular, and useful, tools available. It's a great network discovery tool that can also be used to identify rogue access points, network interference, and signal strength. Kismet, another popular tool, provides many of the same features and is noted as a "passive" network discovery tool. NetSurveyor is a free, easy-to-use Windows-based tool that provides many of the same features as NetStumbler and Kismet and works with virtually every wireless NIC in modern existence. A "professional" version of NetSurveyor is now available (you get 10 uses of it before you're required to buy a license). Lastly, identifying a rogue access point requires the security staff to have knowledge of every access point owned—and its MAC. If it's known there are 10 APs in the network and suddenly an 11th appears, that alone won't help find and disable the bad one. It takes some level of organization to find these things, and that plays into your hands as an ethical hacker. The longer your evil twin is left sitting there, the better chance it will be found, so keep it short and sweet.

☒ **D** is incorrect because Aircrack is used to crack network encryption codes, not to identify rogue access points.

☒ **E** is incorrect because ToneLoc is a tool used for war dialing (identifying open modems within a block of phone numbers). As an aside, this was also the moniker for a 1990s one-hit-wonder rapper, although I can promise that won't be on your exam.

18. A pen test member is running the Airsnarf tool from a Linux laptop. What is she attempting to do?

A. MAC flooding against an AP on the network

B. Denial-of-service attacks against APs on the network

C. Cracking network encryption codes from the WEP AP

D. Stealing usernames and passwords from an AP

☑ **D.** Identifying tools and what they do is a big part of the exam—which is easy enough because it's pure memorization, and this is a prime example. Per the website (http://airsnarf.shmoo.com/), "Airsnarf is a simple rogue wireless access point setup utility designed to demonstrate how a rogue AP can steal usernames and passwords from public wireless hotspots. Airsnarf was developed and released to demonstrate an inherent vulnerability of public 802.11b hotspots—snarfing usernames and passwords by confusing users with DNS and HTTP redirects from a competing AP." It basically turns your laptop into a competing AP in the local area and confuses client requests to send your way.

☒ **A** is incorrect because Airsnarf does not provide MAC flooding. You may want to MAC flood a network switch for easier sniffing, but that doesn't work the same way for an access point on a wireless network.

☒ **B** is incorrect because Airsnarf is not a DoS tool. You can make an argument the clients themselves are denied service while they're erroneously communicating with the Airsnarf laptop, but it's not the intent of the application to perform a DoS attack on the network. Quite the opposite: The longer things stay up and running, the more usernames and passwords that can be gathered.

☒ **C** is incorrect because Airsnarf is not an encryption-cracking tool. It reads a lot like "Air*crack*," so don't get confused (these will be used as distractors against one another on your exam).

19. What frequency does Bluetooth operate in?

   A. 2.4–2.48GHz

   B. 2.5GHz

   C. 2.5–5GHz

   D. 5GHz

   ☑ **A.** Yes, you may actually get a question this "down in the weeds" regarding Bluetooth. As an additional study note, you will commonly see a reference to Bluetooth working at 2.45GHz (it's in the range). Bluetooth is designed to work at around 10 meters of range and can attach up to eight devices simultaneously. It makes use of something call *spread-spectrum frequency hopping*, which significantly reduces the chance that more than one device will use the same frequency in communicating.

   ☒ **B, C,** and **D** are incorrect frequency ranges for Bluetooth.

20. Which of the following is true regarding wireless network architecture?

   A. The service area provided by a single AP is known as an ESS.

   B. The service area provided by a single AP is known as a BSSID.

   C. The service area provided by multiple APs acting within the same network is known as an ESS.

   D. The service area provided by multiple APs acting within the same network is known as an ESSID.

   ☑ **C.** An extended service set (ESS) is created by having multiple access points work within the same network SSID and encryption standard to provide extended, uninterrupted coverage for clients. So long as you have everything configured correctly (SSID, channels, and so on), as a client moves from one AP in your network to another, they'll disassociate from one AP and (re)associate with another seamlessly. This movement across multiple APs within a single ESS is known as *roaming*.

   ☒ **A** is incorrect because a single AP's coverage area is referred to as a basic service set (BSS).

   ☒ **B** is incorrect because the basic service set identification (BSSID) is the MAC address of the access point within the BSS.

   ☒ **D** is incorrect because the extended service set identification (ESSID) is the SSID for an ESS (the up-to-32-bit code that identifies the network you're on as you roam from AP to AP in the organization's wireless network).

21. A pen tester boosts the signal reception capabilities of a laptop. She then drives from building to building in the target organization's campus searching for wireless access points. What attack is she performing?

A. War chalking

B. War walking

C. War driving

D. War moving

☑ **C.** This is one of those easy questions on the exam because the term *war driving* is fairly well known. In war driving, an attacker boosts the reception capability of a laptop as best as possible and installs NetStumbler, Kismet, OmniPeek, NetSurveyor, or any of hundreds of network discovery tools. She then simply drives around, identifying which networks are available and where their signal is the strongest.

☒ **A** is incorrect because *war chalking* is the act of drawing a symbol to indicate wireless hotspot locations. A *war chalk* is a symbol drawn somewhere in a public place indicating the presence of a wireless network. These can indicate free networks, hidden SSIDs, pay-for-use hotspots, and which encryption technique is in use.

☒ **B** is incorrect because *war walking*, sometimes referred to as *war jogging*, is done on foot. In practice, it's no different than war driving—only that the attacker is walking or jogging as opposed to driving a vehicle.

☒ **D** is incorrect because *war moving*, to my knowledge, is not a wireless network discovery term and is included purely as a distractor.

22. You are examining the physical configuration of a target's wireless network. You notice on the site survey that omnidirectional antenna access points are located in the corners of the building. Which of the following statements are true regarding this configuration? (Choose all that apply.)

A. The site may be vulnerable to sniffing from locations outside the building.

B. The site is not vulnerable to sniffing from locations outside the building.

C. The use of dipole antennas may improve the security of the site.

D. The use of directional antennas may improve the security of the site.

☑ **A and D.** There are a couple of problems with an omnidirectional (dipole) antenna. The first is coverage area itself. Because it's *omni*directional, it's sending (and looking for) signals in all directions. Therefore, if the AP is placed in the corner of the building, roughly three-quarters of the coverage space is wasted. Unless, of course, you're an attacker sitting in a car outside, drinking coffee, and happily surfing away on the free wireless the company has so carelessly provided to the parking lot. The second problem is the power consumption needed for this coverage. Because it's designed to send in all directions, the coverage area is reduced, and users on the edges will definitely notice it. Think about it—if your AP is in the corner and three-quarters of its coverage is outside the building, that's three-quarters of the power of the device wasted. If you were to concentrate that power—by focusing the signal with a directional antenna—just think of the range and speed of access you could provide your clients.

Allow me to offer one last thought here, and I promise I'll stop talking about antennas: It is a far greater use of time and resources for an organization to securely implement networking in the first place than it is to worry about antenna types and placement. Your security staff isn't saving money by following some ridiculous bean-counting analysis that results in buying a $100 antenna versus paying for a $200-an-hour security analyst—especially if you wind up getting hacked by some guy in a van using a +40db dish to sniff traffic you failed to protect.

☒ **B** and **C** are incorrect statements regarding this architecture. Because the antenna is omnidirectional, the signals will spill out around the building if the AP is put in the corner. Therefore, the site is susceptible to unauthorized clients accessing the signal from outside. Additionally, a dipole antenna is, by its very design and nature, omnidirectional.

23. Which of the following is a true statement regarding wireless security?

   A. WPA2 is a better encryption choice than WEP.

   B. WEP is a better encryption choice than WPA2.

   C. Cloaking the SSID and implementing MAC filtering eliminate the need for encryption.

   D. Increasing the length of the SSID to its maximum increases security for the system.

☑ **A.** WPA2 is, by far, a better security choice for your system. It makes use of TKIP, to change out the keys every 10,000 packets instead of using one for the entire session (as in WEP). Additionally, WPA2 uses AES for encryption and a 128-bit encryption key, as opposed to RC4 and 24-bit IVs in WEP.

☒ **B** is incorrect because WEP only provides the equivalent privacy of being on a wired network. Its "encryption" is ridiculously easy to crack and is not considered a valid security measure. It's perfectly reasonable to use it if your goal is just to frustrate causal surfers from connecting to your network (such as your neighbors), but it's not a valid encryption method.

☒ **C** is incorrect because these two options do nothing to protect the actual data being transmitted. SSID cloaking is somewhat pointless, given that SSIDs are included in every header of every packet (not to mention that SSIDs aren't designed for security). MAC filtering will frustrate casual observers; however, spoofing a MAC address on the network is relatively easy and eliminates this as a foolproof security method.

    ☒ **D** is incorrect because the length of an SSID has nothing whatsoever to do with security and encryption. Increasing the length of the SSID does not increase network security.

24. A pen test colleague is attempting to use a wireless connection inside the target's building. On his Linux laptop he types the following commands:

```
ifconfig wlan0 down
ifconfig wlan0 hw ether 0A:0B:0C:1A:1B:1C
ifconfig wlan0 up
```

What is the most likely reason for this action?

    A. Port security is enabled on the access point.

    B. The SSID is cloaked from the access point.

    C. MAC filtering is enabled on the access point.

    D. Weak signaling is frustrating connectivity to the access point.

    ☑ **C.** The sequence of the preceding commands has the attacker bringing the wireless interface down, changing its hardware address, and then bringing it back up. The most likely reason for this is MAC filtering is enabled on the AP, which is restricting access to only those machines the administrator wants connecting to the wireless network. The easy way around this is to watch traffic and copy one of the MAC addresses. A quick spoof on your own hardware and—*voilà*—you're connected. As an aside, MAC spoofing isn't just for the wireless world. The command would be slightly different (wlan0 refers to a wireless NIC; eth0 would be an example of a wired port), but the idea is the same.

    ☒ **A** is incorrect because port security isn't an option on wireless access points. Were this attacker connecting to a switch, this might be valid but not on a wireless connection.

    ☒ **B** is incorrect because SSID cloaking has nothing to do with this scenario. The commands are adjusting a MAC address.

    ☒ **D** is incorrect because weak signal strength has nothing to do with this scenario. The commands are adjusting a MAC address.

25. An individual attempts to make a call using his cell phone; however, it seems unresponsive. After a few minutes of effort, he turns it off and turns it on again. During his next phone call, the phone disconnects and becomes unresponsive again. Which Bluetooth attack is underway?

    A. Bluesmacking

    B. Bluejacking

    C. Bluesniffing

    D. Bluesnarfing

☑ **A.** From the description, it appears the phone is either defective or—since it's spelled out so nicely in the question for you—there is a denial-of-service attack against the phone. As stated earlier, bluesmacking is a denial-of-service attack on a Bluetooth device. An attacker somewhere nearby (within 10 meters or, for the real bad guys, farther away using a big enough transmitter, amplifier, and antenna) is using something like the Linux Bluez packages (www.bluez.org) to carry out a DoS against the phone.

☒ **B** is incorrect because bluejacking involves sending unsolicited messages— much like spam—to a Bluetooth device.

☒ **C** is incorrect because bluesniffing is a basic sniffing attempt, where the device's transmissions are sniffed for useful information.

☒ **D** is incorrect because bluesnarfing refers to the actual theft of data directly from the device. This takes advantage of the "pairing" feature of most Bluetooth devices, willingly seeking out other devices to link up with.

26. Which wireless standard achieves high data rate speeds by implementing MIMO antenna technology?

   A. 802.11b

   B. 802.11g

   C. 802.11n

   D. 802.16

☑ **C.** 802.11n boasts speeds faster than 100Mbps, operating in a frequency range from 2.4GHz to 5GHz. One method it uses to achieve this is known as multiple in, multiple out (MIMO). MIMO, not unlike other technologies you're supposed to learn about, has tons of mind-numbing technical minutiae to explore concerning how it works, but basically the thought behind it is to use multiple antennas, in somewhat of an array, to send and receive simultaneously. Also known as *smart antennas*, these greatly speed up wireless communications. Once the technology dropped to a more affordable range, it became more and more prevalent. Another note you may see referenced on this standard has to do with multiplexing used within the transmission: 802.11n uses something called Spatial Division Multiplexing (SDM).

☒ **A and B** are incorrect because neither standard uses MIMO antennas.

☒ **D** is incorrect because 802.16 is a set of IEEE standards for wireless within a metropolitan area network. Referred to as *WiMax* (Worldwide Interoperability for Microwave Access), 802.16 was written for the global development of broadband wireless metropolitan area networks. It provides speeds up to 40Mbps and is moving toward gigabit speed.

Trojans and Other Attacks

This chapter includes questions from the following topics:

- Define Trojans and their purpose
- Identify common Trojan ports
- Identify Trojan deployment methods
- Identify Trojan countermeasures
- Define viruses and worms
- Identify virus countermeasures
- Describe DoS attacks
- Define common DoS attack types
- Describe session hijacking and sequence prediction

When you're a dad, you tend to pile up gross stories of fixing things, savings things, and cleaning up things. By the time your kids get to be 6 or 7 years old, you feel like you probably should've spent half of the previous few years in a hazmat suit or being decontaminated in some full-body spray-down room. Kids have a unique way of taking something simple and turning it into an experience parents need counseling for to deal with in the future. And as bad as it is when they're toddlers, it gets worse as they get older—because they introduce a whole new set of tools to enrich your life.

The first time I ever plunged a toilet I was a 24-year-old father of two little girls. The girls had gotten more than a little carried away with the paper and had to, um, *continue* afterward even though the toilet was clogged. By the time I got in there, it was out of hand, and plunging the thing was inevitable. I didn't want to do it, and I certainly didn't enjoy it, but I grabbed the tool at hand to get the job done and performed the duties I was called upon to complete.

Much like that old wooden-handled plunger I used back in the mid-1990s, your pen test tool set can be augmented by visiting the dark side yourself, wielding tools and actions that may seem a bit unsavory to you. Although you may not think of malware and viruses as pen test methods, they're definitely tools in the arsenal and something you really need to know about—for your job and especially this exam.

STUDY TIPS   Most of the questions from the malware sections—especially those designed to trip you up—will be of the pure memorization type. Stick with key words for each definition (it'll help you in separating good answers from bad ones), especially for the virus types. Don't miss an easy point on the exam because you forgot the difference between polymorphic and multipartite or why a worm is different from a virus. Tool identification should also be relatively straightforward (assuming you commit all those port numbers to memory, like I told you to do).

Finally, as always, get rid of the answers you know to be wrong in the first place. It's actually easier sometimes to identify the ones you downright know aren't relevant to the question. Then, from the remainder, you can scratch your gray matter for the key word that will shed light on the answer.

1. Examine the Wireshark TCP flow capture here:

```
Host A       --- SYN --- >              Host B Seq = 0 Ack = 13425675
Host A       < --- SYN, ACK ---         Host B Seq = 0 Ack = 1
Host A       --- ACK --- >              Host B Seq = 1 Ack = 1
Host A       --- PSH, ACK Len:700 --- > Host B Seq = 1 Ack = 1
Host A       < --- ACK ---              Host B Seq = 1 Ack = 701
Host A       < --- ACK Len:1341 ---     Host B Seq = 1 Ack = 701
Host A       --- ACK --- >              Host B Seq = 701 Ack = 1342
Host A       < --- ACK Len : 1322 ---   Host B Seq = 1342 Ack = 701
Host A       --- ACK --- >              Host B Seq = 701 Ack = 2664
Host A       < --- ACK Len : 1322 ---   Host B Seq = 2664 Ack = 701
```

   Which of the following represents the next appropriate acknowledgment from Host A?

   A. Sequence Number 701, Acknowledgment Number 3986

   B. Sequence Number 701, Acknowledgment Number 2664

   C. Sequence Number 2664, Acknowledgment Number 2023

   D. Sequence Number 2664, Acknowledgment Number 701

2. You have established a Netcat connection to a target machine. Which flag can be used to launch a program?

   A. –p

   B. –a

   C. –l

   D. –e

3. Which database type was targeted by the Slammer worm?

   A. Microsoft SQL

   B. MySQL

   C. Oracle

   D. Sybase

4. Which virus type will rewrite itself after each new infection?

   A. Multipartite

   B. Metamorphic

   C. Cavity

   D. Macro

5. A pen test colleague is carrying out attacks. In one attack, she attempts to guess the ISN for a TCP session. Which attack is she most likely carrying out?

   A. XSS

   B. Session splicing

   C. Session hijacking

   D. Multipartite attack

6. Which of the following malware types does not require user intervention to spread?

   A. Trojan

   B. Virus

   C. Worm

   D. Polymorphic

7. An attacker is attempting a DoS attack against a machine. She first spoofs the target's IP address and then begins sending large amounts of ICMP packets containing the MAC address FF:FF:FF:FF:FF:FF. What attack is underway?

   A. ICMP flood

   B. Ping of death

   C. SYN flood

   D. Smurf

   E. Fraggle

8. Tripwire is one of the most popular tools to protect against Trojans. Which of the following statements best describes Tripwire?

   A. Tripwire is a signature-based antivirus tool.

   B. Tripwire is a vulnerability assessment tool used for port scanning.

   C. Tripwire is a file integrity program.

   D. Tripwire is a session-splicing tool.

9. Which of the following tools are good choices for session hijack attempts? (Choose all that apply.)

   A. Ettercap

   B. Netcat

   C. Hunt

   D. Nessus

10. In regard to Trojans, which of the following best describes a wrapper?

   A. The legitimate file the Trojan is attached to

   B. A program used to bind the Trojan to a legitimate file

   C. Encryption methods used for a Trojan

   D. Polymorphic code used to avoid detection by antivirus programs

11. Which of the following are true regarding BugBear and Pretty Park? (Choose three.)

   A. Both programs make use of e-mail.

   B. Pretty Park propagates via network shares and e-mail.

   C. BugBear propagates via network shares and e-mail.

   D. Pretty Park uses an IRC server to send your personal passwords.

   E. Pretty Park terminates antivirus applications.

12. Which of the following is a legitimate communication path for the transfer of data?

   A. Overt

   B. Covert

   C. Authentic

   D. Imitation

   E. Actual

13. In what layer of the OSI reference model is session hijacking carried out?

   A. Data link layer

   B. Transport layer

   C. Network layer

   D. Physical layer

14. A pen test team member types the following command:

   `nc222.15.66.78 -p 8765`

   Which of the following is true regarding this attempt?

   A. The attacker is attempting to connect to an established listening port on a remote computer.

   B. The attacker is establishing a listening port on his machine for later use.

   C. The attacker is attempting a DoS against a remote computer.

   D. The attacker is attempting to kill a service on a remote machine.

15. Examine the partial command-line output listed here:

```
Active Connections
Proto  Local Address              Foreign Address          State
  TCP    0.0.0.0:912                COMPUTER11:0             LISTENING
  TCP    0.0.0.0:3460               COMPUTER11:0             LISTENING
  TCP    0.0.0.0:3465               COMPUTER11:0             LISTENING
  TCP    0.0.0.0:8288               COMPUTER11:0             LISTENING
  TCP    0.0.0.0:16386              COMPUTER11:0             LISTENING
  TCP    192.168.1.100:139          COMPUTER11:0             LISTENING
  TCP    192.168.1.100:58191        173.194.44.81:https      ESTABLISHED
  TCP    192.168.1.100:58192        173.194.44.81:https      TIME_WAIT
  TCP    192.168.1.100:58193        173.194.44.81:https      TIME_WAIT
  TCP    192.168.1.100:58194        173.194.44.81:https      ESTABLISHED
  TCP    192.168.1.100:58200        bk-in-f138:http          TIME_WAIT
```

Which of the following is a true statement regarding the output?

A. This is output from a netstat –an command.

B. This is output from a netstat –b command.

C. This is output from a netstat –e command.

D. This is output from a netstat –r command.

16. You are discussing malware with a new pen test member who asks about restarting executables. Which registry keys within Windows automatically run executables and instructions? (Choose all that apply.)

A. HKEY_LOCAL_MACHINE\Software\Microsoft\Windows\CurrentVersion\RunServicesOnce

B. HKEY_LOCAL_MACHINE\Software\Microsoft\Windows\CurrentVersion\RunServices

C. HKEY_LOCAL_MACHINE\Software\Microsoft\Windows\CurrentVersion\RunOnce

D. HKEY_LOCAL_MACHINE\Software\Microsoft\Windows\CurrentVersion\Run

17. Which of the following best describes a covert channel?

A. An application using a port number that is not well-known

B. Using a protocol in a way it is not intended to be used

C. Multiplexing a communication link

D. WEP encryption channels

18. Which denial-of-service attack involves sending SYN packets to a target machine but never responding to any of the SYN/ACK replies?

A. SYN flood

B. SYN attack

C. Smurf

D. LOIC

19. Which of the following takes advantage of weaknesses in the fragment reassembly functionality of TCP/IP?

    A. Teardrop

    B. SYN flood

    C. Smurf attack

    D. Ping of death

20. IPSec is an effective preventative measure against session hijacking. Which IPSec mode encrypts only the data payload?

    A. Transport

    B. Tunnel

    C. Protected

    D. Spoofed

21. Which type of session hijacking is displayed in Figure 8-1?

    A. Cross-site scripting attack

    B. SQL injection attack

    C. Token sniffing attack

    D. Session fixation attack

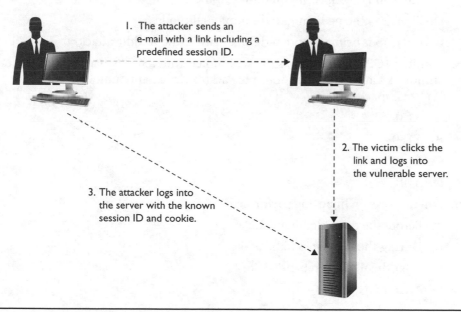

Figure 8-1   Session hijacking example

22. Which of the following best describes the comparison between spoofing and session hijacking?

   A. Spoofing and session hijacking are the same thing.

   B. Spoofing interrupts a client's communication, whereas hijacking does not.

   C. Hijacking interrupts a client's communication, whereas spoofing does not.

   D. Hijacking emulates a foreign IP address, whereas spoofing refers to MAC addresses.

23. Which of the following is an effective deterrent against session hijacking?

   A. Install and use a HIDS on the system.

   B. Install and use Tripwire on the system.

   C. Enforce good password policy.

   D. Use unpredictable sequence numbers.

24. A pen test team member types the following command:

   ```
   ettercap –T –q –M ARP /200.70.55.12
   ```

   Which of the following are true regarding this command? (Choose all that apply.)

   A. Ettercap is being configured for a GUI interface.

   B. Ettercap is being configured as a sniffer.

   C. Ettercap is being configured for text mode.

   D. Ettercap is being configured for manual mode.

   E. Ettercap is being configured for a man-in-the-middle attack.

25. Within a TCP packet dump, a packet is noted with the SYN flag set and a sequence number set at A13F. What should the acknowledgment number in the return SYN/ACK packet be?

   A. A131

   B. A130

   C. A140

   D. A14F

26. When is session hijacking performed?

   A. Before the three-step handshake

   B. During the three-step handshake

   C. After the three-step handshake

   D. After a FIN packet

1. B
2. D
3. A
4. B
5. C
6. C
7. D
8. C
9. A, C
10. B
11. A, C, D
12. A
13. B
14. A
15. A
16. A, B, C, D
17. B
18. A
19. A
20. A
21. D
22. C
23. D
24. C, E
25. C
26. C

1. Examine the Wireshark TCP flow capture here:

```
Host A       --- SYN --- >                Host B Seq = 0 Ack = 13425675
Host A       < --- SYN, ACK ---           Host B Seq = 0 Ack = 1
Host A       --- ACK --- >                Host B Seq = 1 Ack = 1
Host A       --- PSH, ACK Len:700 --- >   Host B Seq = 1 Ack = 1
Host A       < --- ACK ---                Host B Seq = 1 Ack = 701
Host A       < --- ACK Len:1341 ---       Host B Seq = 1 Ack = 701
Host A       --- ACK --- >                Host B Seq = 701 Ack = 1342
Host A       < --- ACK Len : 1322 ---     Host B Seq = 1342 Ack = 701
Host A       --- ACK --- >                Host B Seq = 701 Ack = 2664
Host A       < --- ACK Len : 1322 ---     Host B Seq = 2664 Ack = 701
```

Which of the following represents the next appropriate acknowledgment from Host A?

A. Sequence Number 701, Acknowledgment Number 2664

B. Sequence Number 701, Acknowledgment Number 3986

C. Sequence Number 2664, Acknowledgment Number 2023

D. Sequence Number 2664, Acknowledgment Number 701

☑ **B.** Sequence and acknowledgment number prediction can get really, really confusing when you take all the options into account—acknowledgment numbers, window sizes, and so on—but thankfully it'll be pretty easy on your exam. An acknowledgment packet will recognize the agreed-upon sequence number (in this case, 701) and then acknowledge receipt of the previous packet by incrementing the acknowledgment number with the packet size of the receipt. In this example, the agreed-upon sequence number is 701, and the receipt of the previous packet is acknowledged by adding the previous sequence number (2664) to the packet length (1322): 2664 + 1322 = 3986.

☒ **A, C,** and **D** are incorrect choices because the sequence and acknowledgment numbers do not add up. You can follow the preceding TCP stream and watch the acknowledgment number increment by the packet length. You can also see this at home: Open a Wireshark session and capture a TCP session; then choose Statistics, Flow Graph, and TCP Flow.

2. You have established a Netcat connection to a target machine. Which flag can be used to launch a program?

A. –p

B. –a

C. –l

D. –e

☑ **D.** Netcat is often referred to as the Swiss Army knife of hacking efforts. You can use it to set up a listening port on target machines that you can then revisit to wreak all sorts of havoc. The flag associated with launching a program is –e. For example, issuing the command

```
nc -L -p 12657 -t -e cmd.exe
```

will open a Windows command shell on the target machine; the –t flag sets up a telnet connection over the port you defined with the –p flag (12657).

☒ **A** is incorrect because the –p flag indicates the protocol port you want to use for your session.

☒ **B** is incorrect because –a is not a recognized Netcat flag.

☒ **C** is incorrect because the –l flag indicates Netcat should open the port for listening. As an aside, the –L flag does the same thing; however, it restarts listening after the inbound session completes.

3. Which database type was targeted by the Slammer worm?

   A. Microsoft SQL

   B. MySQL

   C. Oracle

   D. Sybase

   ☑ **A.** The Slammer worm, a.k.a. SQL Slammer, wreaked havoc in Microsoft SQL installations in 2003. It exploited a buffer-overflow vulnerability in SQL Server 2000 and propagated via UDP port 1434. Microsoft's MS02-039 patch resolved the issues but not before thousands of machines were infected.

   ☒ **B, C,** and **D** are incorrect because Slammer did not affect these SQL server types.

4. Which virus type will rewrite itself after each new infection?

   A. Multipartite

   B. Metamorphic

   C. Cavity

   D. Macro

   ☑ **B.** EC-Council defines several different virus types, depending on what the virus does, how it acts, and how it is written. In the case of a metamorphic virus, it will rewrite itself each time it infects a new file. Metamorphic viruses write versions of themselves in machine code, making it easy to port to different machines.

☒ **A** is incorrect because multipartite viruses do not rewrite themselves. They attempt to infect and spread in multiple ways and try to infect files and the boot sector at the same time. They can spread quickly and are notoriously hard to clean.

☒ **C** is incorrect because a cavity virus writes itself into unused space within a file. The idea is to maintain the file's size.

☒ **D** is incorrect because macro viruses do not rewrite themselves. Macro viruses usually attack Microsoft Office files, executing as a macro within the file itself (anyone who's ever been stuck in Excel purgatory should be familiar with macros within a spreadsheet). Melissa (a famous virus attacking Microsoft Word 1997) is a classic example of a macro virus.

5. A pen test colleague is carrying out attacks. In one attack, she attempts to guess the ISN for a TCP session. Which attack is she most likely carrying out?

   A. XSS

   B. Session splicing

   C. Session hijacking

   D. Multipartite attack

   ☑ **C.** The idea behind session hijacking is fairly simple: The attacker waits for a session to begin and, after all the pesky authentication gets done, jumps in to steal the session for herself. In practice, it's a little harder and more complicated than that, but the key to the whole attack is in determining the initial sequence number (ISN) used for the session. The ISN is sent by the initiator of the session in the first step (SYN). This is acknowledged in the second handshake (SYN/ACK) by incrementing that ISN by 1, and then another ISN is generated by the recipient. This second number is acknowledged by the initiator in the third step (ACK) and from there on out communication can occur. Per EC-Council, the following steps describe the session hijack:

   1. Sniff the traffic between the client and the server.

   2. Monitor the traffic and predict the sequence numbering.

   3. Desynchronize the session with the client.

   4. Predict the session token and take over the session.

   5. Inject packets to the target server.

   For what it's worth, pulling this attack off via EC-Council's take on the whole matter requires you to do some fairly significant traffic sniffing. And if you're already positioned to sniff the traffic in the first place, wouldn't the whole scenario possibly be a moot point? You need to know it for the exam, but real-world application may be small and rare.

☒ **A** is incorrect because cross-site scripting is a web application attack.

☒ **B** is incorrect because session splicing is an IDS evasion method. The attacker delivers a payload that the IDS would have otherwise seen by "slicing" it over multiple packets. The payload can be spread out over a long period of time.

☒ **D** is incorrect because *multipartite* refers to a virus type, not an attack that requires ISN determination.

6. Which of the following malware types does not require user intervention to spread?

   A. Trojan

   B. Virus

   C. Worm

   D. Polymorphic

   ☑ **C.** A *worm* is a self-replicating malware computer program that uses a computer network to send copies of itself to other systems without human intervention. Usually it doesn't necessarily alter files, but it resides in active memory and duplicates itself, eating up resources and wreaking havoc along the way. The most common use for a worm in the hacking world is the creation of botnets. A classic worm example you will no doubt see on your exam is Conficker. It targeted Windows machines starting in 2008, infecting millions of computers worldwide, making it the largest computer worm infection in history.

   ☒ **A** is incorrect because Trojans need human interaction to spread. A *Trojan* is software that appears to perform a desirable function for the user prior to running or installation but instead performs a function, usually without the user's knowledge, that steals information or otherwise harms the system (or data). Much like the horse used to fool the people of Troy, Trojan malware is usually hidden inside something that appears totally harmless or even beneficial.

   ☒ **B** is incorrect because viruses do not spread without user intervention. By definition, viruses are attached to other files and are activated when those files are executed. Viruses are spread when users copy infected files from one machine to another.

   ☒ **D** is incorrect because viruses need human interaction to spread. A polymorphic piece of malware (a type of virus) still requires interaction; it just morphs its code along the way.

7. An attacker is attempting a DoS attack against a machine. She first spoofs the target's IP address and then begins sending large amounts of ICMP packets containing the MAC address FF:FF:FF:FF:FF:FF. What attack is underway?

   A. ICMP flood

   B. Ping of death

   C. SYN flood

   D. Smurf

   E. Fraggle

   ☑ **D.** A smurf attack is a generic denial-of-service (DoS) attack against a target machine. The idea is simple: have so many ICMP requests going to the target that all its resources are taken up. To accomplish this, the attacker spoofs the target's IP address and then sends thousands of ping requests from that spoofed IP to the subnet's broadcast address. This, in effect, pings every machine on the subnet. Assuming they're configured to do so, every machine will respond to the request, effectively crushing the target's network resources.

   ☒ **A** is incorrect because an ICMP flood does not act this way. In this attack, the hacker sends ICMP Echo packets to the target with a spoofed (fake) source address. The target continues to respond to an address that doesn't exist and eventually reaches a limit of packets per second sent.

   ☒ **B** is incorrect because a ping of death does not act this way. It's not a valid attack with modern systems because of preventative measures in the OS; in the ping of death, an attacker fragments an ICMP message to send to a target. When the fragments are reassembled, the resulting ICMP packet is larger than the maximum size and crashes the system. As an aside, each OS has its own method of dealing with network protocols, and the implementation of dealing with particular protocols opens up things like this.

   ☒ **C** is incorrect because a SYN flood takes place when an attacker sends multiple SYN packets to a target without providing an acknowledgment to the returned SYN/ACK. This is another attack that does not necessarily work on modern systems.

   ☒ **E** is incorrect because in a fraggle attack, UDP packets are used. The same principle applies—spoofed IP and Echo requests sent to the broadcast address—it's just with UDP.

8. Tripwire is one of the most popular tools to protect against malware. Which of the following statements best describes Tripwire?

   A. Tripwire is a signature-based antivirus tool.

   B. Tripwire is a vulnerability assessment tool used for port scanning.

C. Tripwire is a file integrity program.

D. Tripwire is a session-splicing tool.

☑ **C.** Although it has grown substantially from its early days as nothing more than a file integrity checker, Tripwire is a well-respected integrity verifier that can act as a host-based intrusion detection system (HIDS) in protection against Trojans. Simply put, Tripwire runs a file integrity check against critical files on your system. If they change—because of malware or any other circumstance—Tripwire can alert you and prevent the Trojan from being activated.

☒ **A** and **B** are incorrect because these are not functions Tripwire performs. Per the Tripwire website (www.tripwire.com), "Tripwire offerings solve the security configuration management, continuous monitoring, and incident detection problems facing organizations of all sizes, as stand-alone solutions or in concert with other IT security controls." Antivirus and vulnerability assessment are not functions this particular tool is designed for.

☒ **D** is incorrect because session splicing is an IDS evasion technique, not a function of Tripwire—not to mention session splicing does absolutely nothing to prevent Trojans.

9. Which of the following tools are good choices for session hijack attempts? (Choose all that apply.)

   A. Ettercap

   B. Netcat

   C. Hunt

   D. Nessus

   ☑ **A** and **C.** Both Ettercap and Hunt are good tools for session hijacking. Ettercap is an excellent man in the middle tool and can be run from a variety of platforms (although it is Linux native). Per the Ettercap home page (http://ettercap.sourceforge.net/), "Ettercap is a comprehensive suite for man in the middle attacks. It features sniffing of live connections, content filtering on the fly and many other interesting tricks. It supports active and passive dissection of many protocols and includes many features for network and host analysis." Hunt is probably one of the best-known session-hijacking tools. Hunt can sniff, hijack, and reset connections at will.

   ☒ **B** is incorrect because Netcat is not a session hijack application. It *is* valuable for setting up listening ports and executing commands on target machines, but it's not designed for session hijacking.

   ☒ **D** is incorrect because Nessus is a vulnerability assessment tool.

10. In regard to Trojans, which of the following best describes a wrapper?

   A. The legitimate file the Trojan is attached to

   B. A program used to bind the Trojan to a legitimate file

   C. Encryption methods used for a Trojan

   D. Polymorphic code used to avoid detection by antivirus programs

   ☑ **B.** *Wrappers* are programs that allow you to bind an executable of your choice (Trojan) to an innocent file your target won't mind opening. For example, you might use a program such as EliteWrap to embed a backdoor application with a game file (.exe). A user on your target machine then opens the latest game file (maybe to play a hand of cards against the computer or to fling a bird at pyramids built by pigs) while your backdoor is installing and sits there waiting for your use later. As an aside, many wrappers themselves are considered malicious and will show up on any up-to-date virus signature list.

   ☒ **A, C,** and **D** are all incorrect definitions of a wrapper in regard to Trojans. The wrapper is used to bind the Trojan to the legitimate file and has nothing to do with encryption of the Trojan itself. Polymorphic code deals with a type of virus that changes its code to avoid detection by signature-based antivirus programs.

11. Which of the following are true regarding BugBear and Pretty Park? (Choose three.)

   A. Both programs make use of e-mail.

   B. Pretty Park propagates via network shares and e-mail.

   C. BugBear propagates via network shares and e-mail.

   D. Pretty Park uses an IRC server to send your personal passwords.

   E. Pretty Park terminates antivirus applications

   ☑ **A, C,** and **D.** Believe it or not, you will be asked some rather inane questions regarding specific viruses, worms, and Trojans. While most of the time it'll be silly things like "Which port number is used by _____?" occasionally you'll see one like this. There's no rhyme or reason—it's just the way it is. In this case, both BugBear and Pretty Park use e-mail, but only BugBear can propagate through network shares. BugBear actually tries killing any resident antivirus programs, and Pretty Park uses IRC for all sorts of information-stealing activities.

   ☒ **B** and **E** are incorrect because these are not true statements. Pretty Park cannot use network shares and does not terminate antivirus programs.

12. Which of the following is a legitimate communication path for the transfer of data?

   A. Overt

   B. Covert

   C. Authentic

   D. Imitation

   E. Actual

   ☑ **A.** This is another one of those easy, pure-definition questions you simply can't miss on your exam. Whether the channel is inside a computer, between systems, or across the Internet, any legitimate channel used for communications and data exchange is known as an *overt channel*. And don't let the inherit risk with any channel itself make the decision for you—even if the channel itself is a risky endeavor, if it is being used for its intended purpose, it's still overt. For example, an IRC or a gaming link is still an overt channel, so long as the applications making use of it are legitimate. Overt channels are legitimate communication channels used by programs across a system or a network, whereas covert channels are used to transport data in ways they were not intended for.

   ☒ **B** is incorrect because an overt channel, per EC-Council's own definition, is "a channel that transfers information within a computer system or network in a way that violates security policy." For example, a Trojan might create a channel for stealing passwords or downloading sensitive data from the machine.

   ☒ **C, D,** and **E** are incorrect because none of these is a term for the communications channel; they are included here as distractors.

13. In what layer of the OSI reference model is session hijacking carried out?

   A. Data link layer

   B. Transport layer

   C. Network layer

   D. Physical layer

   ☑ **B.** Think about a session hijack, and this makes sense. Authentication has already occurred, so we know both computers have already found each other. Therefore, the physical, data link, and network layers have already been eclipsed. And what is being altered and played with in these hijacking attempts? Why, the sequence numbers, of course, and sequencing occurs at the transport layer. Now, for all you real-world guys out there screaming that communications can be, and truly are, hijacked at every level, let me caution your outrage with something I've said repeatedly throughout this book: Sometimes the exam and reality are two different things, and if you want to pass the test, you'll need to memorize it the way EC-Council wants you to. Session hijacking is taught in CEH circles as a measure of guessing sequence numbers, and that's a transport layer entity. In the real world, your physical layer interception of a target would result in access to everything above, but on the exam just stick with "session hijacking = transport layer."

☒ **A, C,** and **D** are incorrect because these layers are not where a session hijack attack is carried out.

14. A pen test team member types the following command:

```
nc222.15.66.78 -p 8765
```

Which of the following is true regarding this attempt?

A. The attacker is attempting to connect to an established listening port on a remote computer.

B. The attacker is establishing a listening port on his machine for later use.

C. The attacker is attempting a DoS against a remote computer.

D. The attacker is attempting to kill a service on a remote machine.

☑ **A.** As covered earlier, Netcat is a wonderful tool that allows all sorts of remote access wizardry on a machine, and you'll need to be able to recognize the basics of the syntax. In the command example, Netcat is being told, "Please attempt a connection to the machine with the IP address of 222.15.66.78 on port 8765. I believe you'll find the port in a listening state, waiting for our arrival." Obviously at some point previous to issuing this command on his local machine, the pen tester planted the Netcat Trojan on the remote system (222.15.66.78) and set it up in a listening state. He may have set it up with a command-shell access (allowing a telnet-like connection to issue commands at will) using the following command:

```
nc -L -p 8765 -t -e cmd.exe
```

☒ **B** is incorrect because this command is issued on the client side of the setup, not the server side. At some point previously, the port was set to a listening state, and this Netcat command will access it.

☒ **C** is incorrect because this command is not attempting a denial of service against the target machine. It's included here as a distractor.

☒ **D** is incorrect because this command is not attempting to kill a process or service on the remote machine. It's included here as a distractor.

15. Examine the partial command-line output listed here:

```
Active Connections
Proto  Local Address           Foreign Address        State
  TCP    0.0.0.0:912             COMPUTER11:0           LISTENING
  TCP    0.0.0.0:3460            COMPUTER11:0           LISTENING
  TCP    0.0.0.0:3465            COMPUTER11:0           LISTENING
  TCP    0.0.0.0:8288            COMPUTER11:0           LISTENING
  TCP    0.0.0.0:16386           COMPUTER11:0           LISTENING
  TCP    192.168.1.100:139       COMPUTER11:0           LISTENING
  TCP    192.168.1.100:58191     173.194.44.81:https    ESTABLISHED
  TCP    192.168.1.100:58192     173.194.44.81:https    TIME_WAIT
  TCP    192.168.1.100:58193     173.194.44.81:https    TIME_WAIT
  TCP    192.168.1.100:58194     173.194.44.81:https    ESTABLISHED
  TCP    192.168.1.100:58200     bk-in-f138:http        TIME_WAIT
```

Which of the following is a true statement regarding the output?

A. This is output from a netstat –an command.

B. This is output from a netstat –b command.

C. This is output from a netstat –e command.

D. This is output from a netstat –r command.

☑ **A.** You'll need to get to know Netstat before your exam. It's not a huge thing, and you won't get bogged down in minutiae, but you do need to know the basics. Netstat is a great command-line tool built into every Microsoft operating system. From Microsoft's own description, Netstat "displays active TCP connections, ports on which the computer is listening, Ethernet statistics, the IP routing table, IPv4 statistics (for the IP, ICMP, TCP, and UDP protocols), and IPv6 statistics (for the IPv6, ICMPv6, TCP over IPv6, and UDP over IPv6 protocols)." It's a great, easy way to see which ports you have open on your system, helping you to identify any naughty Trojans that may be hanging around. A netstat –an command will show all connections and listening ports in numerical form.

☒ **B** is incorrect because the –b option displays the executable involved in creating each connection or listening port. Its output appears something like this:

```
Proto  Local Address      Foreign Address   State
  TCP    127.0.0.1:5354     COMPUTER11:49155  ESTABLISHED
[mDNSResponder.exe]
  TCP    127.0.0.1:27015    COMPUTER11:49175  ESTABLISHED
[AppleMobileDeviceService.exe]
  TCP    127.0.0.1:49155    COMPUTER11:5354   ESTABLISHED
[AppleMobileDeviceService.exe]
  TCP    127.0.0.1:49175    COMPUTER11:27015  ESTABLISHED
[iTunesHelper.exe]
```

☒ **C** is incorrect because the –e flag displays Ethernet statistics for the system. The output appears something like this:

```
                      Received          Sent
Bytes                125454856      33551337
Unicast packets         164910        167156
Non-unicast packets        570         15624
Discards                     0             0
Errors                       0           268
Unknown protocols            0
```

☒ **D** is incorrect because the –r flag displays the route table for the system. A sampling of the output looks like this:

```
IPv4 Route Table
===================================================================
Active Routes:
Network Destination        Netmask      Gateway     Interface Metric
          0.0.0.0          0.0.0.0 192.168.1.1 192.168.1.100     25
         15.0.0.0        255.0.0.0      On-link 16.213.104.24     26
   15.195.201.216 255.255.255.255 192.168.1.1 192.168.1.100     26
   15.255.255.255 255.255.255.255      On-link 16.213.104.24    281.
```

16. You are discussing malware with a new pen test member who asks about restarting executables. Which registry keys within Windows automatically run executables and instructions? (Choose all that apply.)

   A. HKEY_LOCAL_MACHINE\Software\Microsoft\Windows\CurrentVersion\ RunServicesOnce

   B. HKEY_LOCAL_MACHINE\Software\Microsoft\Windows\CurrentVersion\ RunServices

   C. HKEY_LOCAL_MACHINE\Software\Microsoft\Windows\CurrentVersion\ RunOnce

   D. HKEY_LOCAL_MACHINE\Software\Microsoft\Windows\CurrentVersion\ Run

   ☑ **A, B, C,** and **D.** Creating malware and infecting a machine with it is accomplishing only the basics. Getting it to hang around by having it restart when the user reboots the machine? Now we're talking. The Run, RunOnce, RunServices, and RunServicesOnce registry keys within the HKEY_LOCAL_ MACHINE hive are great places to stick all sorts of executables. Because of this, it's helpful to run registry monitoring on occasion to check for anything suspicious. Sys Analyzer, Regshot, and TinyWatcher are all options for this.

17. Which of the following best describes a covert channel?

   A. An application using a port number that is not well-known

   B. Using a protocol in a way it is not intended to be used

   C. Multiplexing a communication link

   D. WEP encryption channels

☑ **B.** Yes, this is almost the same question we asked earlier. This means, for those of you paying attention, it's probably important for you to know. A covert channel is, basically, a channel or protocol being used in a manner in which it was never intended to be used. This could be a communication channel exploited by a process to transfer information that violates the system's security policy or making use of a protocol in a way it was not intended to be used. Stuck behind a firewall, but you're using HTTP tunneling to communicate out? Welcome to covert channels.

☒ **A**, **C**, and **D** are all incorrect definitions of a covert channel and are included as distractors.

18. Which denial-of-service attack involves sending SYN packets to a target machine but never responding to any of the SYN/ACK replies?

    A. SYN flood

    B. SYN attack

    C. Smurf

    D. LOIC

☑ **A.** I know some of you are probably wondering whether I'm describing a half-open scan here, and certainly the description meets the criteria: Send a SYN packet and, based on the response, map which ports are open and which are closed. However, the volume, duration, and purpose define this as a SYN flood. In a SYN flood attack, the attacker sends thousands of SYN packets to the target but never responds to any of the return SYN/ACK packets. Because there is a certain amount of time the target must wait to receive an answer to the SYN/ACK (network congestion may be slowing things down, in a legitimate example), it will eventually bog down and run out of available connections.

☒ **B** is incorrect because EC-Council defines a SYN attack and a SYN flood differently. Whereas a SYN flood takes advantage of tons of half-open connections, the SYN attack goes one step further—by spoofing the sending IP address in the first place. The target will attempt to respond with a SYN/ACK but will be unsuccessful because the sending address is false. Eventually, all the machine's resources are engaged, and the DoS is successful.

☒ **C** is incorrect because a smurf attack is a DoS attack making use of ICMP packets and broadcast addresses. The idea is simple: Spoof the target's IP address and send multiple ping requests to the broadcast address of the subnet. The entire subnet will then begin sending ping responses to the target, exhausting the target's resources and rendering it a giant paperweight.

☒ **D** is incorrect because Low Orbit Ion Cannon (LOIC) is a simple-to-use DDoS tool that floods a target with TCP, UDP, or HTTP requests. It was originally written open source to attack various Scientology websites but has since had many people voluntarily joining a botnet to support all sorts of attacks. Recently, LOIC was used in a coordinated attack against Sony's PlayStation network, and the tool has a track record of other successful hits: The Recording Industry Association of America, PayPal, MasterCard, and several other companies have all fallen victim to LOIC.

19. Which of the following takes advantage of weaknesses in the fragment reassembly functionality of TCP/IP?

   A. Teardrop

   B. SYN flood

   C. Smurf attack

   D. Ping of death

   ☑ **A.** It seemed like every study guide and reference material I picked up for version 7 included references to Conficker, but in version 8 the emphasis seems to have shifted to the teardrop attack. In a teardrop attack, overlapping, mangled packet fragments are sent in an effort to confuse a target system, causing it to reboot or crash. Teardrop attacks exploit an overlapping IP fragment bug present in Windows 95, Windows NT, and Windows 3.1 machines, as well as some early versions of Linux. The attack is really more of an annoyance than anything because a reboot clears it all up; however, anything that was open and altered, sitting unsaved on the device, would be lost.

   ☒ **B** is incorrect because a SYN flood attack exhausts connections on a device by flooding it with thousands of open SYN packets, never sending any acknowledgments to the return SYN/ACKs.

   ☒ **C** is incorrect because a smurf attack involves spoofing the target's address and then pinging the broadcast address with it. The resulting responses of thousands of ICMP packets kills the machine.

   ☒ **D** is incorrect because the ping of death attack involves sending a ping request with an unusually large payload. The ping would be fragmented and, when put together, would kill the target machine.

20. IPSec is an effective preventative measure against session hijacking. Which IPSec mode encrypts only the data payload?

   A. Transport

   B. Tunnel

   C. Protected

   D. Spoofed

   ☑ **A.** IPSec is a wonderful encryption mechanism that can rather easily be set up between two endpoints or even across your entire subnet if you configure the hosts appropriately. You won't need to know all the bells and whistles with IPSec (and thank goodness, because there's a lot to write about), but you do need the basics. Transport mode does not affect the header of the packet at all and encrypts only the payload. It's typically used as a secured connection between two endpoints, whereas Tunnel mode creates a VPN-like connection protecting the entire session. Additionally, Transport mode is compatible with conventional Network Address Translation (NAT).

☒ **B** is incorrect because Tunnel mode encapsulates the entire packet, including the header. This is typically used to form a VPN connection, where the tunnel is used across an untrusted network (such as the Internet). For pretty obvious reasons, it's not compatible with conventional NAT; when the packet goes through the router (or whatever is performing NAT for you), the source address in the packet changes because of Tunnel mode and, therefore, invalidates the packet for the receiving end. There are workarounds for this, generally lumped together as NAT traversal (NAT-t). Many home routers take advantage of something referred to as IPSec pass-through to allow just this.

☒ **C** and **D** are invalid terms involving IPSec.

21. What type of session hijacking attack is shown in Figure 8-1?

    A. Cross-site scripting attack

    B. Cookie session attack

    C. Token evasion attack

    D. Session fixation attack

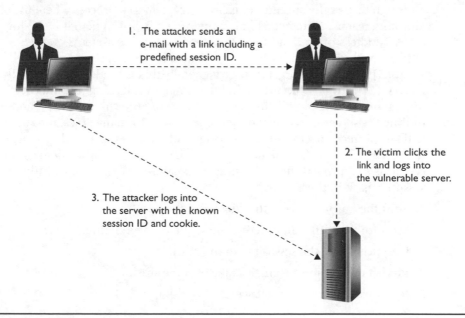

Figure 8-1   Session hijacking example

☑ **D.** This is another example of something new that popped up in version 8: defining a session hijack type. In a session fixation attack, the hacker sends a link (containing an HTTP GET variable identifying the session) to a target. The link points the user to a vulnerable server and contains a predefined session ID (so the hacker knows it without having to sniff). The victim clicks the link and generates a connection and cookie. The attacker connects to the server using the same session ID (passing variables and data as a GET parameter) and *voila*. The attacker must provide a legitimate web application session ID and can do so in a URL, hidden form field, or cookie.

☒ **A** is incorrect because cross-site scripting can be used as part of a session hijack; however, it's not shown in this illustration.

☒ **B** and **C** are incorrect because they are not legitimate attack names and are included solely as distractors.

22. Which of the following best describes the comparison between spoofing and session hijacking?

A. Spoofing and session hijacking are the same thing.

B. Spoofing interrupts a client's communication, whereas hijacking does not.

C. Hijacking interrupts a client's communication, whereas spoofing does not.

D. Hijacking emulates a foreign IP address, whereas spoofing refers to MAC addresses.

☑ **C.** Hijacking and spoofing can sometimes be confused with each other, although they really shouldn't be. *Spoofing* refers to a process where the attacking machine pretends to be something it is not. Whether by faking a MAC address or an IP address, the idea is that other systems on the network will communicate with your machine (that is, set up and tear down sessions) as if it's the target system: Generally this is used to benefit sniffing efforts. Hijacking is a totally different animal. In hijacking, the attacker jumps into an already existing session, knocking the client out of it and fooling the server into continuing the exchange. In many cases, the client will simply reconnect to the server over a different session, with no one the wiser: The server isn't even aware of what happened, and the client simply connects again in a different session. As an aside, EC-Council describes the session hijack in these steps:

1. Sniff the traffic between the client and the server.

2. Monitor the traffic and predict the sequence numbering.

3. Desynchronize the session with the client.

4. Predict the session token and take over the session.

5. Inject packets to the target server.

⊠ **A** is incorrect because spoofing and hijacking are different. An argument can be made that hijacking makes use of some spoofing, but the two attacks are separate entities: Spoofing pretends to be another machine, eliciting (or setting up) sessions for sniffing purposes, whereas hijacking takes advantage of existing communications sessions.

⊠ **B** is incorrect because spoofing doesn't interrupt a client's existing session at all; it's designed to sniff traffic and/or set up its own sessions.

⊠ **D** is incorrect because spoofing isn't relegated to MAC addresses only. You can spoof almost anything, from MAC and IP addresses to system names and services.

23. Which of the following is an effective deterrent against session hijacking?

    A. Install and use a HIDS on the system.

    B. Install and use Tripwire on the system.

    C. Enforce good password policy.

    D. Use unpredictable sequence numbers.

    ☑ **D.** As noted already, session hijacking requires the attacker to guess the proper upcoming sequence number(s) to pull off the attack, pushing the original client out of the session. Using unpredictable session IDs (or, better stated in the real world, using a modern operating system with less predictable sequence numbers) in the first place protects against this. Other countermeasures for session hijacking are fairly common sense: Use encryption to protect the channel, limit incoming connections, minimize remote access, and regenerate the session key after authentication is complete. And, lastly, don't forget user education: If the users don't know any better, they might not think twice about clicking past the security certificate warning or reconnecting after being suddenly shut down.

    ⊠ **A** is incorrect because a host-based intrusion detection system may not deter session hijacking at all.

    ⊠ **B** is incorrect because Tripwire is a file integrity application and won't do a thing for session hijacking prevention.

    ⊠ **C** is incorrect because system passwords have nothing to do with session hijacking.

24. A pen test team member types the following command:

    ```
    ettercap -T -q -M ARP /200.70.55.12
    ```

Which of the following are true regarding this command? (Choose all that apply.)

A. Ettercap is being configured for a GUI interface.

B. Ettercap is being configured as a sniffer.

C. Ettercap is being configured for text mode.

D. Ettercap is being configured for manual mode.

E. Ettercap is being configured for a man-in-the-middle attack.

☑ **C and E.** Ettercap is defined as a "comprehensive suite for man-in-the-middle attacks" by nearly every website devoted to it (do a search for *Ettercap*, and you'll see what I mean), and it's almost universally recognized as one of—if not *the*—best man-in-the-middle attack suites on the planet. Because of this, you'll need to know some basics about it (not much but some). Ettercap can run in one of four user interfaces: text only (–T), something called curses (–C), a GUI (known as GTK, and using the –G flag), and daemon mode (–D). In this example, text mode is enabled, the –q flag sets things "quiet," and the –M flag sets up man-in-the-middle ARP poisoning.

☒ **A** is incorrect because the –T flag is used to put Ettercap in text mode. –G would put Ettercap in GTK mode.

☒ **B** is incorrect because Ettercap isn't being configured as a sniffer here. It's being set up to perform an MITM attack, not to log packets.

☒ **D** is incorrect because there is no "manual" mode in Ettercap. This is included as a distractor.

25. Within a TCP packet dump, a packet is noted with the SYN flag set and a sequence number set at A13F. What should the acknowledgment number in the return SYN/ACK packet be?

A. A131

B. A130

C. A140

D. A14F

☑ **C.** We've been over the need for predicting sequence numbers before, so I won't bore you with it again other than to restate the salient point here: The ISN is incremented by 1 in the SYN/ACK return packet. Because these values were given in hex instead of decimal, all you need to know is what the next hex value after A13F is. You could split it out into binary (each hex digit is four bits, so this would equate to 1010000100111111) and then pick the next available number (1010000101000000) and split it back into hex (1010 = A, 0001 = 1, 0100 = 4, and 0000 = 0). Alternatively, you could convert directly to decimal (41279), add 1, and then convert back to hex. And, yes, you do need to know number conversion from decimal to binary to hex, so stop complaining.

☒ **A, B,** and **D** are incorrect hex equivalents for decimal 41280 (the next number acknowledgment for the ISN).

26. When is session hijacking performed?

    A. Before the three-step handshake

    B. During the three-step handshake

    C. After the three-step handshake

    D. After a FIN packet

    ☑ **C.** This question should be an easy one for you, but it's included here to reinforce the point that you need to understand session hijacking steps well for the exam. Of course, session hijacking should occur after the three-step handshake. As a matter of fact, you'll probably need to wait quite a bit after the three-step handshake so that everything on the session can be set up—authentication and all that nonsense should be taken care of before you jump in and take over.

    ☒ **A** and **B** are incorrect because session hijacking occurs after a session is already established, and the three-step handshake must obviously occur first for this to be true.

    ☒ **D** is incorrect because the FIN packet brings an orderly close to the TCP session. Why on Earth would you wait until it's over to start trying to hijack it?

Cryptography 101

This domain includes questions from the following topics:

- Identify fundamentals of cryptography and encryption techniques
- Learn about cryptographic algorithms
- Learn about how public and private keys are generated
- Get an overview of MD5, SHA, RC4, RC5, and Blowfish algorithms
- Learn about the digital signature and its components
- Learn about the method and application of digital signature technology
- Get an overview of digital certificates
- Learn about cryptanalysis and code-breaking methodologies
- Understand the types of cryptography attacks
- Describe a PKI system

I've lived in four different states and two foreign countries, and each stop along the way in my life offered something irreplaceable, unique, and downright cool. And almost without fail, I didn't appreciate that irreplaceable, unique, and cool thing until I left for a new locale. Maybe it's just human nature to look backward and romanticize the things no longer yours, but I think it's valuable to pause where you're at right now and take stock of the things you do have available to you and to sometimes marvel at how it's all put together.

Technology is no different, and we're all guilty of taking it for granted. When you examine how nearly anything in technology works, though, it's almost a miracle to behold and something definitely not to be taken lightly or just accepted as a given, like gravity or rain. Cryptography is a prime example.

Consider the document I am typing right now. It's made up of a bunch of 1s and 0s arranged in such a way as to present the text in a readable format on the screen—not to mention all the font formats, bolding, spacing, and other goodies I type in here to make it more pleasing to the eye. Just pause for a moment and consider the simple act of typing this sentence and how many bits it takes, properly formatted to display it onscreen or to save and transport it. Then figure out a way to encrypt it, also using a bunch of 1s and 0s.

The entire concept is mind-boggling if you really think about it and something we should all be grateful for. I mean, replacing a letter with a different one based on a number wheel *as you write* is one thing, and maybe replacing characters with symbols as you jot down on a sheet of paper doesn't seem so exciting to you. But consider how this document's 1s and 0s can be altered in such a way that they make no sense to an outsider but are perfectly readable for anyone I provide the key to. It's downright magical, I tell you. Cryptography and cryptanalysis are big parts of the security world and have been ever since the earliest known communication between people. If you're going to be an ethical hacker, you're going to have to at least know the basics. The good news is, you are not required to break down the mathematics of the algorithms. The bad news, though, is that you need to know pretty much everything else about them.

 STUDY TIPS You'll be asked a variety of questions about cryptography on the exam, ranging from simple identification to mind-altering questions you won't even believe are part of this certification. The biggest thing you can do to prepare for the CEH cryptography questions is plain old organization: Commit to memory the categories (block and stream, symmetric and asymmetric, and so on) and get all your key words together.

Also, make use of an old test-taking trick: Eliminating those answers you absolutely know to be wrong is faster and easier than trying to figure out which one is right. As an example, if you simply remember which algorithms are symmetric and which are asymmetric, you can oftentimes eliminate half the answers based on that qualifier in the question. Focus on the characteristics of algorithms—symmetric versus asymmetric, block versus stream—and you're well on your way. And don't forget your key lengths—you'll be asked about them a lot.

Lastly, when it comes to encrypted messaging, PKI is always going to be high on the testing list. Simply remembering that you encrypt with a public key and decrypt with a private key will nab you a couple questions without fail, but you'll definitely need to have a solid understanding of the entire system and what makes it: Questions on certificate authorities, trust systems, and cross-certification will undoubtedly show up. And, for goodness sake, be sure to know the difference between a digital certificate and a digital signature.

1. Which of the following describes the major difference between SSL and S-HTTP?

    A. SSL operates at the network layer, and S-HTTP operates at the application layer.

    B. SSL operates at the application layer, and S-HTTP operates at the network layer.

    C. SSL operates at the transport layer, and S-HTTP operates at the application layer.

    D. SSL operates at the application layer, and S-HTTP operates at the transport layer.

2. Which of the following would be the best choice to guarantee the integrity of messages in transit or storage?

    A. Block cipher

    B. Symmetric algorithm

    C. Asymmetric algorithm

    D. Hash algorithm

3. Which of the following are true regarding a PKI system? (Choose two.)

    A. The CA encrypts all messages.

    B. The CA is the trusted root that issues certificates.

    C. The CA is the recovery agent for lost certificates.

    D. The RA verifies an applicant to the system.

    E. The RA issues all certificates.

    F. The RA encrypts all messages.

4. A person approaches a network administrator and wants advice on how to send encrypted e-mail from home. The end user does not want to have to pay for any license fees or manage server services. Which of the following offers a method for sending encrypted e-mail without having to pay for license fees or to manage a server?

    A. IP Security (IPSec)

    B. Multipurpose Internet Mail Extensions (MIME)

    C. Pretty Good Privacy (PGP)

    D. Hyper Text Transfer Protocol with Secure Socket Layer (HTTPS)

5. Which of the following encryption algorithms is your best choice if your primary need is bulk encryption and you need fast, strong encryption?

   A. AES

   B. ECC

   C. RSA

   D. MD5

6. You're describing a basic PKI system to a new member of the team. He asks how the public key can be distributed within the system in an orderly, controlled fashion so that the users can be sure of the sender's identity. Which of the following would be your answer?

   A. Digital signature

   B. Hash value

   C. Private key

   D. Digital certificate

   E. Nonrepudiation

7. You are discussing hash values with a CEH instructor. Immediately after telling you the hash is a one-way algorithm and cannot be reversed, he explains that you can still discover the value entered into the hash, given enough time and resources. Which of the following hash anomalies might allow this?

   A. L0phtCrack

   B. Hash value compromise

   C. Chosen plain text

   D. Collision

8. What is the standard format for digital certificates?

   A. X.500

   B. X.25

   C. XOR

   D. X.509

9. An organization is concerned about corporate espionage and has evidence suggesting an internal employee has been communicating trade secrets to a competitor. After some investigation, the employee trading secrets was identified. Monitoring of the employee's previous communications outside the company revealed nothing out of the ordinary, save for some large unencrypted e-mails

containing image files of humorous pictures to external addresses. Which of the following is the most logical conclusion based on these facts?

A. E-mail encryption allowed the user to hide files.

B. The user hid information in the image files using steganography.

C. Logical watermarking of images and e-mails fed the sensitive files piece by piece to the competitor.

D. SMTP transport fuzzing was used.

10. A hacker has gained access to several files. Many are encrypted, but one is not, and it happens to be an unencrypted version of an encrypted file. Which of the following is the best choice for possibly providing a successful break into the encrypted files?

A. Cipher text only

B. Known plain text

C. Chosen cipher text

D. Replay

11. You are discussing a steganography tool that takes advantage of the nature of "white space" to conceal information. Which tool are you referring to?

A. Snow

B. GifShuffle

C. White Wipe

D. Tripwire

12. At the basic core of encryption approaches, two main methods are in play: substitution and transposition. Which of the following best describes transposition?

A. Bits are replaced with a different value.

B. Bits are removed.

C. The order of bits is changed.

D. The parity bits are changed.

13. Jack and Jill work in an organization that has a PKI system in place for securing messaging. Jack encrypts a message for Jill and sends it on. Jill receives the message and decrypts it. Within a PKI system, which of the following statements is true?

A. Jack encrypts with his private key. Jill decrypts with her private key.

B. Jack encrypts with his public key. Jill decrypts with her public key.

C. Jack encrypts with Jill's private key. Jill decrypts with her public key.

D. Jack encrypts with Jill's public key. Jill decrypts with her private key.

14. Which of the following would you find in an X.509 digital certificate? (Choose all that apply.)

    A. Version

    B. Algorithm ID

    C. Private key

    D. Public key

    E. Key usage

    F. PTR record

15. Which of the following is a secure substitute for Telnet?

    A. SHA-1

    B. RSA

    C. SSL

    D. SSH

16. An SSL session requires a client and a server to handshake information between each other and agree on a secured channel. Which of the following best describes the session key creation during the setup of an SSL session?

    A. The server creates the key after verifying the client's identity.

    B. The server creates the key immediately on the client connection.

    C. The client creates the key using the server's public key.

    D. The client creates the key after verifying the server's identity.

17. Which encryption algorithm uses variable block sizes (from 32 to 128 bits)?

    A. SHA-1

    B. RC5

    C. 3DES

    D. AES

18. Which hash algorithm was developed by the NSA and produces output values up to 512 bits?

    A. MD5

    B. SHA-1

    C. SHA-2

    D. SSL

19. A hacker is attempting to uncover the key used in a cryptographic encryption scheme. Which attack vector is the most resource intensive and usually takes the longest amount of time?

    A. Social engineering

    B. Known plain text

    C. Frequency analysis

    D. Brute force

20. Which of the following best describes session key creation in SSL?

    A. It is created by the server after verifying the user's identity.

    B. It is created by the server as soon as the client connects.

    C. It is created by the client using the server's public key.

    D. It is created by the client after verifying the server's identity.

21. In a discussion on symmetric encryption, a friend mentions that one of the drawbacks with this system is scalability. He goes on to say that for every person you add to the mix, the number of keys increases dramatically. If seven people are in a symmetric encryption pool, how many keys are necessary?

    A. 7

    B. 14

    C. 21

    D. 28

22. Which of the following is a true statement?

    A. Symmetric encryption scales easily and provides for nonrepudiation.

    B. Symmetric encryption does not scale easily and does not provide for nonrepudiation.

    C. Symmetric encryption is not suited for bulk encryption.

    D. Symmetric encryption is slower than asymmetric encryption.

23. The PKI system you are auditing has a certificate authority (CA) at the top that creates and issues certificates. Users trust each other based on the CA. Which trust model is in use here?

    A. Stand-alone CA

    B. Web of trust

    C. Single authority

    D. Hierarchical trust

24. A portion of a digital certificate is shown here:

```
Version                    V3
Serial Number              26 43 03 62 e9 6b 39 a4 9e 15 00 c7 cc 21 a2 20
Signature Algorithm        sha1RSA
Signature Hash Algorithm   sha1
Issuer                     VeriSign Class 3 Secure Server
Valid From                 Monday, October 17, 2011 8:00 PM
Valid To                   Wednesday, October 17, 2012 7:59:59 PM
.
Public Key                 RSA (2048)
.
```

Which of the following statements is true?

A. The hash created for the digital signature holds 160 bits.

B. The hash created for the digital signature holds 2,048 bits.

C. RSA is the hash algorithm used for the digital signature.

D. This certificate contains a private key.

25. Two bit strings are run through an XOR operation. Which of the following is a true statement for each bit pair regarding this function?

A. If the first value is 0 and the second value is 1, then the output is 0.

B. If the first value is 1 and the second value is 0, then the output is 0.

C. If the first value is 0 and the second value is 0, then the output is 1.

D. If the first value is 1 and the second value is 1, then the output is 0.

26. Which of the following attacks attempts to re-send a portion of a cryptographic exchange in hopes of setting up a communications channel?

A. Known plain text

B. Chosen plain text

C. Man in the middle

D. Replay

27. Within a PKI system, which of the following is an accurate statement?

A. Bill can be sure a message came from Sue by using his public key to decrypt it.

B. Bill can be sure a message came from Sue by using his private key to decrypt it.

C. Bill can be sure a message came from Sue by using her private key to decrypt the digital signature.

D. Bill can be sure a message came from Sue by using her public key to decrypt the digital signature.

28. Which of the following could be considered a drawback to using AES with a 256-bit key to share sensitive data?

   A. The key size requires a long time to encrypt and decrypt messages.

   B. It's a complex algorithm that requires intense system configuration.

   C. AES is a weak cypher.

   D. Each recipient must receive the key through a different channel than the message.

29. One use of hash algorithms is for the secure storage of passwords: The password is run through a one-way hash, and the value is stored instead of the plain-text version. If a hacker gains access to these hash values and knows the hash algorithm used to create them, which of the following could be used to speed up his effort in cracking them?

   A. Salt

   B. Rainbow tables

   C. Steganography

   D. Collision

1. C
2. D
3. B, D
4. C
5. A
6. D
7. D
8. D
9. B
10. B
11. A
12. C
13. D
14. A, B, D, E
15. D
16. D
17. B
18. C
19. D
20. D
21. C
22. B
23. C
24. A
25. D
26. D
27. D
28. D
29. B

1. Which of the following describes a major difference between SSL and S-HTTP?

   A. SSL operates at the network layer, and S-HTTP operates at the application layer.

   B. SSL operates at the application layer, and S-HTTP operates at the network layer.

   C. SSL operates at the transport layer, and S-HTTP operates at the application layer.

   D. SSL operates at the application layer, and S-HTTP operates at the transport layer.

   ☑ **C.** OK, I'll grant you the wording in this question is a little...weird, but I promise it's apropos for your exam. Apparently EC-Council thinks writing S-HTTP will confuse you about HTTPS, which uses SSL for encryption. The differences? Well, S-HTTP and HTTPS (SSL) have a couple big ones. The first is the layer at which they operate: SSL works at the transport layer, and S-HTTP operates at the application layer. SSL tends to be application-independent, while S-HTTP is limited to the specific application using it. Lastly, SSL encrypts the entire communications channel, and S-HTTP encrypts each message independently. As an aside, S-HTTP is rarely (if ever) implemented in the real world.

   ☒ **A, B,** and **D** are incorrect because SSL does not work at the network or application layer.

2. Which of the following would be the best choice to guarantee the integrity of messages in transit or storage?

   A. Block cipher

   B. Symmetric algorithm

   C. Asymmetric algorithm

   D. Hash algorithm

   ☑ **D.** Although it's nice to know the terms *block*, *stream*, *asymmetric*, and *asymmetric*, they're all irrelevant to this question. The key is the word *integrity*, and as you should already know from your study for this exam, that equates to a hash every time. Hash algorithms don't encrypt anything at all. They're *one-way* mathematical functions that take an input and typically produce a fixed-length string (usually a hex number), known as a *hash*, based on the arrangement of the data bits in the input. The sole purpose of a hash is to provide a means to verify the integrity of a piece of data—change a single bit in the arrangement of the original data, and you'll get a different response.

☒ **A** is incorrect because block ciphers are not designed for integrity checks. They use methods such as substitution and transposition in their algorithms and are considered simpler, and slower, than stream ciphers. Data bits are split up into blocks and fed into the cipher, with each block of data (usually 64 bits at a time) then encrypted with the key and algorithm.

☒ **B** is incorrect because a symmetric algorithm is not designed to provide integrity checks. Also known as *single key* and *shared key*, *symmetric encryption* simply means one key is used both to encrypt and to decrypt the data. Therefore, as long as both the sender and the receiver know and have the secret key, communication can be encrypted between the two.

☒ **C** is incorrect because asymmetric algorithms are not designed for integrity checks. Asymmetric encryption uses two keys—what the one key encrypts, the other key decrypts. The "public" key is the one used for encryption, whereas the "private" key is used for decryption.

3. Which of the following is true regarding a PKI system? (Choose two.)

   A. The CA encrypts all messages.

   B. The CA is the trusted root that issues certificates.

   C. The CA is the recovery agent for lost certificates.

   D. The RA verifies an applicant to the system.

   E. The RA issues all certificates.

   F. The RA encrypt all messages.

   ☑ **B** and **D**. A PKI system consists of a bunch of parts, but the certificate authority is right at the top. The CA issues all the certificates for the system and is the one place everything in the system can go to for protected data. The registration authority does all sorts of stuff to take the load off the CA, and verifying the identity of an applicant wanting to use the system is one of the major tasks.

   ☒ **A, C, E,** and **F** are all incorrect because they do not correctly describe a PKI environment. The CA does not encrypt messages and is not a recovery agent for lost ones. The RA does not issue certificates or encrypt messages.

4. A person approaches a network administrator and wants advice on how to send encrypted e-mail from home. The end user does not want to have to pay for any license fees or manage server services. Which of the following offers a method for sending encrypted e-mail without having to pay for license fees or to manage a server?

   A. IP Security (IPSec)

   B. Multipurpose Internet Mail Extensions (MIME)

C. Pretty Good Privacy (PGP)

D. Hyper Text Transfer Protocol with Secure Socket Layer (HTTPS)

☑ **C.** I'm pretty sure you understand this comment already, but I'll say it again here to reinforce it: Sometimes things on your CEH exam simply don't match up with reality. This question is a prime example. EC-Council, and its documentation up through version 8, defines Pretty Good Privacy (PGP) as a free, open source e-mail encryption method available for all to use. In truth, PGP is now synonymous with a single company's offering, based on the original PGP. The true open source, free side of it now is known more by OpenPGP (www.openpgp.org). OpenPGP uses a decentralized system of trusted introducers, which act in the same way as a certificate authority. Basically, in this web of trust relationship, if User A signs User B's certificate, then anyone who trusts User A will also trust User B. You can find downloads for software still using the free, open PGP at www.pgpi.org/.

☒ **A** is incorrect because IPSec is not intended as an e-mail encryption standard; it creates tunnels for the secure exchange of data from one system to another.

☒ **B** is incorrect because MIME is an Internet standard that allows the text-only protocol SMTP to transport nontext entities, such as pictures and non-ASCII character sets.

☒ **D** is incorrect because HTTPS is not intended as an e-mail encryption standard. It sets up a secured means of transporting data within a session and is *usually* associated with web traffic.

5. Which of the following encryption algorithms is your best choice if your primary need is bulk encryption and you need fast, strong encryption?

A. AES

B. ECC

C. RSA

D. MD5

☑ **A.** Questions like this on the exam are to be celebrated because they are easy—assuming you paid attention to my study tips at the beginning of this chapter. The question references bulk encryption—something fast and strong. This screams symmetric all the way, and the only symmetric algorithm listed here is AES.

☒ **B** is incorrect because Elliptic Curve Cryptosystem (ECC) is not symmetric in nature. It's primarily used for mobile devices and uses points on an elliptical curve, in conjunction with logarithmic problems, for encryption and signatures.

☒ **C** is incorrect because RSA is an asymmetric choice, not a symmetric one. RSA achieves strong encryption through the use of two large prime numbers. Factoring these numbers creates key sizes up to 4,096 bits. RSA can be used for encryption and digital signatures, and it's the modern de facto standard for those purposes.

☒ **D** is incorrect because MD5 is a hash algorithm, and as we all know, hash algorithms don't encrypt anything. Sure, they're great at integrity checks, and, yes, you can pass a hash of something in place of the original (sending a hash of a stored password, for instance, instead of the password itself). However, this is not true encryption.

6. You're describing a basic PKI system to a new member of the team. He asks how the public key can be distributed within the system in an orderly, controlled fashion so that the users can be sure of the sender's identity. Which of the following would be your answer?

   A. Digital signature

   B. Hash value

   C. Private key

   D. Digital certificate

   E. Nonrepudiation

☑ **D.** This one is actually easy yet is confusing to a lot of folks. You have to remember the goal of this little portion of a PKI system—how does one *know* this public key really belongs to User Joe and not User Mike, and how can it be delivered safely to everyone? A digital certificate is the answer because it contains the sender's public key and can be used to identify the sender. Because the CA provides the certificate and key (public), the user can be certain the public key actually belongs to the intended recipient. This simplifies distribution of keys as well, because users can go to a central authority—a key store, if you will—instead of directly to each user in the organization. Without central control and digital certificates, it would be a madhouse, with everyone chucking public keys at one another with wild abandon. And PKI is no place for Mardi Gras, my friend.

☒ **A** is incorrect because although a digital signature does provide a means for verifying an identity (encryption with your private key, which can be decrypted only with your corresponding public key, proves you are indeed you), it doesn't provide any means of sending keys anywhere. A digital signature is nothing more than an algorithmic output that is designed to ensure the authenticity (and integrity) of the sender. You need it to prove your certificate's authenticity, but you need the certificate in order to send keys around.

☒ **B** is incorrect because a hash value has nothing to do with sending public keys around anywhere. Yes, hash values are "signed" to verify authenticity, but that's it. There is no transport capability in a hash. It's just a number and, in this case, a distractor answer.

☒ **C** is incorrect for a number of reasons, but one should be screaming at you from the page right now: You never, *never*, send a private key anywhere. If you did send your private key off, it wouldn't be private anymore, now would it? The private key is simply the part of the pair used for encryption. It is never shared with anyone.

☒ **E** is incorrect because nonrepudiation is a definition term and has nothing to do with the transport of keys. Nonrepudiation is the means by which a recipient can ensure the identity of the sender and neither party can deny having sent or received the message.

7. You are discussing hash values with a CEH instructor. Immediately after telling you the hash is a one-way algorithm and cannot be reversed, he explains that you can still discover the value entered into the hash, given enough time and resources. Which of the following hash anomalies might allow this?

   A. L0phtCrack

   B. Hash value compromise

   C. Chosen plain text

   D. Collision

   ☑ **D.** A collision, in the world of hashes, occurs when plain text is fed into a hash until, eventually, two or more entries are found that create the same fixed-value hash result. In short, a collision occurs when two or more files create the same output. When a hacker can create a second file that produces the same hash value output as the original, he may be able to pass off the fake file as the original. This can obviously cause all sorts of problems, and when you think about what hashes are sometimes used for (such as storing hashes of passwords in a file instead of the passwords themselves), you can certainly understand where collisions are concerning. As an aside, it is just as likely you would find a *new* collision than the original collision, and without the knowledge of the original text, your results would be nothing more than an educated guess. For the purposes of the exam, though, just remember what a collision is and means.

   ☒ **A** is incorrect because L0phtCrack really has nothing to do with this question. It is a good-old password cracker in the Windows world, but it's not a collision of hash values in any sense. It's a "password auditing and recovery application" used to test password strength and "recover" lost passwords on Windows machines. It uses dictionary, brute-force, and hybrid attacks, as well as rainbow tables.

☒ **B** is incorrect for a couple of reasons. First, the term *hash value compromise* sounds really cool but has no meaning in the CEH world. This term could be construed to mean lots of things, but if you run a quick Google check (go ahead, I'll wait), you'll see that it's not a definition term you'll need to know. It's a pretty good distractor, yes, but not a viable answer.

☒ **C** is incorrect because chosen plain text is an attack used to determine the key used for encryption. It's a variant of known plain text, where the hacker has both plain-text and corresponding cipher-text messages and scans them for repeatable sequences. These are compared to the cipher-text versions and—*voilà*—key found.

8. What is the standard format for digital certificates?

   A. X.500

   B. X.25

   C. XOR

   D. X.509

   ☑ **D.** This is a quick, simple question you'll see on pretty much every study guide and practice test for CEH. It's just something you're going to need in your memory bank—one of those things you just know without thinking about it. The X.509 standard is a part of a much bigger series of standards, and it defines what should and should not be in a digital certificate. Because of the standard, any system complying with X.509 can exchange and use digital certificates to establish authenticity.

   ☒ **A** is incorrect because X.500 has nothing to do with digital certificates. It's actually a *series* of standards covering directory services, and it's more applicable to things such as Active Directory in Windows-based networks. On a related but completely worthless note, it was developed by ITU-T way back in 1988.

   ☒ **B** is incorrect because X.25 has nothing to do with digital certificates. X.25 is a protocol suite from ITU-T defining wide area network (WAN) communication.

   ☒ **C** is incorrect because XOR refers to a mathematical function. An XOR operation requires two inputs, which are compared by the operation. If the bits match, the output is 0; if they don't, it's 1.

9. An organization is concerned about corporate espionage and has evidence suggesting an internal employee has been communicating trade secrets to a competitor. After some investigation, the employee trading secrets was identified. Monitoring of the employee's previous communications outside the company revealed nothing out of the ordinary, save for some large unencrypted

e-mails containing image files of humorous pictures to external addresses. Which of the following is the most logical conclusion based on these facts?

A. E-mail encryption allowed the user to hide files.

B. The user hid information in the image files using steganography.

C. Logical watermarking of images and e-mails fed the sensitive files piece by piece to the competitor.

D. SMTP transport fuzzing was used.

☑ B. In this circumstance, we know the employee has been sending sensitive documents out of the network. IDS obviously hasn't picked up on anything, and there was nothing overtly done to give away the intent. The only thing out of the ordinary turned out to be large e-mail files holding nothing but images. Steganography is the most logical choice here, and the user simply folded the sensitive data into the latest joke image he found and sent it on its merry way.

☒ A is incorrect because e-mail encryption isn't in place—it's specifically called out in the question and wouldn't necessarily allow external encryption or hide the information from later forensics examinations.

☒ C and D are incorrect because logical watermarking and SMTP transport fuzzing, so far as I know, don't even exist. They sound cool and may appear legitimate, but they're definitely not the answers we're looking for.

10. A hacker has gained access to several files. Many are encrypted, but one is not, and it happens to be an unencrypted version of an encrypted file. Which of the following is the best choice for possibly providing a successful break into the encrypted files?

A. Cipher text only

B. Known plain text

C. Chosen cipher text

D. Replay

☑ B. There is definitely some room for argument on this question: Who's to say all the files were encrypted in the same way? However, of the options presented, known plain text is the one that makes the most sense. In this attack, the hacker has both plain-text and cipher-text messages. Plain-text copies are scanned for repeatable sequences, which are then compared to the cipher-text versions. Over time, and with effort, this can be used to decipher the key.

☒ A is incorrect, but just barely so. I'm certain some of you are arguing that a cipher-text-only attack could also be used here because in that attack several messages encrypted in the same way are run through statistical analysis to eventually reveal repeating code, which may be used to decode messages later. Sure, an attacker might just ignore the plain-text copy in there, but the inference in the question is that he'd use both. You'll often see questions like this where you'll need to take into account the inference without over-thinking the question.

☒ **C** is incorrect because chosen cipher text works almost exactly like a cipher-text-only attack. Statistical analysis without a plain-text version for comparison can be performed, but it's only for *portions* of gained cipher text. That's the key word to look for.

☒ **D** is incorrect because it's irrelevant to this scenario. Replay attacks catch streams of data and replay them to the intended recipient from another sender.

11. You are discussing a steganography tool that takes advantage of the nature of "white space" to conceal information. Which tool are you discussing?

    A. Snow

    B. GifShuffle

    C. White Wipe

    D. Tripwire

    ☑ **A.** Snow is one of the steganography tools the CEH exam covers. The following is from the Snow website: "The program snow is used to conceal messages in ASCII text by appending whitespace to the end of lines. Because spaces and tabs are generally not visible in text viewers, the message is effectively hidden from casual observers. And if the built-in encryption is used, the message cannot be read even if it is detected."

    ☒ **B** is incorrect because GifShuffle is used to conceal messages in GIF images by shuffling bits in the color map. Because these changes are minutely small, GifShuffle leaves the image visibly unchanged. It's also an open source tool.

    ☒ **C** is incorrect because White Wipe is not a steganography tool. In fact, as far as I know, it's not a tool at all. This is simply a distractor answer.

    ☒ **D** is incorrect because Tripwire is not a steganography tool either. Rather, it's a conglomeration of tool actions that perform the overall IT security efforts for an enterprise. It provides for integrity checks, regulatory compliance, configuration management, and all other sorts of goodies.

12. At the basic core of encryption approaches, two main methods are in play: substitution and transposition. Which of the following best describes transposition?

    A. Bits are replaced with a different value.

    B. Bits are removed.

C. The order of bits is changed.

D. The parity bits are changed.

☑ C. This is just a different way of asking you to define substitution and transposition. Substitution is exactly what it sounds like. Transposition doesn't substitute at all; it changes the bit order altogether.

☒ A is incorrect because this is the definition for substitution. Substitution is exactly what it sounds like—bits are simply replaced by other bits.

☒ B is incorrect because bits aren't technically removed with either function. They may be replaced, or reordered, but they are not removed.

☒ D is incorrect because this answer has nothing, really, to do with encryption. *Parity bits* sounds sexy and exciting, but it's meaningless in this context. Parity bits are used for basic error correction, not encryption.

13. Jack and Jill work in an organization that has a PKI system in place for securing messaging. Jack encrypts a message for Jill and sends it on. Jill receives the message and decrypts it. Within a PKI system, which of the following statements is true?

A. Jack encrypts with his private key. Jill decrypts with her private key.

B. Jack encrypts with his public key. Jill decrypts with her public key.

C. Jack encrypts with Jill's private key. Jill decrypts with her public key.

D. Jack encrypts with Jill's public key. Jill decrypts with her private key.

☑ D. When it comes to PKI encryption questions, remember the golden rule: Encrypt with public, decrypt with private. In this instance, Jack wants to send a message to Jill. He will use Jill's public key—which everyone can get—to encrypt the message, knowing that only Jill, with her corresponding private key, can decrypt it.

☒ A is incorrect because you do not encrypt with a private key in a PKI system. Yes, you *can* encrypt with it, but what would be the point? Anyone with your public key—which everyone has—could decrypt it! Remember, private = decrypt, public = encrypt.

☒ B is incorrect because, in this case, Jack has gotten his end of the bargain correct, but Jill doesn't seem to know what she's doing. PKI encryption is done in key pairs—what one key encrypts, the other decrypts. So, her use of her own public key to decrypt something encrypted with Jack's key—a key from a completely different pair—is baffling.

☒ C is incorrect because there is no way Jack should have anyone's private key, other than his own. That's kind of the point of a private key—you keep it to yourself and don't share it with anyone. As a note here, the stated steps would actually work—that is, one key encrypts, so the other decrypts—but it's completely backward for how the system is supposed to work. It's an abomination to security, if you will.

14. Which of the following would you find in an X.509 digital certificate? (Choose all that apply.)

   A. Version

   B. Algorithm ID

   C. Private key

   D. Public key

   E. Key usage

   F. PTR record

   ☑ **A, B, D,** and **E.** You are definitely going to need to know the digital certificate and what it contains. A *digital certificate* is an electronic file that is used to verify a user's identity, providing nonrepudiation throughout the system. The certificate contains standard fields used for specific purposes. Those fields are Version, Serial Number, Subject, Algorithm ID (or Signature Algorithm), Issuer, Valid From and Valid To, Key Usage, Subject's Public Key, and Optional.

   ☒ **C** is incorrect because a private key is never shared. The certificate usually is "signed" with an encrypted hash by the private key, but the key itself is never shared.

   ☒ **F** is incorrect because a PTR record is a part of the Domain Name System (DNS), not a digital certificate. A PTR record provides a reverse DNS lookup as a pointer to a canonical name.

15. Which of the following is a secure substitute for Telnet?

   A. SHA-1

   B. RSA

   C. SSL

   D. SSH

   ☑ **D.** Secure Shell (SSH) was created to fill a security need. Telnet provides easy administrative access, but it's in the clear and ripe for theft. SSH performs the same functions—providing a channel for command execution and remote logging—but does so in a secured method, over a secured channel with strong authentication. As an aside, Telnet can do lots of things SSH cannot (providing some marginal interaction with generic TCP services, serving as a poor hacker's web browser, and so on). Therefore, SSH is to be thought of as a secure alternative to Telnet, not a replacement.

   ☒ **A** is incorrect because SHA-1 is a hashing algorithm, not a means for encrypting a channel for communication exchange. It was published by the National Institute of Standards and Technology (NIST) as a better, stronger hash alternative and is now in its third cycle of development (SHA-2 and SHA-3 have been released).

☒ **B** is incorrect because RSA is an encryption algorithm, achieving strong encryption through the use of two large prime numbers. Factoring these numbers creates key sizes up to 4,096 bits. RSA can be used for encryption and digital signatures and is the modern de facto standard.

☒ **C** is incorrect because SSL is an application layer protocol for managing security on Internet message transit. It uses RSA asymmetric encryption to encrypt data transferred over its connection.

16. An SSL session requires a client and a server to handshake information between each other and agree on a secured channel. Which of the following best describes the session key creation during the setup of an SSL session?

   A. The server creates the key after verifying the client's identity.

   B. The server creates the key immediately on the client connection.

   C. The client creates the key using the server's public key.

   D. The client creates the key after verifying the server's identity.

   ☑ **D.** In the CEH world, SSL has six major steps (others claim seven or more, but we're studying for the CEH certification here, so we'll stick with theirs). The six steps are (1) Client hello, (2) Server hello and certificate, (3) Server hello done message, (4) Client verifies server identity and sends Client Key Exchange message, (5) Client sends Change Cipher Spec and Finish message, and (6) Server responds with Change Cipher Spec and Finish message. The session key is created by the client after it verifies the server identity (using the certificate provided in step 2).

   ☒ **A** is incorrect because the server does not create the session key.

   ☒ **B** is incorrect for the same reason—the client creates the key, not the server.

   ☒ **C** is incorrect because the client does not use a "public key" for an SSL session. It's a great distractor, trying to confuse you with PKI terms in an SSL question.

17. Which encryption algorithm uses variable block sizes (from 32 to 128 bits)?

   A. SHA-1

   B. RC5

   C. 3DES

   D. AES

   ☑ **B.** Questions on identifying encryption algorithms really come down to memorization of some key terms. Rivest Cipher (RC) encompasses several versions, from RC2 through RC6. It is an asymmetric block cipher that uses a variable key length up to 2,040 bits. RC6, the latest version, uses 128-bit blocks, whereas RC5 uses variable block sizes (32, 64, or 128).

☒ **A** is incorrect because SHA-1 is a hash algorithm, not an encryption algorithm. If this question were about verifying integrity, this would be a good choice. However, in this case, it is a distractor.

☒ **C** is incorrect because although 3DES is a symmetric block cipher, it does not use variable block sizes. 3DES (called *triple* DES) uses a 168-bit key and can use up to three keys in a multiple-encryption method. It's much more effective than DES but is much slower.

☒ **D** is incorrect because AES, another symmetric block cipher, uses key lengths of 128, 192, or 256 bits. It effectively replaces DES and is much faster than either DES or its triplicate cousin (3DES).

18. Which hash algorithm was developed by the NSA and produces output values up to 512 bits?

    A. MD5

    B. SHA-1

    C. SHA-2

    D. SSL

☑ **C.** Both SHA-1 and SHA-2 were developed by the NSA; however, SHA-1 produced only a 160-bit output value. SHA-2 was developed to rectify the shortcomings of its predecessor and is capable of producing outputs of 224, 256, 384, and 512 bits. Although it was designed as a replacement for SHA-1 (which was supposed to have been phased out in 2010), SHA-2 is still not as widely used.

☒ **A** is incorrect because MD5 produces 128-bit output. It was created by Ronald Rivest for ensuring file integrity; however, serious flaws in the algorithm, and the advancement of other hashes, have resulted in this hash being rendered obsolete (U.S. CERT, August 2010). Despite this, you'll find MD5 is still used for file verification on downloads and, in many cases, to store passwords.

☒ **B** is incorrect because SHA-1 produces a 160-bit value output. It was created by NSA and used to be required by law for use in U.S. government applications. However, serious flaws became apparent in late 2005, and the U.S. government began recommending the replacement of SHA-1 with SHA-2 after 2010 (see FIPS PUB 180-1).

☒ **D** is incorrect because SSL isn't even a hash algorithm. If you picked this one, you have some serious studying to do.

19. A hacker is attempting to uncover the key used in a cryptographic encryption scheme. Which attack vector is the most resource intensive and usually takes the longest amount of time?

A. Social engineering

B. Known plaintext

C. Frequency analysis

D. Brute force

☑ D. I know you probably weren't expecting a brute-force definition to show up so early, but sometimes this exam will throw terms in and out of objectives to see whether you're paying attention. Brute-force attacks—whether attempting to crack a password or, in this case, to determine a key used in cryptography— are the longest and most resource intensive. If you think about what the attack is doing, this makes perfect sense. Although, eventually, every brute-force attack will be successful, the length of the key can make the length of time necessary to go through all possible iterations unacceptable. For example, if it takes your supercomputer 12 years to crack an algorithm key, it's probably a safe bet that the target has changed it within that time span.

☒ A is incorrect because social engineering requires little to no resources at all, and given the right individual on the phone (or sitting behind a desk), it could be pretty quick. Granted, this is a ridiculous answer here—who is actually going to hand over a cryptographic key to someone? —but stranger things have happened.

☒ B is incorrect because known plain text takes at least some of the time-crunching out for you. Remember in this attack that the hacker has both plain-text and cipher-text messages. Plain-text copies are scanned for repeatable sequences, which are then compared to the cipher-text versions. Over time, and with effort, this can be used to decipher the key; however, it is not as resource intensive as brute force.

☒ C is incorrect because, although this answer sounds really cool, it doesn't fit with the question criteria (time and resource intensive). Frequency analysis relies on the fact that, in any given sample of English writing, there will be certain letters (and combinations of letters) that occur with more frequency than others. This kind of attack appeals to the math geeks in our field—and to those who tech-edit hacking books.

20. Which of the following best describes session key creation in SSL?

A. It is created by the server after verifying the user's identity.

B. It is created by the server as soon as the client connects.

C. It is created by the client using the server's public key.

D. It is created by the client after verifying the server's identity.

☑ **D.** Depending on the book you're reading, an SSL session can have anywhere from five to ten steps. For our purposes, there are six defined steps that start with an exchange of hello packets that allows the server to authenticate itself to the client (using public-key techniques and providing SSL version, session ID, and certificate). After these three handshake messages are exchanged, the client verifies the certificate and generates a secret key, which it then encrypts using the server's public key. Finally, a finish message from the client is sent, and the server compares hashes, sending its own finish message to start the session.

☒ **A** and **B** are incorrect because the server does not create the secret key.

☒ **C** is incorrect because the public key is used to *encrypt* the key, not to *create* it.

21. In a discussion on symmetric encryption, a friend mentions that one of the drawbacks with this system is scalability. He goes on to say that for every person you add to the mix, the number of keys increases dramatically. If seven people are in a symmetric encryption pool, how many keys are necessary?

    A. 7

    B. 14

    C. 21

    D. 28

    ☑ **C.** Symmetric encryption is really fast and works great with bulk encryption; however, scalability and key exchange are huge drawbacks. To determine the number of keys you need, use the formula $N (N - 1) / 2$. Plugging 7 into this, we have $7 (7 - 1) / 2 = 21$.

    ☒ **A** is incorrect because although symmetric key does use the same key for encryption and decryption, each new node requires a different key. Seven keys simply isn't enough.

    ☒ **B** is incorrect because 14 keys isn't enough.

    ☒ **D** is incorrect because 28 keys is too many. Stick with the formula $N (N - 1) / 2$.

22. Which of the following is a true statement?

    A. Symmetric encryption scales easily and provides for nonrepudiation.

    B. Symmetric encryption does not scale easily and does not provide for nonrepudiation.

    C. Symmetric encryption is not suited for bulk encryption.

    D. Symmetric encryption is slower than asymmetric encryption.

☑ **B.** Symmetric encryption has always been known for strength and speed; however, scalability and key exchange are big drawbacks. Additionally, there is no way to provide for nonrepudiation (within the confines of the encryption system). Symmetric encryption is good for a great many things when you don't want all the overhead of key management.

☒ **A** is incorrect because symmetric encryption does not scale easily and does not provide for nonrepudiation. The single key used for each channel makes scalability an issue. Remember, the formula for number of keys is $N (N − 1) / 2$.

☒ **C** is incorrect because symmetric encryption is perfectly designed for bulk encryption. Assuming you can find a way to ensure the key exchange is protected, speed makes this the best choice.

☒ **D** is incorrect because one of the benefits of symmetric encryption is its speed. It is much faster than asymmetric encryption but doesn't provide some of the benefits asymmetric provides us (scalability, nonrepudiation, and so on).

23. The PKI system you are auditing has a certificate authority (CA) at the top that creates and issues certificates. Users trust each other based on the CA. Which trust model is in use here?

    A. Stand-alone CA

    B. Web of trust

    C. Single authority

    D. Hierarchical trust

☑ **C.** Trust models within PKI systems provide a standardized method for certificate and key exchanges. The valid trust models include web of trust, single authority, and hierarchical. The single authority system has a CA at the top that creates and issues certs. Users then trust each other based on the CA at the top vouching for them. Assuming a single authority model is used, it's of vital importance to protect it. After all, if it is compromised, your whole system is kaput.

☒ **A** is incorrect because "stand-alone CA" doesn't refer to a trust model. It instead defines a single CA that is usually set up as a trusted offline root in a hierarchy or when extranets and the Internet are involved.

☒ **B** is incorrect because web of trust refers to a model where users create and manage their own certificates and key exchange and multiple entities sign certificates for one another. In other words, users within this system trust each other based on certificates they receive from other users on the same system.

☒ **D** is incorrect because although a hierarchical trust system also has a CA at the top (which is known as the *root CA*), it makes use of one or more intermediate CAs underneath it—known as *RAs*—to issue and manage certificates. This system is the most secure because users can track the certificate back to the root to ensure authenticity without a single point of failure.

24. A portion of a digital certificate is shown here:

```
Version                     V3
Serial Number               26 43 03 62 e9 6b 39 a4 9e 15 00 c7 cc 21 a2 20
Signature Algorithm         sha1RSA
Signature Hash Algorithm    sha1
Issuer                      VeriSign Class 3 Secure Server
Valid From                  Monday, October 17, 2011 8:00 PM
Valid To                    Wednesday, October 17, 2012 7:59:59 PM
.
Public Key                  RSA (2048)
.
```

Which of the following statements is true?

A. The hash created for the digital signature holds 160 bits.

B. The hash created for the digital signature holds 2,048 bits.

C. RSA is the hash algorithm used for the digital signature.

D. This certificate contains a private key.

☑ **A.** Questions on the digital certificate are usually easy enough, and this is no exception. The algorithm used to create the hash is clearly defined as Signature Hash Algorithm (SHA-1), and, as we already know, SHA-1 creates a 160-bit hash output. This will then be encrypted by the sender's private key and decrypted on the recipient's end with the public key, thus verifying identity.

☒ **B** is incorrect as a distractor because the RSA key size of 2,048 is listed in the public key section of the certificate.

☒ **C** incorrect because RSA is not a hash algorithm. It is, without doubt, used as an encryption algorithm with this certificate (and uses a 2,048-bit key to do so) but does not hash anything.

☒ **D** is incorrect because (as I'm certain you are already aware) a private key is *never* shared. The public key is contained for recipients to use if they want to encrypt something to send back to the originator, but the private key is never shared.

25. Two bit strings are run through an XOR operation. Which of the following is a true statement for each bit pair regarding this function?

A. If the first value is 0 and the second value is 1, then the output is 0.

B. If the first value is 1 and the second value is 0, then the output is 0.

C. If the first value is 0 and the second value is 0, then the output is 1.

D. If the first value is 1 and the second value is 1, then the output is 0.

☑ **D.** An XOR operation requires two inputs, and in the case of encryption algorithms, this would be the data bits and the key bits. Each bit is fed into the operation—one from the data, the next from the key—and then XOR makes a determination: If the bits match, the output is 0; if they don't, it's 1.

☒ **A** is incorrect because the two values being compared are different; therefore, the output would be 1.

☒ **B** is incorrect because the two values being compared are different; therefore, the output would be 1.

☒ **C** is incorrect because the two values being compared are the same; therefore, the output should be 0.

26. Which of the following attacks attempts to re-send a portion of a cryptographic exchange in hopes of setting up a communications channel?

    A. Known plain text

    B. Chosen plain text

    C. Man in the middle

    D. Replay

    ☑ **D.** Replay attacks are most often performed within the context of a man-in-the-middle attack and not necessarily just for communications channel setup. They're also used for DoS attacks against a system, to feed bad data in hopes of corrupting a system, to try to overflow a buffer (send more encrypted data than expected), and so on. The hacker repeats a portion of a cryptographic exchange in hopes of fooling the system into setting up a communications channel. The attacker doesn't really have to know the actual data (such as the password) being exchanged; he just has to get the timing right in copying and then replaying the bit stream. Session tokens can be used in the communications process to combat this attack.

    ☒ **A** is incorrect because known plain text doesn't really have anything to do with this scenario. Known plain text refers to having both plain-text and corresponding cipher-text messages, which are scanned for repeatable sequences and then compared to the cipher-text versions.

    ☒ **B** is incorrect because it simply doesn't apply to this scenario. In a chosen plain-text attack, a hacker puts several encrypted messages through statistical analysis to determine repeating code.

    ☒ **C** is incorrect because, in this instance, replay refers to the attack being described in the question, not man in the middle. I know you think this is confusing, and I do understand. However, this is an example of CEH wordplay you'll need to be familiar with. Man in the middle is usually listed as an attack by every security guide; however, within the context of the exam, it may also refer solely to where the attacker has positioned himself. From this location, he can launch a variety of attacks—replay being one of them.

27. Within a PKI system, which of the following is an accurate statement?

   A. Bill can be sure a message came from Sue by using his public key to decrypt it.

   B. Bill can be sure a message came from Sue by using his private key to decrypt it.

   C. Bill can be sure a message came from Sue by using her private key to decrypt the digital signature.

   D. Bill can be sure a message came from Sue by using her public key to decrypt the digital signature.

   ☑ **D.** Remember, a digital signature is a hash value that is encrypted with the user's private key. Because the corresponding public key can decrypt it, this provides the nonrepudiation feature we're looking for. This is the only instance on the exam where the private key is used for encryption. In general, public encrypts, and private decrypts.

   ☒ **A** is incorrect because not only does this have nothing to do with proving identity, but it also cannot work. Bill can't use his own public key to decrypt a message sent to him. The keys work in pairs—if the message is encrypted with his public key, only his private key can decrypt it.

   ☒ **B** is incorrect because this has nothing to do with proving Sue's identity. Sure, Bill will be using his own private key to decrypt messages sent to him by other users; however, it doesn't provide any help in proving identity.

   ☒ **C** is incorrect because there is no way Bill should have Sue's private key. Remember, private keys are not shared with anyone, for any reason. This is why encrypting a hash with it works so well for the digital signing process.

28. Which of the following could be considered a drawback to using AES with a 256-bit key to share sensitive data?

   A. The key size requires a long time to encrypt and decrypt messages.

   B. It's a complex algorithm that requires intense system configuration.

   C. AES is a weak cypher.

   D. Each recipient must receive the key through a different channel than the message.

   ☑ **D.** AES is a strong and fast encryption algorithm established by NIST and adopted by the U.S. government to replace DES. The only real drawback is it is symmetric in nature, meaning the key used to encrypt and decrypt is the same.

To use AES, you'd have to find some other way to exchange the key securely, separate from the message itself. This is why most secured communications make use of both symmetric and asymmetric cyphers to get a job done.

☒ **A** is incorrect because symmetric algorithms are fast, and the key size of 256 does not slow it down at all.

☒ **B** is incorrect because there is no more configuration efforts required for AES than there is for any other.

☒ **C** is incorrect because AES is not a weak cypher. It's adopted by the U.S. government and recognized as a strong encryption method—so long as the key is transmitted appropriately.

29. One use of hash algorithms is for the secure storage of passwords: The password is run through a one-way hash, and the value is stored instead of the plain-text version. If a hacker gains access to these hash values and knows the hash algorithm used to create them, which of the following could be used to speed up his effort in cracking them?

    A. Salt

    B. Rainbow tables

    C. Steganography

    D. Collision

    ☑ **B.** Rainbow tables are the result of a lot of effort in putting all known combinations of plain-text entries into a hash, one at a time, and capturing the hash value that's created. Then, instead of having to brute force your way in and spending countless computational cycles, you can simply compare the hash value you stole from the password file to the rainbow table—once you find a match, *voilà*! Rainbow tables may be largely replaced in the real world, with the advent of massive computational offerings like FPGAs and GPUs, but they're still relevant for your exam.

    ☒ **A** is incorrect because a salt is used to increase security on a password hash, not to crack it. A *salt* is a collection of random bits used as a key in addition to the hashing algorithm. Because the bits, and length, are random, a good salt makes a collision attack difficult to pull off.

    ☒ **C** is incorrect because steganography simply makes no sense here. *Steganography* involves hiding messages inside another medium—for example, hiding a message inside a .jpg file.

    ☒ **D** is incorrect because although the entire effort is in finding the correct collision to unlock the plain-text version, the collision itself isn't an effort to speed things up.

Low Tech: Social Engineering and Physical Security

This chapter includes questions from the following topics:

- Define social engineering
- Describe the different types of social engineering attacks
- Describe insider attacks, reverse social engineering, dumpster diving, social networking, and URL obfuscation
- Describe phishing attacks and countermeasures
- List social engineering countermeasures
- Describe physical security measures

I know a lot of people will pick up books like this in an effort to train themselves to be a "hacker," but I've got some news for you: You were already partway there. You are a born social engineer, and you've been doing some of this stuff since you could walk. In fact, I'll bet serious cash you'll probably employ at least some manipulation of your fellow human beings *today*, maybe without even thinking about it.

Don't believe me? I guarantee if you search your memory banks there was at least once in your childhood where you talked your way into another piece of candy or few minutes playing with a toy, just because you were cute. If you had siblings, I bet all of you conspired—at least once—to cover up something bad or to convince Mom you really need more ice cream. And the old trick of employing the "Well, Dad said it was OK" trick, pitting Mom versus Dad? Oldest one in the book....

We all work the system every day because it's how we are wired, and there's not a person reading this book who doesn't try to influence and manipulate the people around them to gain an advantage or accomplish a goal. You've been doing it since you were born, and you will continue to do so until you shed this mortal coil. All we're doing with pen testing and ethical hacking is bringing those same thoughts and actions to influence our virtual workplace and adding one slight twist: While most of your manipulation of others isn't consciously purposeful, it *has to be* in the virtual world.

There's a lot of acting, a lot of intuition, and a lot of lying involved, and to be successful in this area you have to be *convincing* to pull it off.

The entire subject is fascinating, and there are endless articles, studies, and books devoted to it. A Kapersky blog dubbed it "Hacking the Human OS," which is about as apt a description as I could ever come up with myself. Social engineering and physical security measures are those obvious and simple solutions you may accidentally overlook. Why spend all the effort to hack into a system and crack passwords offline when you can just call someone up and ask for them? Why bother with trying to steal sensitive business information from encrypted shares when you can walk into the building and sit in on a sales presentation? Sure, you occasionally almost get arrested shuffling around in a dumpster for good information (our esteemed technical editor can attest to this), but most of social engineering is easy, simple, and effective.

 STUDY TIPS Social engineering is part of the Security segment of the exam, which comprises 25 percent of the questions (31 out of 125 will be in this area). The Security segment covers all sorts of stuff, and social engineering makes up a large part of that. Thankfully, most questions you'll see about these topics are of the straightforward, definition-based variety, so you may not find this chapter's questions as challenging as some from previous offerings.

One note of caution, though: Be careful with the wording in some of these questions. For example, tailgating and piggybacking mean the same thing to us in the real world, but there's a significant difference when it comes to your exam. It's true that most of these are fairly easy to decipher, but EC-Council sometimes likes to focus on minutia.

1. An organization's building has a guard posted at the lone entrance. A door leads into a smaller room with a second door heading into the interior of the building. Which physical security measure is in place?

   A. Guard shack

   B. Turnstile

   C. Man shack

   D. Man trap

2. In your social engineering efforts, you call the company help desk and pose as a user who has forgotten a password. You ask the technician to help you reset your password, which they happily comply with. Which social engineering attack is in use here?

   A. Piggybacking

   B. Reverse social engineering

   C. Technical support

   D. Halo effect

3. Which of the following is a true statement regarding biometric systems?

   A. The lower the CER, the better the biometric system.

   B. The higher the CER, the better the biometric system.

   C. The higher the FRR, the better the biometric system.

   D. The higher the FAR, the better the biometric system.

4. A pen tester sends an unsolicited e-mail to several users on the target organization. The e-mail is well crafted and appears to be from the company's help desk, advising users of potential network problems. The e-mail provides a contact number to call in the event a user is adversely affected. The pen tester then performs a denial of service on several systems and receives phone calls from users asking for assistance. Which social engineering practice is in play here?

   A. Technical support

   B. Impersonation

   C. Phishing

   D. Reverse social engineering

5. A pen test member has gained access to a building and is observing activity as he wanders around. In one room of the building, he stands just outside a cubicle wall opening and watches the onscreen activity of a user. Which social engineering attack is in use here?

   A. Eavesdropping

   B. Tailgating

   C. Shoulder surfing

   D. Piggybacking

6. A recent incident investigated by the local IR team involved a user receiving an e-mail that appeared to be from the U.S. Postal Service, notifying her of a package headed her way and providing a link for tracking the package. The link provided took the user to what appeared to be the USPS site, where she input her user information to learn about the latest shipment headed her way. Which attack did the user fall victim to?

   A. Phishing

   B. Internet level

   C. Reverse social engineering

   D. Impersonation

7. Which type of social engineering attacks uses phishing, pop-ups, and IRC channels?

   A. Technical

   B. Computer based

   C. Human based

   D. Physical

8. An e-mail sent from an attacker to a known hacking group contains a reference stating, "Rebecca works for the finance department at *business-name* and is the administrative assistant to the chief. She can be reached at *phone-number*." What is most likely being communicated here?

   A. The name of an administrative assistant is being published to simplify later social engineering attacks.

   B. The administrative assistant for the chief of the finance department at this business is easily swayed by social engineering efforts.

   C. The finance department has a lax security policy in place.

   D. None of the above. There is not enough information to form a conclusion.

9. Which of the following constitutes the highest risk to the organization?

   A. Black-hat hacker

   B. White-hat hacker

   C. Gray-hat hacker

   D. Disgruntled employee

10. After observing a target organization for several days, you discover that finance and HR records are bagged up and placed in an outside storage bin for later shredding/recycling. One day you simply walk to the bin and place one of the bags in your vehicle, with plans to rifle through it later. Which social engineering attack was used here?

    A. Offline

    B. Physical

    C. Piggybacking

    D. Dumpster diving

11. An attacker waits outside the entry to a secured facility. After a few minutes an authorized user appears with an entry badge displayed. He swipes a key card and unlocks the door. The attacker, with no display badge, follows him inside. Which social engineering attack just occurred?

    A. Tailgating

    B. Piggybacking

    C. Identity theft

    D. Impersonation

12. Which threat presents the highest risk to an organization's resources?

    A. Government-sponsored hackers

    B. Social engineering

    C. Disgruntled employees

    D. Script kiddies

13. Which of the following may be effective countermeasures against social engineering? (Choose all that apply.)

    A. Security policies

    B. Operational guidelines

    C. Appropriately configured IDS

    D. User education and training

    E. Strong firewall configuration

14. Which of the following are indicators of a phishing e-mail? (Choose all that apply.)

    A. It does not reference you by name.

    B. It contains misspelled words or grammatical errors.

    C. It contains spoofed links.

    D. It comes from an unverified source.

15. You are discussing physical security measures and are covering background checks on employees and policies regarding key management and storage. Which type of physical security measures are being discussed?

    A. Physical

    B. Technical

    C. Operational

    D. Practical

16. Which of the following resources can assist in combating phishing in your organization? (Choose all that apply.)

    A. Phishkill

    B. Netcraft

    C. Phishtank

    D. IDA Pro

17. In order, what are the three steps in a reverse social engineering attack?

    A. Technical support, marketing, sabotage

    B. Sabotage, marketing, technical support

    C. Marketing, technical support, sabotage

    D. Marketing, sabotage, technical support

18. Which type of social engineering makes use of impersonation, dumpster diving, shoulder surfing, and tailgating?

    A. Physical

    B. Technical

    C. Human based

    D. Computer based

19. In examining the About Us link in the menu of a target organization's website, an attacker discovers several different individual contacts within the company. She crafts an e-mail asking for information to one of the contacts that appears

to come from an individual within the company who would be expected to make such a request. The e-mail provides a link to click, which then prompts for the contact's user ID and password. Which of the following best describes this attack?

A. Trojan e-mailing

B. Spear phishing

C. Social networking

D. Operational engineering

20. A security admin has a control in place that embeds a unique image into e-mails on specific topics, which verifies the message as authentic and trusted. Which antiphishing method is being used?

A. Steganography

B. Sign-in seal

C. PKI

D. Captcha

21. Which of the following should be in place to assist as a social engineering countermeasure? (Choose all that apply.)

A. Classification of information

B. Strong security policy

C. User education

D. Strong change management process

22. Joe uses a user ID and password to log into the system every day. Jill uses a PIV card and a PIN. Which of the following statements is true?

A. Joe and Jill are using single-factor authentication.

B. Joe and Jill are using two-factor authentication.

C. Joe is using two-factor authentication.

D. Jill is using two-factor authentication.

23. A system owner has implemented a retinal scanner at the entryway to the data floor. Which type of physical security measure is this?

A. Technical

B. Single factor

C. Computer based

D. Operational

24. Which of the following is the best representation of a technical control?

    A. Air conditioning

    B. Security tokens

    C. Automated humidity control

    D. Fire alarms

    E. Security policy

25. A security admin at an organization boasts that her security measures are top notch and cannot be breached. In discussing their biometric authentication mechanisms, which of the following presents a reason biometric systems may still fall under successful attack?

    A. The digital representation of the biometric entry may not be unique, even if the physical characteristic is.

    B. Biometric compares a copy to a copy instead of the original to a copy.

    C. The stored hash in biometric systems is no longer "something you are" and instead becomes "something you have."

    D. A stored biometric can be stolen and used by an attacker to impersonate the individual.

1. D
2. C
3. A
4. D
5. C
6. A
7. B
8. B
9. D
10. D
11. B
12. C
13. A, B, D
14. A, B, C, D
15. C
16. B, C
17. D
18. C
19. B
20. B
21. A, B, C, D
22. D
23. A
24. B
25. D

1. An organization's building has a guard posted at the lone entrance. A door leads into a smaller room with a second door heading into the interior of the building. Which physical security measure is in place?

   A. Guard shack

   B. Turnstile

   C. Man shack

   D. Man trap

   ☑ **D.** If you took a test on college football history, you know it would contain a question about Alabama. If you took one on trumpet players, there'd be one about Dizzy Gillespie. And if you take a test on physical security measures for Certified Ethical Hacker, you're going to be asked about the man trap. They love it that much.

   A *man trap* is nothing more than a locked space you can hold someone in while verifying their right to proceed into the secured area. It's usually a glass (or clear plastic) walled room that locks the exterior door as soon as you enter. Then there is some sort of authentication mechanism, such as a smartcard with a PIN or a biometric system. Assuming the authentication is successful, the second door leading to the interior of the building will unlock, and the person is allowed to proceed. If it's not successful, the doors will remain locked until the guard can check things out. As an aside, in addition to authentication, some man traps add all sorts of extra fun, such as checking your weight to see if you've mysteriously gained or lost 20 pounds since Friday.

   A few other notes here may be of use to you: First, I've seen a man trap defined as either manual or automatic, where manual has a guard locking and unlocking the doors, and automatic has the locks tied to the authentication system, as described previously. Second, a man trap is also referred to in some definitions as an *air lock*. Should you see that term on the exam, know that it is referring to the man trap. Lastly, man traps in the real world can sometimes come in the form of a rotating door or turnstyle, locking partway around if you don't authenticate properly. And, on some of the really fancy ones, sensors will lock it if you're trying to smuggle two people through.

   ☒ **A** is incorrect because this question is not describing a small location at a gate where guards are stationed. Traditionally, these are positioned at gates to the exterior wall or the gate of the facility, where guards can verify identity and so on before allowing people through to the parking lot.

   ☒ **B** is incorrect because a turnstile is not described here and, frankly, does absolutely nothing for physical security. Anyone who has spent any time in subway systems knows this is true: Watching people jump the turnstiles is a great spectator sport.

☒ C is incorrect because, so far as I know, this term *man shack* is not a physical security term within CEH. It's maybe the title of a 1970s disco hit but not a physical security term you'll need to know for the exam.

2. In your social engineering efforts you call the company help desk and pose as a user who has forgotten a password. You ask the technician to help you reset your password, which they happily comply with. Which social engineering attack is in use here?

   A. Piggybacking

   B. Reverse social engineering

   C. Technical support

   D. Halo effect

   ☑ C. Although it may seem silly to label social engineering attacks (because many of them contain the same steps and bleed over into one another), you'll need to memorize them for your exam. A technical support attack is one in which the attacker calls the support desk in an effort to gain a password reset or other useful information. This is a valuable method because if you get the right help desk person (that is, someone susceptible to a smooth-talking social engineer), you can get the keys to the kingdom.

   ☒ A is incorrect because *piggybacking* refers to a method to gain entrance to a facility—not to gain passwords or other information. Piggybacking is a tactic whereby the attacker follows authorized users through an open door without any visible authorization badge at all.

   ☒ B is incorrect because *reverse social engineering* refers to a method where an attacker convinces a target to call him with information. The method involves marketing services (providing the target with your phone number or e-mail address in the event of a problem), sabotaging the device, and then awaiting for a phone call from the user.

   ☒ D is incorrect because *halo effect* refers to a psychological principle that states a person's overall impression (appearance or pleasantness) can impact another person's judgment of them. For example, a good-looking, pleasant person will be judged as more competent and knowledgeable simply because of their appearance. The lesson here is to look good and act nice while you're trying to steal all the target's information.

3. Which of the following is a true statement regarding biometric systems?

   A. The lower the CER, the better the biometric system.

   B. The higher the CER, the better the biometric system.

   C. The higher the FRR, the better the biometric system.

   D. The higher the FAR, the better the biometric system.

☑ **A.** The crossover error rate (CER) is the point on a chart where the false acceptance rate (FAR) and false rejection rate (FRR) meet, and the lower the number, the better the system. It's a means by which biometric systems are calibrated—getting the FAR and FRR the same. All that said, though, keep in mind that in certain circumstances a client may be more interested in a lower FAR than FRR, or vice versa, and therefore the CER isn't as much a concern. For example, a bank may be far more interested in preventing false acceptance than it is in preventing false rejection. In other words, so what if a user is upset they can't log on, so long as their money is safe from a false acceptance?

☒ **B** is incorrect because this is exactly the opposite of what you want. A high CER indicates a system that more commonly allows unauthorized users through and rejects truly authorized people from access.

☒ **C** is incorrect because the false rejection rate needs to be as low as possible. The FRR represents the amount of time a true, legitimate user is denied access by the biometric system.

☒ **D** is incorrect because false acceptance rate needs to be as low as possible. The FAR represents the amount of time an unauthorized user is allowed access to the system.

4. A pen tester sends an unsolicited e-mail to several users on the target organization. The e-mail is well crafted and appears to be from the company's help desk, advising users of potential network problems. The e-mail provides a contact number to call in the event a user is adversely affected. The pen tester then performs a denial of service on several systems and receives phone calls from users asking for assistance. Which social engineering practice is in play here?

A. Technical support

B. Impersonation

C. Phishing

D. Reverse social engineering

☑ **D.** This may turn out to be a somewhat confusing question for some folks, but it's actually pretty easy. Reverse social engineering involves three steps. First, in the marketing phase, an attacker advertises himself as a technical point of contact for problems that may be occurring soon. As an aside, be sure to market to the appropriate audience: Attempting this against IT staff probably won't work as well as the "average" user and may get you caught. Second, in the sabotage phase, the attacker performs a denial of service or other attack on the user. Third, in the tech support phase, the user calls the attacker and freely hands over information, thinking they are being assisted by company's technical support team.

☒ **A is incorrect** because a technical support attack involves the attacker calling a technical support help desk, not having the user calling back with information.

☒ **B is incorrect** because this is not *just* impersonation—the attack described in the question revolves around the user contacting the attacker, not the other way around. Impersonation can cover anybody, from a "normal" user to a company executive. And impersonating a technical support person can result in excellent results; just remember if you're going through steps to have the user call you back, you've moved into reverse social engineering.

☒ **C is incorrect** because a phishing attack is an e-mail crafted to appear legitimate but in fact contains links to fake websites or to download malicious content. In this example, there is no link to click—just a phone number to call in case of trouble. Oddly enough, in my experience people will question a link in an e-mail far more than just a phone number.

5. A pen test member has gained access to a building and is observing activity as he wanders around. In one room of the building, he stands just outside a cubicle wall opening and watches the onscreen activity of a user. Which social engineering attack is in use here?

   A. Eavesdropping

   B. Tailgating

   C. Shoulder surfing

   D. Piggybacking

   ☑ **C.** This one is so easy I hope you maintain your composure and stifle the urge to whoop and yell in the test room. Shoulder surfing doesn't necessarily require you to actually be on the victim's shoulder—you just have to be able to watch their onscreen activity. I once shoulder surfed *in front of* someone (a mirror behind her showed her screen clear as day). As an aside, in the real world if you're close enough to see someone's screen, you're probably close enough to listen to them as well. EC-Council puts the emphasis of shoulder surfing on the visual aspect—eavesdropping would be auditory.

   ☒ **A is incorrect** because *eavesdropping* is a social engineering method where the attacker simply remains close enough to targets to overhear conversations. Although it's doubtful users will stand around shouting passwords at each other, you'd be surprised how much useful information can be gleaned by just listening in on conversations.

   ☒ **B is incorrect** because *tailgating* is a method for gaining entrance to a facility by flashing a fake badge and following an authorized user through an open door.

   ☒ **D is incorrect** because *piggybacking* is another method to gain entrance to a facility. In this effort, though, you don't have a badge at all; you just follow people through the door.

6. A recent incident investigated by the local IR team involved a user receiving an e-mail that appeared to be from the U.S. Postal Service, notifying her of a package headed her way and providing a link for tracking the package. The link provided took the user to what appeared to be the USPS site, where she input her user information to learn about the latest shipment headed her way. Which attack did the user fall victim to?

   A. Phishing

   B. Internet level

   C. Reverse social engineering

   D. Impersonation

   ☑ **A.** Phishing is one of the most pervasive and effective social engineering attacks on the planet. It's successful because crafting a legitimate-looking e-mail that links a user to an illegitimate site or malware package is easy to do, is easy to spread, and preys on our human nature to trust. If the source of the e-mail looks legitimate or the layout looks legitimate, most people will click away without even thinking about it. Phishing e-mails can often include pictures lifted directly off the legitimate website and use creative means of spelling that aren't easy to spot: www.regions.com is a legitimate bank website that could be spelled in a phishing e-mail as www.regi0ns.

   One last note here that our beloved tech editor begged me to include: Phishing has an extreme liability aspect to it when spoofing a legitimate business. If you're pen testing an organization and phish using a variant of a real business name, you could be opening yourself up to some serious costs: The first time someone calls the *real* Regions bank to complain is the moment that the attacker just became liable for the costs associated with the attack.

   ☒ **B** is incorrect because *Internet level* is not a recognized form of social engineering attack by this exam. It's included here as a distractor.

   ☒ **C** is incorrect because reverse social engineering is an attack where the attacker cons the target into calling back with useful information.

   ☒ **D** is incorrect because this particular description does not cover impersonation. *Impersonation* is an attack where a social engineer pretends to be an employee, a valid user, or even an executive (or other V.I.P.). Generally speaking, when it comes to the exam, any impersonation question will revolve around an in-person visit or a telephone call.

7. Which type of social engineering attacks uses phishing, pop-ups, and IRC?

   A. Technical

   B. Computer based

   C. Human based

   D. Physical

☑ **B.** All social engineering attacks fall into one of two categories: human based or computer based. Computer-based attacks are those carried out with the use of a computer or other data-processing device. Examples include, but are not limited to, fake pop-up windows, SMS texts, e-mails, and chat rooms or services. Social media sites (such as Facebook or LinkedIn) are consistent examples as well, and spoofing entire websites isn't out of the realm here either.

☒ **A** is incorrect because *technical* is not a social engineering attack type and is included here as a distractor.

☒ **C** is incorrect because *human-based* social engineering involves the art of human interaction for information gathering. Human-based social engineering uses interaction in conversation or other circumstances between people to gather useful information.

☒ **D** is incorrect because *physical* is not a social engineering attack type and is included here as a distractor.

8. An e-mail sent from an attacker to a known hacking group contains a reference stating, "Rebecca works for the finance department at *business-name* and is the administrative assistant to the chief. She can be reached at *phone-number*." What is most likely being communicated here?

   A. The name of an administrative assistant is being published to simplify later social engineering attacks.

   B. The administrative assistant for the chief of the finance department at this business is easily swayed by social engineering efforts.

   C. The finance department has lax security policy in place.

   D. None of the above. There is not enough information to form a conclusion.

   ☑ **B.** Within the confines of this exam, you need to remember the names Rebecca and Jessica as potential targets of social engineering. According to CEH documentation, these names are used to refer to individuals who are easy targets for social engineering efforts. The reality of your day-to-day work in the field might be that you'll never hear this mentioned this way (I had never heard these names used this way before studying for this exam); however, you need to memorize it for your exam. Jessica and Rebecca are easily swayed by social engineering and are targets for your efforts.

   ☒ **A** is incorrect because, frankly, there's a better answer here (B) *as far as EC-Council and your exam are concerned.* Is it possible the person sending this e-mail knows the assistant's first name is Rebecca? Sure, it is; however, it's unlikely to be shared in this manner, and, more importantly here, this just is not the "most likely" answer. On your exam, when you see Rebecca or Jessica, note it as a notification of an easy target and just move on to the next question.

☒ **C** is incorrect because the name Rebecca is not associated with security policy in any way. The company may well have a lax policy, but there's just nothing here to indicate that. As an aside (that is, it really has nothing to do with the question itself), whether the policy is weak or strong, an individual susceptible to social engineering *almost* makes the policy moot. Security policy is one of those things that has to be supported and enforced from the top down and made part of the culture of the organization. If you have those things, it's a great countermeasure to a whole assortment of security issues. If you don't, it's a big waste of time.

☒ **D** is incorrect because there is a correct answer to the question. This answer is included as a distractor.

9. Which of the following constitutes the highest risk to the organization?

   A. Black-hat hacker

   B. White-hat hacker

   C. Gray-hat hacker

   D. Disgruntled employee

   ☑ **D.** When considering security measures, most of the attention is usually aimed outside, where all the bad guys are, right? Unfortunately this line of thinking leads to all sorts of exposure, for a whole lot of reasons, and is more common than you might think. A disgruntled employee is, well, an employee. He's already inside and already has credentials to at least some of the organizational resources. The idea that someone wanting to do harm to an organization's network not only already has the access to do so but has it because we gave it to him and we're not watching him should be frightening to all.

   ☒ **A** is incorrect because black-hat hackers aren't necessarily already inside the network. They have a lot of work to do in getting access and a lot of security levels to wade through to do it.

   ☒ **B** is incorrect because a white-hat hacker is one of the good guys—an ethical hacker, hired for a specific purpose.

   ☒ **C** is incorrect because a gray-hat (or grey-hat) hacker falls somewhere between white and black. They may be hacking without express consent, but doing so with good intentions (not that good intentions will keep you out of jail). Supposedly they're not hacking for personal gain; they just don't bother to get permission and occasionally dance on the dark side of legality.

10. After observing a target organization for several days, you discover that finance and HR records are bagged up and placed in an outside storage bin for later shredding/recycling. One day you simply walk to the bin and place one of the

bags in your vehicle, with plans to rifle through it later. Which social engineering attack was used here?

A. Offline

B. Physical

C. Piggybacking

D. Dumpster diving

☑ **D.** Dumpster diving doesn't necessarily mean you're actually taking a header into a dumpster outside. It could be any waste canister, in any location, and you don't even have to place any more of your body in the canister than you need to extract the old paperwork with. And you'd be amazed what people just throw away without thinking about it: password lists, network diagrams, employee name and number listings, and financial documents are all examples. Lastly, don't forget that EC-Council defines this as a passive activity. Sure, in the real world, you run a real risk of discovery and questioning by any number of the organization's staff, but on your exam it's considered passive.

☒ **A** is incorrect because offline is not a social engineering attack and is used here as a distractor.

☒ **B** is incorrect because physical is not a social engineering attack type.

☒ **C** is incorrect because piggybacking is a social engineering attack that allows entry into a facility and has nothing to do with digging through trash for information.

11. An attacker waits outside the entry to a secured facility. After a few minutes an authorized user appears with an entry badge displayed. He swipes a key card and unlocks the door. The attacker, with no display badge, follows him inside. Which social engineering attack just occurred?

A. Tailgating

B. Piggybacking

C. Identity theft

D. Impersonation

☑ **B.** This is one of those questions that just drives everyone batty—especially people who actually perform pen tests for a living. Does knowing that gaining entry without flashing a fake ID badge of any kind is called piggy-backing make it any easier or harder to pull off? I submit having two terms for what is essentially the same attack, separated by one small detail, is unfair, in the least, but there's not a whole lot we can do about it. If it makes it easier to memorize, just keep in mind that pigs wouldn't wear a badge—they don't have any clothes to attach it to.

☒ **A** is incorrect because a tailgating attack requires the attacker to be holding a fake badge of some sort. I know it's silly, but that's the only differentiation between these two items: tailgaters have badges, piggybackers do not. If it makes it any easier, just keep in mind a lot of tailgaters at football games should have a badge on them—to prove they are of legal drinking age.

☒ **C** is incorrect because this attack has nothing to do with identity theft. Identity theft occurs when an attacker uses personal information gained on an individual to assume that person's identity. Although this is normally thought of in the criminal world (stealing credit cards, money, and so on), it has its uses elsewhere.

☒ **D** is incorrect because impersonation is not in play here. The attacker isn't pretending to be anyone else at all—he's just following someone through an open door.

12. Which threat presents the highest risk to an organization's resources?

    A. Government-sponsored hackers

    B. Social engineering

    C. Disgruntled employees

    D. Script kiddies

    ☑ **C.** I can almost guarantee you'll see this on your exam. EC-Council made a big point of stressing this in the CEH version 7 documentation, so I in turn will stress it to you. Disgruntled employees can cause all sorts of havoc for a security team. The main reason is location: They're *already* inside the network. Inside attacks are generally easier to launch, are more successful, and are harder to prevent. When you add a human element of having an axe to grind, this can boil over quickly—whether the employee has the technical knowledge to pull it off or not.

    ☒ **A** is incorrect because most organizations won't have government-sponsored hackers knocking at their virtual front door, and, even if they do, the attacks still generate from outside. Now I'm not saying a sponsored hacker group wouldn't seek out a disgruntled employee inside a government organization, but that proves the answer in itself.

    ☒ **B** is incorrect because social engineering as a whole is not the greatest threat. It is a major concern, though, because most people are susceptible to it, and, frankly, users can't be trusted.

    ☒ **D** is incorrect because script kiddies by definition are relatively easy to find and squash. A *script kiddy* is someone who goes out and steals hack codes and techniques right off the Web, flinging them around wildly in an attempt to succeed. They don't really understand what the attack vector is, how the code works, or (usually) what to do if they actually find success, which makes them easy to spot.

13. Which of the following may be effective countermeasures against social engineering? (Choose all that apply.)

   A. Security policies

   B. Operational guidelines

   C. Appropriately configured IDS

   D. User education and training

   E. Strong firewall configuration

   ☑ **A, B,** and **D.** The problem with countermeasures against social engineering is they're almost totally out of your control. Sure you can draft strong policy requiring users to comply with security measures, implement guidelines on everything imaginable to reduce risks and streamline efficiency, and hold educational briefings and training sessions for each and every user in your organization, but when it comes down to it, it's the user who has to do the right thing. All countermeasures for social engineering have something to do with the users themselves because they are the weak link here.

   ☒ **C and E** are both incorrect for the same reason: A social engineering attack doesn't target the network or its defenses; it targets the users. Many a strongly defended network has been compromised because a user inside was charmed by a successful social engineer.

14. Which of the following are indicators of a phishing e-mail? (Choose all that apply.)

   A. It does not reference you by name.

   B. It contains misspelled words or grammatical errors.

   C. It contains spoofed links.

   D. It comes from an unverified source.

   ☑ **A, B, C,** and **D.** One of the objectives of CEH version 7 is, and I quote, to "understand phishing attacks." Part of the official curriculum to study for the exam covers detecting phishing e-mail in depth, and all of these answers are indicators an e-mail may not be legitimate. First, most companies now sending e-mail to customers will reference you *by name* and sometimes by account number. An e-mail starting with "Dear Customer" or something to that effect may be an indicator something is amiss. Misspellings and grammatical errors from a business are usually dead giveaways because companies do their best to proofread things before they are released. There are, occasionally, some slip-ups (Internet search some of these; they're truly funny), but those are definitely the exception and not the rule. Spoofed links can be found by hovering a mouse over them (or by looking at their properties). The link text may read www.yourbank.com, but the hyperlink properties will be sending you to some IP address you don't want to go to.

Finally, while these are all great answers to a question on an exam, don't let them dictate your day-to-day Internet life outside of your exam. A perfectly written, grammatically correct e-mail containing real links and originating from someone you trust could *still* be part of a spear-phishing campaign.

15. You are discussing physical security measures and are covering background checks on employees and policies regarding key management and storage. Which type of physical security measure is being discussed?

    A. Physical

    B. Technical

    C. Operational

    D. Practical

    ☑ **C.** Physical security has three major facets: physical measures, technical measures, and operational measures. Operational measures (sometimes referred to as *procedural* controls) are the policies and procedures you put into place to assist with security. Background checks on employees and any kind of written policy for operational behaviors are prime examples.

    ☒ **A** is incorrect because physical measures can be seen or touched. Examples include guards (although you probably would want to be careful touching one of them), fences, and locked doors.

    ☒ **B** is incorrect because technical measures include things such as authentication systems (biometrics anyone?) and specific permissions you assign to resources.

    ☒ **D** is incorrect because, although these may seem like practical measures to put into place, there is simply no category named such. It's included here as a distractor, nothing more.

16. Which of the following resources can assist in combating phishing in your organization? (Choose all that apply.)

    A. Phishkill

    B. Netcraft

    C. Phishtank

    D. IDA Pro

    ☑ **B and C.** For obvious reasons, there are not a lot of questions from these objectives concerning tools—mainly because social engineering is all about the human side of things, not necessarily using technology or tools.

However, you can put into place more than a few protective applications to help stem the tide. There are innumerable e-mail filtering applications and appliances you can put on an e-mail network boundary to cut down on the vast amount of traffic (spam or otherwise) headed to your network. Additionally, Netcraft's phishing toolbar and Phishtank are two client-side, host-based options you can use (there are others, but these are pointed out specifically in EC-Council's official courseware).

Netcraft's (http://toolbar.netcraft.com/) and Phishtank's (www.phishtank.com/) toolbars are like neighborhood watches on virtual steroids, where eagle-eyed neighbors can see naughty traffic and alert everyone else. From the Netcraft site: "Once the first recipients of a phishing mail have reported the target URL, it is blocked for community members as they subsequently access the URL."

These tools, although useful, are not designed to completely protect against phishing. Much like antivirus software, they will act on attempts that match a signature file. This, sometimes, makes it even easier on the attacker—because they know which phishing will *not* work right off the bat.

☒ **A** is incorrect because phishkill is not an antiphishing application.

☒ **D** is incorrect because IDA Pro is a debugger tool you can use to analyze malware (viruses).

17. In order, what are the three steps in a reverse social engineering attack?

    A. Technical support, marketing, sabotage

    B. Sabotage, marketing, technical support

    C. Marketing, technical support, sabotage

    D. Marketing, sabotage, technical support

    ☑ **D.** Reverse engineering occurs when the attacker creates a circumstance or situation that makes users call him with information. This is carried out in three steps. First, the attacker will market his skills, position, and impending problem (for example, the attacker may send e-mails promoting himself as help desk personnel to call in the event of problems next Wednesday when the server is rebooted). Second, the attacker performs sabotage against the user or network segment (a denial-of-service attack to take users off network confirms with the user that the original e-mail must have been correct). Lastly, the attacker provides "technical support" to the users calling in for assistance (by stealing all their account information, which is gladly being handed over the phone by panicked users).

    ☒ **A, B,** and **C** are incorrect because the order presented is not correct.

18. Which type of social engineering makes use of impersonation, dumpster diving, shoulder surfing, and tailgating?

    A. Physical

    B. Technical

    C. Human based

    D. Computer based

    ☑ C. Once again, we're back to the two major forms of social engineering: human based and computer based. Human-based attacks include all the attacks mentioned here and a few more. Human-based social engineering uses interaction in conversation or other circumstances between people to gather useful information. This can be as blatant as simply asking someone for their password or pretending to be a known entity (authorized user, tech support, or company executive) in order to gain information.

    ☒ A is incorrect because social engineering attacks do not fall into a physical category.

    ☒ B is incorrect because social engineering attacks do not fall into a technical category.

    ☒ D is incorrect because computer-based social engineering attacks are carried out with the use of a computer or other data-processing device. These attacks can include everything from specially crafted pop-up windows, tricking the user into clicking through to a fake website, to SMS texts, which provide false technical support messages and dial-in information to a user.

19. In examining the About Us link in the menu of a target organization's website, an attacker discovers several different individual contacts within the company. She crafts an e-mail asking for information to one of the contacts that appears to come from an individual within the company who would be expected to make such a request. The e-mail provides a link to click, which then prompts for the contact's user ID and password. Which of the following best describes this attack?

    A. Trojan e-mailing

    B. Spear phishing

    C. Social networking

    D. Operational engineering

    ☑ B. Yes, sometimes you'll get an easy one, and this question is no exception. Phishing is using e-mail to accomplish the social engineering task. Spear phishing is actually targeting those e-mails to specific individuals or groups within an organization. This usually has a much higher success rate than just a blind-fire phishing effort.

☒ **A, C,** and **D** are incorrect because they are all added as distractors and do not match the circumstances listed. Trojan e-mailing and operational engineering aren't valid terms in regard to social engineering attacks. A social networking attack, per EC-Council, is one that involves using Facebook, LinkedIn, Twitter, or some other social media to elicit information or credentials from a target.

20. A security admin has a control in place that embeds a unique image into e-mails on specific topics, which verifies the message as authentic and trusted. Which antiphishing method is being used?

    A. Steganography

    B. Sign-in seal

    C. PKI

    D. Captcha

    ☑ **B.** Sign-in seal is an e-mail protection method in use at a variety of business locations. The practice is to use a secret message or image that can be referenced on any official communication with the site. If you receive an e-mail purportedly from the business but it does not include the image or message, you're aware it's probably a phishing attempt. This sign-in seal is kept locally on your computer, so the theory is that no one can copy or spoof it.

    ☒ **A** is incorrect because steganography is not used for this purpose. As we know, steganography is a method of hiding information inside another file—usually an image file.

    ☒ **C** is incorrect because PKI refers to an encryption system using public and private keys for security of information between members of an organization.

    ☒ **D** is incorrect because a captcha is an authentication test of sorts, which I am sure you've seen hundreds of times already. Captcha (actually an acronym meaning Completely Automated Public Turing test to tell Computers and Humans Apart) is a challenge-response-type method where an image is shown, and the client is required to type the word from the image into a challenge box. An example is on a contest entry form—you type in your information at the top and then see an image with a word (or two) in a crazy font at the bottom. If you type the correct word in, it's somewhat reasonable for the page to assume you're a human (as opposed to a script), and the request is sent forward.

21. Which of the following should be in place to assist as a social engineering countermeasure? (Choose all that apply.)

    A. Classification of information

    B. Strong security policy

    C. User education

    D. Strong change management process

☑ **A, B, C, and D.** All of the answers are correct, but let's get this out of the way up front: You'll never be able to put anything whatsoever into place that will effectively render *all* social engineering attacks moot. You can do some things to limit them, and those on this list can definitely help in that regard, but a security organization that responds to social engineering concerns with "We have a strong policy and great user education" is probably one that'll see a high turnover rate.

Classification of information is seen as a strong countermeasure because the information—and access to it—is stored and processed according to strict definitions of sensitivity. In the government/DoD world, you'd see labels such as Confidential, Secret, and Top Secret. In the commercial world, you might see Public, Sensitive, and Confidential. I could write an entire chapter on the difference between DoD and commercial labels and have all sorts of fun arguing the finer points of various access control methods, but we'll stick just to this chapter and what you need here. As a side note, classification of information won't do you a bit of good if the enforcement of access to that information, and the protection of it in storage or transit, is lax.

Strong security policy has been covered earlier in the chapter, so I won't waste much print space here on it. You must have a good one in place to help prevent all sorts of security failures; however, you can't *rely* on it as a countermeasure on its own.

User education is not only a viable social engineering countermeasure, but according to EC-Council it's the best measure you can take. Anyone reading this book who has spent any time at all trying to educate users on a production-enterprise-level network is probably yelling right now because results can sometimes be spotty. However, the weak point in the chain *is* the user, so we must do our best to educate users on what to look for and what to do as they see it. There simply is no better defense than a well-educated user (and by well-educated I mean a user who absolutely refuses to participate in a social engineering attempt). There's just not that many of them out there.

A change management process helps to organize change to a system or organization by providing a standardized, reviewable process to any major change. In other words, if you allow changes to your financial system, IT services, HR processes, or *fill-in-the-blank* without any review or control process, you're basically opening Pandora's box. Change can be made on a whim (sometimes at the behest of a social engineer, maybe?), and there's no control or tracking of it.

22. Joe uses a user ID and password to log into the system every day. Jill uses a PIV card and a PIN. Which of the following are true?

   A. Joe and Jill are using single-factor authentication.

   B. Joe and Jill are using two-factor authentication.

   C. Joe is using two-factor authentication.

   D. Jill is using two-factor authentication.

☑ **D.** When it comes to authentication systems, you can use three factors to prove your identity to a system: something you *know*, something you *have*, and something you *are*. Items you know are, basically, a password or PIN. Something you have is a physical token of some sort—usually a smartcard—that is presented as part of the authentication process. Something you are relates to biometrics—a fingerprint or retinal scan, for instance. Generally speaking, the more factors you have in place, the better (more secure) the authentication system. In this example, Joe is using only something he knows, whereas Jill is using something she has (PIV card) *and* something she knows (PIN).

☒ **A** is incorrect because Jill is using two-factor authentication.

☒ **B** is incorrect because Joe is using single-factor authentication.

☒ **C** is incorrect because Joe is using single-factor authentication.

23. A system owner has implemented a retinal scanner at the entryway to the data floor. Which type of physical security measure is this?

    A. Technical

    B. Single factor

    C. Computer based

    D. Operational

☑ **A.** Physical security measures are characterized as physical (door locks, guards), operational (policies, procedures), and technical (authentications systems, permissions). This example falls into the technical security measure category. Sure, the door itself is physical, but the question centers on the biometric system itself—clearly technical in origin.

☒ **B** is incorrect because single factor refers to the method the authentication system uses, not the physical security measure itself. In this case, the authentication is using something you are—a biometric retina scan.

☒ **C** is incorrect because computer based refers to a social engineering attack type, not a physical security measure.

☒ **D** is incorrect because an operational physical security measure deals with policy and procedure.

24. Which of the following is the best representation of a technical control?

    A. Air conditioning

    B. Security tokens

    C. Automated humidity control

    D. Fire alarms

    E. Security policy

☑ **B.** All security controls are put into place to minimize, or to avoid altogether, the probability of a successful exploitation of a risk or vulnerability.

Logical (logical is the other name used for technical) controls do this through technical, system-driven means. Examples include security tokens, authentication mechanisms, and antivirus software.

☒ **A, C, D,** and **E** are incorrect because they are not logical (technical) controls. Air conditioning and humidity fall under the physical controls. A policy would fall under procedural controls.

25. A security admin at an organization boasts that her security measures are top notch and cannot be breached. In discussing their biometric authentication mechanisms, which of the following presents a reason biometric systems may still fall under successful attack?

A. The digital representation of the biometric entry may not be unique, even if the physical characteristic is.

B. Biometric compares a copy to a copy instead of the original to a copy.

C. The stored hash in biometric systems is no longer "something you are" and instead becomes "something you have."

D. A stored biometric can be stolen and used by an attacker to impersonate the individual.

☑ **D.** I think I'm safe in thinking most of you will agree with this statement: Passwords stink. We all hate them, and they're notoriously easy to crack or attain. But when you consider that passwords at least *change* over time, they may not seem so horrible after all. See, the hash that matches your fingerprint will never change, which puts the odds considerably in the bad guy's corner. Tell a hacker your passwords are at least 16 characters long and change every 30 days and she's liable to get too frustrated to even start. Hand her a hash and tell her she has *eternity* to crack it? No worries.

On a side note here, Windows authentication doesn't really care if you're using biometrics, passwords, or smartcards—you're a *hash* to the system in all of them. Whether your hash was the result of a password, a thumbprint, a smartcard, or a token, when it comes to how Windows passes you around, you're a hash. Some things change your hash more often—a 30-day password change is different than, say, a thumbprint that never changes.

☒ **A** is incorrect because the digital representation is built off the physical, which ensures it's unique. If it weren't, what's the point?

☒ **B** is incorrect because the original *is* your biometric. When you use a fingerprint, or iris scanner, or *fill-in-the-biometric-blank-here*, you are providing an original to compare against the stored hash.

☒ **C.** "Something you have" generally refers to a physical item you carry with you, like a token or a card. The hash is stored somewhere in the system as a means of comparison with your biometric authentication, and is therefore not 'something you have.'

The Pen Test: Putting It All Together

This chapter includes questions from the following topics:
- Describe penetration testing, security assessments, and risk management
- Define automatic and manual testing
- List pen test methodology and deliverables

I used to work in a paint and body auto shop when I was a teenager and saw some amazing work come out of the place. The proprietor, Rob Dunne, seemingly knew everything about cars—from the minutiae of the internal engine to the right buffing, sanding, paint, and clear coat on the exterior—and taught me more about vehicles than anyone else on the planet. He also taught me some important work lessons, such as preparing correctly for a job, organizing and planning the steps, working hard and smart through a job, and, possibly just as importantly, finishing the right way.

On many jobs we performed during my time there, especially early on, I just couldn't wait to finish things off. After all that taping and paper, sanding and buffing, and finally painting the darned thing, I couldn't wait to rip off all the tape and paper and see the final product. But, as I learned several times over before the lesson finally sank into my head, rushing the final steps of a job can ruin the whole thing. The paint needed time to cure, and as exciting as it is to pull everything off and see your work come to life, it's far better to see things through to the end, all the way, with all the patience and care you started with.

This chapter is, admittedly, short and sweet, but don't go ripping off the tape and paper just yet—there's a little bit more curing to be done. The questions and answers here should be on the easy side (if memorizing terms is easy for you, that is), and the write-ups on what's correct and what's false will reflect that as well. Sure, I might sneak in a question from earlier in the book—just to see whether you're paying attention and to wrap up terms EC-Council throws into this section—but these are all supposed to be about the pen test itself. We've already covered the nuts and bolts, so now we're going to spend some time on the finished product. And, yes, you will see this stuff on your exam. But I hope, when that time comes, you'll confidently and patiently finish it off, just as well as you started it.

STUDY TIPS The information covered in this chapter, that you'll find on the exam, generally boils down to basic memorization. While that may sound easy enough to you, I think you'll find that some of these terms are so closely related that questions on the exam referencing them will be confusing in the least—and most likely rage-inducing by the time the exam ends. Pay close attention to the details and key words for definitions (in particular the *insiders*, *outsiders*, and *affiliates* definitions), and take the time to memorize the phases involved with a pen test and an actual attack. Lastly, and I think I've said this before, it's sometimes easier to eliminate wrong answers than it is to choose the correct one. When you're looking at one of these questions that seems totally out of left field, spend your time eliminating the choices you know aren't correct. Eventually all that's left must be the correct answer. After all, the mechanism scoring the test doesn't care *how* you got to the answer, only that the right one is chosen.

1. Which of the following would be found in a final report from a full penetration test? (Choose all that apply.)

   A. The names of all the participants

   B. A list of findings from the assessments

   C. An executive summary of the assessments

   D. A list of vulnerabilities that were patched by the team

2. A team is starting a security assessment and has been provided a system on an internal subnet. No other previous knowledge of any pertinent information has been given. Which of the following best describes the type of test the team will be performing?

   A. Internal, white box

   B. Internal, black box

   C. External, white box

   D. External, black box

3. Which of the following provide automated pen test–like results for an organization? (Choose all that apply.)

   A. Metasploit

   B. Nessus

   C. Core Impact

   D. CANVAS

   E. SAINT

   F. GFI Languard

4. Which of the following best describes an assessment against a network segment that tests for existing vulnerabilities but does not attempt to exploit any of them?

   A. Penetration test

   B. Partial penetration test

   C. Vulnerability assessment

   D. Security scan

5. A spouse of an employee illegally uses the employee's credentials to gain access to the organization and carry out an attack. Which of the following best defines the attacker?

   A. Outside affiliate

   B. Outside associate

   C. Insider affiliate

   D. Insider associate

6. In which phase of a pen test is scanning performed?

    A. Pre-attack

    B. Attack

    C. Post-attack

    D. Reconnaissance

7. Which of the following tests is generally faster and costs less than a manual pen test?

    A. Automatic

    B. Internal

    C. Black box

    D. External

8. Which of the following best defines an attack against the organization by an internal user?

    A. External, black box

    B. Internal, gray box

    C. Internal, announced

    D. External, white box

9. Brad is part of an environmental group protesting SomeBiz, Inc., for the company's stance on a variety of issues. Frustrated by the failure of multiple attempts to raise awareness of his cause, Brad launches sophisticated web defacement and denial-of-service attacks against the company, without attempting to hide the attack source and with no regard to being caught. Which of the following terms best defines Brad?

    A. Hactivism

    B. Ethical hacker

    C. Script kiddie

    D. Suicide hacker

10. A security team has been hired by upper management to assess the organization's security. The assessment is designed to emulate an Internet hacker and to test the behavior of the security devices and policies in place as well as the IT security staff. Which of the following best describe this test? (Choose all that apply.)

    A. Internal

    B. External

    C. Announced

    D. Unannounced

11. In which phase of a pen test will the team penetrate the perimeter and acquire targets?

    A. Pre-attack

    B. Attack

    C. Post-attack

    D. None of the above

12. Which of the following test types presents a higher probability of encountering problems and takes the most amount of time?

    A. Black box

    B. Gray box

    C. White box

    D. Internal

13. Which of the following best describes the difference between a professional pen test team member and a hacker?

    A. Ethical hackers are paid for their time.

    B. Ethical hackers never exploit vulnerabilities; they only point out their existence.

    C. Ethical hackers do not use the same tools and actions as hackers.

    D. Ethical hackers hold a predefined scope and agreement from the system owner.

14. Sally is part of a penetration test team and is starting a test. The client has provided a network drop on one of their subnets for Sally to launch her attacks from. However, they did not provide any authentication information, network diagrams, or other notable data concerning the systems. Which type of test is Sally performing?

    A. External, white box

    B. External, black box

    C. Internal, white box

    D. Internal, black box

15. Joe is part of a pen test team that has been hired by AnyBiz to perform testing under a contract. As part of the defined scope and activities, no IT employees within AnyBiz know about the test. After some initial information gathering, Joe strikes up a conversation with an employee in the cafeteria and steals the employee's access badge. Joe then uses this badge to gain entry to secured areas of AnyBiz's office space. Which of the following best defines Joe in this scenario?

    A. Outside affiliate

    B. Outside associate

    C. Insider affiliate

    D. Insider associate

16. In which phase of a penetration test would you compile a list of vulnerabilities found?

    A. Pre-attack

    B. Attack

    C. Post-attack

    D. Reconciliation

17. Which of the following has a database containing thousands of signatures used to detect vulnerabilities in multiple operating systems?

    E. Nessus

    F. Hping

    G. LOIC

    H. SNMPUtil

18. Cleaning registry entries and removing uploaded files and tools are part of which phase of a pen test?

    A. Covering tracks

    B. Pre-attack

    C. Attack

    D. Post-attack

19. Jake, an employee of AnyBiz, Inc., parks his vehicle outside the corporate offices of SomeBiz, Inc. He turns on a laptop and connects to an open wireless access point internal to SomeBiz's network. Which of the following best defines Jake?

    A. Outside affiliate

    B. Outside associate

    C. Insider affiliate

    D. Insider associate

20. Which of the following are true regarding a pen test? (Choose all that apply.)

    A. Pen tests do not include social engineering.

    B. Pen tests may include unannounced attacks against the network.

    C. During a pen test, the security professionals can carry out any attack they choose.

    D. Pen tests always have a scope.

    E. The client is not notified of the vulnerabilities the team chooses to exploit.

21. Which of the following causes a potential security breach?

    A. Vulnerability

    B. Threat

    C. Exploit

    D. Zero day

22. Which Metasploit payload type operates via DLL injection and is difficult for antivirus software to pick up?

    A. Inline

    B. Meterpreter

    C. Staged

    D. Remote

23. Metasploit is a framework allowing for the development and execution of exploit code against a remote host and is designed for use in pen testing. The framework consists of several libraries, each performing a specific task and set of functions. Which library is considered the most fundamental component of the Metasploit framework?

    A. MSF Core

    B. MSF Base

    C. MSF Interfaces

    D. Rex

24. EC-Council defines six stages of scanning methodology. Which of the following correctly lists the six steps?

    A. Scan for vulnerabilities, check for live systems, check for open ports, perform banner grabbing, draw network diagrams, prepare proxies

    B. Perform banner grabbing, check for live systems, check for open ports, scan for vulnerabilities, draw network diagrams, prepare proxies

    C. Check for live systems, check for open ports, perform banner grabbing, scan for vulnerabilities, draw network diagrams, prepare proxies

    D. Prepare proxies, check for live systems, check for open ports, perform banner grabbing, scan for vulnerabilities, draw network diagrams

25. Which of the following may be effective countermeasures against an inside attacker? (Choose all that apply.)

    A. Enforce elevated privilege control.

    B. Secure all dumpsters and shred collection boxes.

    C. Enforce good physical security practice and policy.

    D. Perform background checks on all employees.

26. The IP address 132.58.90.55/20 is given for a machine your team is to test. Which of the following represents an address within the same subnet?

    A. 132.58.88.254

    B. 132.58.96.20

    C. 132.58.254.90

    D. 132.58.55.90

1. A, B, C
2. B
3. A, C, D
4. C
5. C
6. A
7. A
8. B
9. D
10. B, D
11. B
12. A
13. D
14. D
15. C
16. C
17. A
18. D
19. A
20. B, D
21. B
22. B
23. D
24. C
25. A, B, C, D
26. A

1. Which of the following would be found in a final report from a full penetration test? (Choose all that apply.)

   A. The names of all the participants

   B. A list of findings from the assessments

   C. An executive summary of the assessments

   D. A list of vulnerabilities that were patched by the team

   ☑ **A, B, and C.** It seems fairly obvious that if you hire someone to perform a security audit of your organization that you would expect a report at the end of it. Pen tests vary from company to company and from test to test, but some basics are part of every pen test final report to the customer. The basics that are part of every report are listed here:

   - An executive summary of the organization's overall security posture (if testing under the auspices of FISMA, DIACAP, HIPAA, or other standard, this will be tailored to the standard)
   - The names of all participants as well as the dates of all tests
   - A list of findings, usually presented in order of highest risk
   - An analysis of each finding as well as recommended mitigation steps (if available)
   - Log files and other evidence from your toolset

   ☒ **D** is incorrect because a pen test is not designed to repair or mitigate security problems as they are discovered. The point of a pen test is to identify these potential security shortcomings so the organization can make a determination on repair or mitigation: There may be an acceptable level of risk versus the cost to fix for certain findings that the customer is perfectly comfortable with. Something that may seem to you, the pen tester, as a glaring security hole dooming the organization to certain virtual death simply may not matter to the client—no matter how clearly and forcefully you try to stress that point.

2. A team is starting a security assessment and has been provided a system on an internal subnet. No other previous knowledge of any pertinent information has been given. Which of the following best describes the type of test the team will be performing?

   A. Internal, white box

   B. Internal, black box

   C. External, white box

   D. External, black box

☑ **B.** EC-Council defines two types of penetration tests: external and internal. An external assessment analyzes publicly available information and conducts network scanning, enumeration, and testing from the network perimeter—usually from the Internet. An internal assessment, as you might imagine, is performed from within the organization, from various network access points. On your exam, just as it is here, this pure definition term may be combined with the white-, gray-, and black-box testing terms you're already familiar with.

☒ **A** is incorrect because although the test is indeed internal, it is not a white-box test—where the team would be provided with all knowledge of the inner workings of the system.

☒ **C and D** are incorrect because this is not an external test.

3. Which of the following provide automated pen test–like results for an organization? (Choose all that apply.)

   A. Metasploit

   B. Nessus

   C. Core Impact

   D. CANVAS

   E. SAINT

   F. GFI Languard

   ☑ **A, C, and D.** Automated tool suites for pen testing can be viewed as a means to save time and money by the client's management, but (in my opinion, at least) these tools do not provide the same quality results as a test performed by security professionals. Automated tools can provide a lot of genuinely good information but are also susceptible to false positives and false negatives and don't necessarily care what your agreed-upon scope says is your stopping point. Metasploit has a free, open source version and an insanely expensive "Pro" version for developing and executing exploit code against a remote target machine. Metasploit offers an autopwn module that can automate the exploitation phase of a penetration test.

   Core Impact is probably the best-known, all-inclusive automated testing framework. From its website (www.coresecurity.com/content/core-impact-overview), Core Impact "takes security testing to the next level by safely replicating a broad range of threats to the organization's sensitive data and mission-critical infrastructure—providing extensive visibility into the cause, effect, and prevention of data breaches." Core Impact tests everything from web applications and individual systems to network devices and wireless.

   Per the Immunity Security website (www.immunitysec.com), CANVAS "makes available hundreds of exploits, an automated exploitation system, and a comprehensive, reliable exploit development framework to penetration testers and security professionals." Additionally, the company claims CANVAS's Reference Implementation (CRI) is "the industry's first open platform for IDS and IPS testing."

For you real-world purists out there and for those reading this who don't have any experience with any of this just quite yet, it's important to note that *no* automated testing suite provides anything close to the results you'd gain from a real pen test. Core Impact provides a one-step automated pen test result feature (and probably offers the best result and report features), Metasploit offers autopwn, and CANVAS has a similar "run everything" mode; however, all lack the ability to provide results that a true pen test would provide. In the truest sense of "automated pen test," you simply can't do it in the real world. However, for your exam stick with the three listed here.

☒ **B, E,** and **F** are incorrect for the same reason: They are all vulnerability assessment tool suites, not automated pen test frameworks. Nessus is probably the most recognizable of the three, but SAINT and GFI Languard are both still listed as top vulnerability assessment applications.

4. Which of the following best describes an assessment against a network segment that tests for existing vulnerabilities but does not attempt to exploit any of them?

   A. Penetration test

   B. Partial penetration test

   C. Vulnerability assessment

   D. Security scan

   ☑ **C.** A vulnerability assessment is exactly what it sounds like: the search for and identification of potentially exploitable vulnerabilities on a system or network. These vulnerabilities can be poor security configurations, missing patches, or any number of other weaknesses a bad guy might exploit. The two keys to a vulnerability assessment are that the vulnerabilities are identified, not exploited, and the report is simply a snapshot in time. The organization will need to determine how often they want to run a vulnerability assessment. Lastly, it's important to note that there are some vulnerabilities that simply can't be confirmed without exploiting them. For example, the act of infecting SQL statements to expose a SQL injection vulnerability may very well constitute an exploit action, but it's the only way to prove it exists. For your exam, though, stick with no exploitation during this assessment and move on with your life.

   ☒ **A** is incorrect because team members on a pen test not only discover vulnerabilities but also actively exploit them (within the scope of their prearranged agreement, of course).

   ☒ **B** and **D** are incorrect because they are not valid terms associated with assessment types and are included as distractors.

5. A spouse of an employee illegally uses the employee's credentials to gain access to the organization and carry out an attack. Which of the following best defines the attacker?

A. Outside affiliate

B. Outside associate

C. Insider affiliate

D. Insider associate

☑ **C.** There are few truisms in life, but this is one of them: You will need to memorize certain terms that are important for the exam you are taking but probably don't amount to a hill of Skittles in the real world (and this memorization will infuriate and frustrate you to no end). This is a prime example. In the CEH world, you can define attackers by a lot of different criteria (for example, white hat versus black hat). When it comes to these terms, you differentiate attackers by who they are in relation to the company and how they gain access.

Defining inside versus outside may seem simple, but you have to be careful. It has nothing to do with where the attack is coming from, but everything to do with the person's relationship to the company. *All company employees (including contractors)* are considered "inside." Anyone who is not an employee is considered "outside," with one notable exception: An inside affiliate is a spouse, friend, or acquaintance of an employee who makes use of the employee's credentials to gain access and cause havoc. It's a tricky little differentiation that you'll definitely see on your test somewhere. For memorization purposes, know the following:

- Insiders are employees and contractors of the organization.

- Outsiders are everyone else attempting to get in (hackers and so on).

- *Affiliate* deals with the credentials used in the attack. An insider affiliate is the employee's credentials (most often used by a spouse, friend, or client), and an outsider affiliate is the use of open access (such as open wireless).

- *Insider associates* are contractors, janitors, and so on, who may have limited access to resources. This authorized access isn't necessarily to IT resources, but it does allow the attacker to roam freely into and out of organization offices and buildings—which makes things such as social engineering attacks easier.

☒ **A** is incorrect because an outside affiliate is someone who is not employed with the company in any way (a hacker or maybe a corporate spy) and makes use of open access to the organization's network. For example, a corporate spy may park his car close to a building and tie in to an unsecured WAP to look for information on the network.

☒ **B** is incorrect because *outside associate* isn't a term EC-Council defines.

☒ **D** is incorrect because an *insider associate* is someone who has limited access to resources, such as a guard or a contractor.

6. In which phase of a pen test is scanning performed?

   A. Pre-attack

   B. Attack

   C. Post-attack

   D. Reconnaissance

   ☑ **A.** I know you're sick of CEH definitions, terms, and phases of attacks, but this is another one you'll just need to commit to memory. Per EC-Council, there are three phases of a pen test: pre-attack, attack, and post-attack. The pre-attack phase is where you'd find scanning and other reconnaissance (competitive intelligence, website crawling, and so on).

   ☒ **B** is incorrect because scanning is completed in the pre-attack phase. The attack phase holds four areas of work: penetrate the perimeter, acquire targets, execute attack, and escalate privileges.

   ☒ **C** is incorrect because scanning is completed long before the post-attack phase. Actions accomplished in post-attack include removing all uploaded files and tools, restoring (if needed) to the original state, analyzing results, and preparing reports for the customer.

   ☒ **D** is incorrect because reconnaissance is not a phase of pen testing.

7. An organization wants a security test but is concerned about time and cost. Which of the following tests is generally faster and costs less than a manual pen test?

   A. Automatic

   B. Internal

   C. Black box

   D. External

   ☑ **A.** Automated tests—using tools such as CANVAS and Core Impact—are generally faster and cheaper than manual pen testing, which involve a professional team and a predefined scope/agreement. These automated tests are more susceptible to false positives and false negatives. Perhaps more importantly, though, they also don't necessarily care about any scope or test boundary. With a manual pen test, you have a predetermined scope and agreement in place. With an automated tool, you risk it running past the boundary of your test. While setting the software to stay within a predetermined IP subnet range is easy enough, boundaries don't always follow those clear-cut guidelines in the real world. Additionally, automated pen tests suffer the same flaw as most virus scanners: They rarely find anything a real hacker would use. Automated tools are dependent on the same signature-based mind-set of most antivirus software, so if you really want to know whether your custom application, your complex architecture, your websites, and your users are vulnerable, you should hire a professional.

☒ **B** is incorrect because this definition doesn't match an internal test. Internal testing is performed from inside the organization's network boundary. Internal testing can be announced (IT staff know it's going on) or unannounced (IT staff is kept in the dark and only management knows the test is being performed).

☒ **C** is incorrect because black box doesn't necessarily have anything to do with cost. It generally takes longer than, say, white-box testing, but it doesn't fit this question.

☒ **D** is incorrect because this definition doesn't match external testing. External testing is all about publicly available information and attempts to enumerate targets and other goodies from outside the network boundary.

8. Which of the following best defines an attack against the organization by an internal user?

   A. External, black box

   B. Internal, gray box

   C. Internal, announced

   D. External, white box

☑ **B.** I understand some of you are going to try arguing semantics with me on this one, but trust me, the "best" designator in this question covers me here. *Most* employees are going to have at least some idea of internal networks or operations within the company—even if it's just the domain to log into, password policy, or lockout policy. The internal gray box test best describes this: an attack inside the network by someone who has some information or knowledge about the network and resources being attacked. As an aside, these insider attacks may very well be the work of the "disgruntled employee," whom EC-Council has dubbed as the most dangerous threat to an organization's security.

☒ **A** is incorrect because a disgruntled employee would not need to perform an external test—much less a black-box (no knowledge) one. Is it possible a disgruntled employee wouldn't take advantage of his internal knowledge? Is it possible he would ignore the built-in advantage of already being on the network and having login credentials there? Sure, it is—it's just not likely.

☒ **C** is incorrect because the attack most certainly will not be announced (that is, the IT security staff is notified it is being conducted). It's highly unlikely the disgruntled employee will want to assist the IT security team in noting and patching security problems within the network.

☒ **D** is incorrect but just barely so. It is possible that this particular employee has all the knowledge of the network segment he's attacking. And it's plausible he may even decide to run an attack externally. However, ignoring the advantage of being inside the network to launch an attack—even if it's simply to set up a listening port to be used from a remote location—is highly unlikely. This choice simply isn't the best description of the disgruntled employee attack.

9. Brad is part of an environmental group protesting SomeBiz, Inc., for the company's stance on a variety of issues. Frustrated by the failure of multiple attempts to raise awareness of his cause, Brad launches sophisticated web defacement and denial-of-service attacks against the company, without attempting to hide the attack source and with no regard to being caught. Which of the following terms best defines Brad?

   A. Hactivism

   B. Ethical hacker

   C. Script kiddie

   D. Suicide hacker

   ☑ **D.** This is another definition term from EC-Council you'll see on your exam. And, much like in this question, you'll almost always see it paired with "hactivism" as an answer. A suicide hacker is an attacker who is so wrapped up in promoting their cause they do not care about the consequences of their actions. If defacing a website or blowing up a company server results in 30 years of prison time, so be it—as long as the cause has been promoted. In some instances (I've seen this in practice test exams before), the suicide hacker even *wants* to be caught to serve as a martyr for the cause.

   ☒ **A** is incorrect because *hactivism* refers to the act, not the attacker. Hactivism is the act of hacking for a cause, but those participating may very well want to avoid jail time. Suicide hackers don't care.

   ☒ **B** is incorrect for obvious reasons. As a matter of fact, if you chose this answer, stop right now and go back to page 1—you need to start the whole thing over again. An ethical hacker is employed as part of a team of security professionals and works under strict guidelines and agreed-upon scope.

   ☒ **C** is incorrect because a script kiddie is a point-and-shoot type of "hacker" who simply pulls information off the Internet and fires away.

10. A security team has been hired by upper management to assess the organization's security. The assessment is designed to emulate an Internet hacker and to

test the behavior of the security devices and policies in place as well as the IT security staff. Which of the following best describe this test? (Choose all that apply.)

A. Internal

B. External

C. Announced

D. Unannounced

☑ **B** and **D.** An external test is designed to mirror steps a hacker might take from outside the company perimeter. The team will start, of course, with publicly available information and ratchet up attempts from there. Because the question states it's testing security devices, policies, and the IT staff, the indication is this is an unannounced test. After all, if the IT staff knew the attack was going to occur in advance, it wouldn't be a true test of their ability to detect and react to an actual, real attack.

☒ **A** and **C** are incorrect because this attack is not internal to the organization's network perimeter, nor has it been announced to the IT staff.

11. In which phase of a pen test will the team penetrate the perimeter and acquire targets?

A. Pre-attack

B. Attack

C. Post-attack

D. None of the above

☑ **B.** EC-Council splits a pen test into three phases: pre-attack, attack, and post-attack. In the attack phase, the team will attempt to penetrate the network perimeter, acquire targets, execute attacks, and elevate privileges. Getting past the perimeter might take into account things such as verifying ACLs by crafting packets as well as checking the use of any covert tunnels inside the organization. Attacks such as XSS, buffer overflows, and SQL injections will be used on web-facing applications and sites. After acquiring specific targets, password cracking, privilege escalation, and a host of other attacks will be carried out.

☒ **A** is incorrect because these actions do not occur in the pre-attack phase. Per EC-Council, pre-attack includes planning, reconnaissance, scanning, and gathering competitive intelligence.

☒ **C** is incorrect because these actions do not occur in the post-attack phase. Per EC-Council, post-attack includes removing all files, uploaded tools, registry entries, and other items installed during testing from the targets. Additionally, your analysis of findings and creation of the pen test report will occur here.

☒ **D** is incorrect because there is an answer for the question listed.

12. Which of the following test types presents a higher probability of encountering problems and takes the most amount of time?

   A. Black box

   B. Gray box

   C. White box

   D. Internal

   ☑ **A.** Tests can be internal or external, can be announced or unannounced, and can be classified by the knowledge the team has before the test occurs. A black-box test, whether internal or external, is designed to simulate a hacker's attempts at gaining entry into the organization. Obviously this usually starts as an external test but can become internal as time progresses (depending on the pen test team's scope and agreement). Because it's a test with no prior knowledge to simulate that true outsider threat, black-box testing provides more opportunity for problems along the way and takes the most amount of time. External, black-box testing takes the longest because the tester has to plan higher-risk activities.

   Lastly (and a fun little nugget added by our renowned tech editor), in the real world the attacker has to figure out what is *important* to the target. What actions would damage or cause harm to the target? Where are critical files, folders, data, and other resources held? It's targeted reconnaissance and prepares your "battlespace" for attack.

   ☒ **B** and **C** are incorrect for the same reason: In both cases, the information provided to the team greatly reduces the amount of time and effort needed to gain entry.

   ☒ **D** is incorrect because there is no reference in the question to where this attack is actually taking place. As an aside, an internal test, where the team is given a network access point inside the network to start with, should obviously provide a leg up in both time and effort compared to an external one.

13. Which of the following best describes the difference between a professional pen test team member and a hacker?

   A. Ethical hackers are paid for their time.

   B. Ethical hackers never exploit vulnerabilities; they only point out their existence.

   C. Ethical hackers do not use the same tools and actions as hackers.

   D. Ethical hackers hold a predefined scope and agreement from the system owner.

   ☑ **D.** This one is a blast from the book's past and will pop up a couple of times on your exam. The only true difference between a professional pen test team member (an ethical hacker) and the hackers of the world is the existence of the formally approved, agreed-upon scope and contract before any attacks begin.

☒ **A** is incorrect because although professional ethical hackers are paid for their efforts during the pen test, it's not necessarily a delineation between the two (ethical and nonethical). Some hackers may be paid for a variety of illicit activities. For one example, maybe a company wants to cause harm to a competitor, so they hire a hacker to perform attacks.

☒ **B** and **C** are incorrect for the same reason. If a pen test team member never exploited an opportunity and refused to use the same tools and techniques that the hackers of the world have at their collective fingertips, what would be the point of an assessment? A pen test is designed to show true security weaknesses and flaws, and the only way to do that is to attack it just as a hacker would.

14. Sally is part of a penetration test team and is starting a test. The client has provided a network drop on one of their subnets for Sally to launch her attacks from. However, they did not provide any authentication information, network diagrams, or other notable data concerning the systems. Which type of test is Sally performing?

    A. External, white box

    B. External, black box

    C. Internal, white box

    D. Internal, black box

    ☑ **D.** Sally was provided a network drop inside the organization's network, so we know it's an internal test. Additionally, no information of any sort was provided—from what we can gather, she knows nothing of the inner workings, logins, network design, and so on. Therefore, this is a black-box test— an internal black-box test.

    ☒ **A** and **B** are incorrect because this is an internal test, not an external one.

    ☒ **C** is incorrect because a white-box test would have included all the information Sally wanted about the network—designed to simulate a disgruntled internal network or system administrator.

15. Joe is part of a pen test team that has been hired by AnyBiz to perform testing under a contract. As part of the defined scope and activities, no IT employees within AnyBiz know about the test. After some initial information gathering, Joe strikes up a conversation with an employee in the cafeteria and steals the employee's access badge. Joe then uses this badge to gain entry to secured areas of AnyBiz's office space. Which of the following best defines Joe in this scenario?

    A. Outside affiliate

    B. Outside associate

    C. Insider affiliate

    D. Insider associate

☑ **C.** You had to know I would check to see whether you're paying attention, right? Otherwise, there would be no explanation for asking nearly the same question twice within one chapter, unless, of course, I was trying to make a point about how important these definitions are. Remember, an insider affiliate is someone—a spouse, friend, or acquaintance—who uses the employee's access credentials to further their attack.

☒ **A** is incorrect because an outside affiliate is someone who is not employed with the company who makes use of open access (such as unsecured wireless) to the organization's network.

☒ **B** is incorrect because "outside associate" isn't a term within CEH study.

☒ **D** is incorrect because an insider associate is a member of the organization—such as a guard or a subcontractor—who has limited access to resources.

16. In which phase of a penetration test would you compile a list of vulnerabilities found?

   A. Pre-attack

   B. Attack

   C. Post-attack

   D. Reconciliation

☑ **C.** This is another simple definition question you're sure to see covered on the exam. You compile the results of all testing in the post-attack phase of a pen test so you can create and deliver the final report to the customer.

☒ **A and B** are incorrect because this action does not occur in the pre-attack or attack phase.

☒ **D** is incorrect because reconciliation is not a phase of a pen test as defined by EC-Council.

17. Which of the following has a database containing thousands of signatures used to detect vulnerabilities in multiple operating systems?

   A. Nessus

   B. Hping

   C. LOIC

   D. SNMPUtil

☑ **A.** Nessus is probably the best-known, most-utilized vulnerability assessment tool on the planet—even though it's not necessarily free anymore. Nessus works on a server-client basis and provides "plug-ins" to test everything from Cisco devices, Mac OS, and Windows machines to SCADA devices, SNMP, and VMware ESX (you can find a list of plug-in families here: www.tenable.com/plugins/index.php?view=all). It's part of virtually every security team's portfolio, and you should definitely spend some time learning how to use it.

As an aside—not necessarily because it has anything to do with your test but because I am all about informing you to become a good pen tester— Openvas (www.openvas.org) is the open source community's attempt to have a free vulnerability scanner. Nessus was a free scanner for the longest time. However, once purchased by Tenable Network Security, it, for lack of a better term, angered a lot of people in the security community because it became a for-profit entity instead of a for-security one. Don't get me wrong—Nessus is outstanding in what it does; it just costs you money. Openvas is attempting to do the same thing for free because the community wants security over profit.

Just keep in mind that most vulnerabilities that are actually capable of causing harm to your systems probably won't be found by any scanner. The recent Heartbleed vulnerability, taking advantage of an SSL issue, was a prime example: scanners simply can't find vulnerabilities we don't already know about.

☒ **B** is incorrect because Hping is not a vulnerability assessment tool. Per Hping's website (www.hping.org), it is "a command line-oriented TCP/IP packet assembler/analyzer" used to test firewalls, to fingerprint operating systems, and even to perform man-in-the-middle (MITM) attacks.

☒ **C** is incorrect because Low Orbit Ion Cannon (LOIC) is a distributed interface denial-of-service tool. It's open source and can be used, supposedly legitimately, to test "network stress levels."

☒ **D** is incorrect because SNMPUtil is an SNMP security verification and assessment tool.

18. Cleaning registry entries and removing uploaded files and tools are part of which phase of a pen test?

    A. Covering tracks

    B. Pre-attack

    C. Attack

    D. Post-attack

    ☑ **D.** Cleaning up all your efforts occurs in the post-attack phase, alongside analyzing the findings and generating the final report. The goal is to put things back exactly how they were before the assessment.

    ☒ **A** is incorrect because covering tracks is part of the phases defining a hacking attack, not a phase of a pen test.

    ☒ **B** and **C** are incorrect because these steps do not occur in the pre-attack or attack phase.

19. Jake, an employee of AnyBiz, Inc., parks his vehicle outside the corporate offices of SomeBiz, Inc. He turns on a laptop and connects to an open wireless access point internal to SomeBiz's network. Which of the following best defines Jake?

A. Outside affiliate

B. Outside associate

C. Insider affiliate

D. Insider associate

☑ **A.** Here we are again, back at a pure memorization question you're sure to see on your exam. EC-Council defines four types of attackers in this scenario: a pure insider (easy enough to figure out), an insider associate, an insider affiliate, and an outside affiliate. In this example, Jake best fits outside affiliate. He is a nontrusted outsider: He's not an employee or employed contractor, and he's not using credentials stolen from one. His access is from an unsecured, open access point (usually wireless but doesn't have to be).

☒ **B** is incorrect because EC-Council does not define an outside associate.

☒ **C** is incorrect because an insider affiliate is someone who does not have actual, authorized, direct access to the company's network, but they use credentials they've stolen from a pure insider to gain entry and launch attacks.

☒ **D** is incorrect because an insider associate is defined as someone who has limited access (to the network or to the facility itself) and uses that access to elevate privileges and launch attacks. The most common examples of this you'll see are subcontractors, janitors, and guards.

20. Which of the following are true regarding a pen test? (Choose all that apply.)

A. Pen tests do not include social engineering.

B. Pen tests may include unannounced attacks against the network.

C. During a pen test, the security professionals can carry out any attack they choose.

D. Pen tests always have a scope.

E. A list of all personnel involved in the test is not included in the final report.

☑ **B and D.** Pen tests are carried out by security professionals who are bound by a specific scope and rules of engagement, which must be carefully crafted, reviewed, and agreed on before the assessment begins. This agreement can allow for unannounced testing, should upper management of the organization decide to test their IT security staff's reaction times and methods.

☒ **A, C, and E** are incorrect because these are false statements concerning a pen test. Unless expressly forbidden in the scope agreement, social engineering is a big part of any true pen test. The scope agreement usually defines how far a pen tester can go—for example, no intentional denial-of-service attacks and so on. Clients are provided a list of discovered vulnerabilities after the test, even if the team did not exploit them: There's not always time to crack into every security flaw during an assessment, but that's no reason to hide it from the customer. Lastly, the final report includes a list of all personnel taking part in the test.

21. Which of the following causes a potential security breach?

    A. Vulnerability

    B. Threat

    C. Exploit

    D. Zero day

    ☑ **B.** A *threat* is something that could potentially take advantage of an existing vulnerability. Threats can be intentional, accidental, human, or even an "act of God." A hacker is a threat to take advantage of an open port on a system and/or poor password policy. A thunderstorm is a threat to exploit a tear in the roof, leaking down to your systems. Heck, a rhinoceros is a threat to bust down the door and destroy all the equipment in the room. Whether those threats have intent, are viable, and are willing/able to take up the vulnerability is a matter for risk assessment to decide; they'll probably beef up password policy and fix the roof, but I doubt much will be done on the rhino front.

    ☒ **A** is incorrect because a vulnerability is a weakness in security. A vulnerability may or may not necessarily be a problem. For example, your system may have horribly weak password policy or even a missing security patch, but if it's never on the network and is locked in a guarded room accessible by only three people who must navigate a biometric system to even open the door, the existence of those vulnerabilities is moot.

    ☒ **C** is incorrect because an exploit is what is or actually can be done by a threat agent to utilize the vulnerability. Exploits can be local or remote, a piece of software, a series of commands, or anything that actually uses the vulnerability to gain access to, or otherwise affect, the target.

    ☒ **D** is incorrect because a zero-day exploit is simply an exploit that most of us don't really know much about at the time of its use. For instance, a couple years back some bad guys discovered a flaw in Adobe Reader and developed an exploit for it. From the time the exploit was created to the time Adobe finally recognized its existence and built a fix action to mitigate against it, the exploit was referred to as *zero day*.

22. Which Metasploit payload type operates via DLL injection and is difficult for antivirus software to pick up?

A. Inline

B. Meterpreter

C. Staged

D. Remote

☑ **B.** For those of you panicking over this question, relax. You do not have to know all the inner workings of Metasploit, but it does appear enough—in the variety of study materials available for the version 7 exam—that EC-Council wants you to know some basics, and this question falls in that category. There are a bunch of different payload types within Metasploit, and *meterpreter* (short for meta-interpreter) is one of them. The following is from Metasploit's website: "Meterpreter is an advanced payload that is included in the Metasploit Framework. Its purpose is to provide complex and advanced features that would otherwise be tedious to implement purely in assembly. The way that it accomplishes this is by allowing developers to write their own extensions in the form of shared object (DLL) files that can be uploaded and injected into a running process on a target computer after exploitation has occurred. Meterpreter and all of the extensions that it loads are executed entirely from memory and never touch the disk, thus allowing them to execute under the radar of standard anti-virus detection."

☒ **A** is incorrect because inline payloads are single payloads that contain the full exploit and shell code for the designed task. They may be more stable than other payloads, but they're easier to detect and, because of their size, may not be viable for many attacks.

☒ **C** is incorrect because staged payloads establish a connection between the attacking machine and the victim. They then will read in a payload to execute on the remote machine.

☒ **D** is incorrect because remote isn't a recognized payload type.

23. Metasploit is a framework allowing for the development and execution of exploit code against a remote host and is designed for use in pen testing. The framework consists of several libraries, each performing a specific task and set of functions. Which library is considered the most fundamental component of the Metasploit framework?

A. MSF Core

B. MSF Base

C. MSF Interfaces

D. Rex

☑ **D.** Once again, this is another one of those weird questions you may see (involving any of the framework components) on your exam. It's included here so you're not caught off guard in the actual exam room and freak out over not hearing it before. Don't worry about learning all the nuances of Metasploit and its architecture before the exam—just concentrate on memorizing the basics of the framework (key words for each area will assist with this), and you'll be fine.

Metasploit, as you know, is an open source framework allowing all sorts of automated (point-and-shoot) pen test methods. The framework is designed in a modular fashion, with each library and component responsible for its own function. The following is from the Metasploit's development guide (http://dev.metasploit.com/redmine/projects/framework/wiki/DeveloperGuide#12-Design-and-Architecture): "The most fundamental piece of the architecture is the *Rex* library, which is short for the Ruby Extension Library. Some of the components provided by Rex include a wrapper socket subsystem, implementations of protocol clients and servers, a logging subsystem, exploitation utility classes, and a number of other useful classes." Rex provides critical services to the entire framework.

☒ **A** is incorrect because the MSF Core "is responsible for implementing all of the required interfaces that allow for interacting with exploit modules, sessions, and plugins." It interfaces directly with Rex.

☒ **B** is incorrect because the MSF Base "is designed to provide simpler wrapper routines for dealing with the framework core as well as providing utility classes for dealing with different aspects of the framework, such as serializing module state to different output formats." The Base is an extension of the Core.

☒ **C** is incorrect because the MSF Interfaces are the means by which you (the user) interact with the framework. Interfaces for Metasploit include Console, CLI, Web, and GUI.

24. EC-Council defines six stages of scanning methodology. Which of the following correctly lists the six steps?

   A. Scan for vulnerabilities, check for live systems, check for open ports, perform banner grabbing, draw network diagrams, prepare proxies

   B. Perform banner grabbing, check for live systems, check for open ports, scan for vulnerabilities, draw network diagrams, prepare proxies

   C. Check for live systems, check for open ports, perform banner grabbing, scan for vulnerabilities, draw network diagrams, prepare proxies

   D. Prepare proxies, check for live systems, check for open ports, perform banner grabbing, scan for vulnerabilities, draw network diagrams

☑ **C.** I can hear the complaints now: "You mean to tell me I have yet another list of steps to remember? Another methodology I've got to commit to memory?" Unfortunately, the answer to that question is yes, Dear Reader. I would apologize, but you're probably used to at least a little bit of CEH madness by now.

EC-Council defines the process of scanning by splitting it into six steps. First, you determine which hosts are alive on the network, followed by a check to see which ports they may have open. Next, a little perform banner grabbing will help in identifying operating systems and such. In step 4, you'll turn your attention to vulnerabilities that may be present on these systems. Next (and the step I, personally, find humorous to be involved in this particular methodology), you'll put all this together in a neat little network drawing for future reference. Lastly (in another step I find to be a weird addition), you'll start preparing proxies from which you will launch attacks later.

These six steps are outlined in EC-Council's official study preparation for the exam. Get to know them because you'll see a question like this somewhere on your exam.

☒ **A, B,** and **D** are all incorrect because they do not list the correct steps in order.

25. Which of the following may be effective countermeasures against an inside attacker? (Choose all that apply.)

   A. Enforce elevated privilege control.

   B. Secure all dumpsters and shred collection boxes.

   C. Enforce good physical security practice and policy.

   D. Perform background checks on all employees.

   ☑ **A, B, C,** and **D.** All of the answers are correct. Admittedly there's nothing you can really do to completely prevent an inside attack. There's simply no way to ensure every single employee is going to remain happy and satisfied, just as there's no way to tell when somebody might just up and decide to turn to crime. It happens all the time, in and out of Corporate America, so the best you can do is, of course, the best you can do.

   Enforcing elevated privilege control (that is, ensuring users have only the amount of access, rights, and privileges to get their job done, and no more) seems like a commonsense thing, but it's amazing how many enterprise networks simply ignore this, and a disgruntled employee with administrator rights on his machine can certainly do more damage than one with just plain user rights. Securing dumpsters and practicing good physical security should help protect against an insider who wants to come back after hours and snoop around. And background checks on employees, although by no means a silver bullet in this situation, can certainly help to ensure you're hiring the right people in the first place (in many companies a background check is a requirement of *law*). Other steps include, but are not limited to, the following:

- Monitoring user network behavior
- Monitoring user computer behavior
- Disabling remote access
- Disabling removable drive use on all systems (USB drives and so on)
- Shredding all discarded paperwork
- Conducting user education and training programs

26. The IP address 132.58.90.55/20 is given for a machine your team is to test. Which of the following represents an address within the same subnet?

A. 132.58.88.254

B. 132.58.96.20

C. 132.58.254.90

D. 132.58.55.90

☑ **A.** Truth being told here, you will not see many subnetting questions on your exam. As a matter of fact, many of you won't have to do any math on your exam at all. But some of you will see it, and all of you had better know it before entering the workplace. Subnetting can be a gigantic pain, but once you're used to seeing it, the process gets easier and easier. There are hundreds of different tips and tricks to make it all easier and quicker for you, but the best and most foolproof way to handle it is to break it all down to bits and do some good old math.

In this case, the subnet is /20, meaning the first 20 bits of the address belong to the network, and the remaining 12 bits constitute hosts in that network. If you break down the address from decimal to binary, 132.58.90.55 equates to the following:

10000100.00111010.01011010.00110111

The first 20 bits of this equate to 10000100.00111010.0101xxxx.xxxxxxxx (where x represents a host bit), and breaking this down to decimal shows us that everything from 132.58.80.1 through 132.58.95.254 would be a valid host within this subnet.

☒ **B, C,** and **D** are all incorrect because they do not fit the subnet. When looking at the third octet of each address in bits, you can clearly see none matches the static four-bit set in the subnet mask. The first four bits of 96, 254, and 55 do not match the static four-bit set for the subnet: The first four bits of the octet for 96 (0110), 254 (1111), and 55 (0011) do not match the first four bits of 0101.

Pre-assessment Test

This pre-assessment test is designed to help you prepare to study for the CEH Certified Ethical Hacker examination. You should take this test to identify the areas where you should focus your study and preparation.

The pre-assessment test includes 55 questions that are similar in style and format to the questions on the exam. As you prepare to take this test, try to simulate the actual exam conditions as closely as possible. Go to a quiet place and be sure that you will not be interrupted for the full length of time it will take to complete the test. You should give yourself one hour and 45 minutes. Do not use any reference materials or other assistance while taking the pre-assessment—remember, the idea is to help you determine what areas you need to focus on during your preparation for the actual exam.

The pre-assessment test contains questions divided in proportion to the CEH exam. Here is a breakdown of the exam content:

Chapter	Exam Weight	Number of Pre-assessment Questions
1: Getting Started: Essential Knowledge	8 percent	4
2: Reconnaissance: Information Gathering for the Ethical Hacker	10 percent	6
3: Scanning and Enumeration	13 percent	7
4: Sniffing and Evasion	13 percent	7
5: Attacking a System	13 percent	7
6: Web-Based Hacking: Servers and Applications	13 percent	7
7: Wireless Network Hacking	10 percent	5
8: Trojans and Other Attacks	5 percent	3
9: Cryptography 101	5 percent	3
10: Low Tech: Social Engineering and Physical Security	5 percent	3
11: The Pen Test: Putting It All Together	5 percent	3

Complete the entire pre-assessment test before checking your results. Once you have finished, use both the "Quick Answer Key" and the "Answers" sections to score your test. Use the table in the "Analyzing Your Results" section to determine how well you performed. The objective map at the end of the appendix will help you identify those areas that require the most attention while you prepare for the exam.

Are you ready? Set your clock for one hour and 45 minutes and begin!

1. A vendor is alerted of a newly discovered flaw in its software that presents a major vulnerability to systems. While working to prepare a fix action, the vendor releases a notice alerting the community of the discovered flaw and providing best practices to follow until the patch is available. Which of the following best describes the discovered flaw?

   A. Input validation flaw

   B. Shrink-wrap vulnerability

   C. Insider vulnerability

   D. Zero-day

2. A security professional applies encryption methods to communication channels. Which security control role is she attempting to meet?

   A. Preventive

   B. Detective

   C. Defensive

   D. Corrective

3. Which of the following comes after scanning in the CEH methodology for testing a system?

   A. Gaining access

   B. Reconnaissance

   C. Maintaining access

   D. Covering tracks

4. An organization allows the data owner to set security permissions on an object. Which access control mechanism is in place?

   A. Mandatory access control

   B. Role-based access control

   C. Discretionary access control

   D. Authorized access control

5. Which of the following is true regarding MX records?

   A. MX records require an accompanying CNAME record.

   B. MX records point to name servers.

   C. MX record priority increases as the preference number decreases.

   D. MX record entries are required for every namespace.

6. From the partial e-mail header provided, which of the following represents the true originator of the e-mail message?

```
...
Return-path: <SOMEONE@anybiz.com>
Delivery-date: Wed, 13 Apr 2011 00:31:13 +0200
Received: from mailexchanger.anotherbiz.com([185.213.4.77])
by mailserver.anotherbiz.com running ExIM with esmtp
id xxxxxx-xxxxxx-xxx; Wed, 13 Apr 2011 01:39:23 +0200
Received: from mailserver.anybiz.com ([177.190.50.254] helo=mailserver
.anybiz.com)
by mailexchanger.anotherbiz.com with esmtp id xxxxxx-xxxxxx-xx
for USERJOE@anotherbiz.com; Wed, 13 Apr 2011 01:39:23 +0200
Received: from SOMEONEComputer [229.88.53.154] (helo=[SOMEONEcomputer])
by mailserver.anybiz.com with esmtpa (Exim x.xx)
(envelope-from <SOMEONE@anybiz.com) id xxxxx-xxxxxx-xxxx
for USERJOE@anotherbiz.com; Tue, 12 Apr 2011 20:36:08 -0100
Message-ID: <xxxxxxxx.xxxxxxxx@anybiz.com>
Date: Tue, 12 Apr 2011 20:36:01 -0100
X-Mailer: Mail Client
From: SOMEONE Name <SOMEONE@anybiz.com>
To: USERJOE Name <USERJOE@anotherbiz.com>
Subject: Something to consider
...
```

   A. The originator is 185.213.4.77.

   B. The originator is 177.190.50.254.

   C. The originator is 229.88.53.154.

   D. The e-mail header does not show this information.

7. What is the primary service of the U.S. Computer Security Incident Response Team (CSIRT)?

   A. CSIRT provides an incident response service to enable a reliable and trusted single point of contact for reporting computer security incidents worldwide.

   B. CSIRT provides computer security surveillance to governments, supplying important intelligence information on individuals traveling abroad.

   C. CSIRT provides pen testing services to individuals and multinational corporations.

   D. CSIRT provides vulnerability assessment services to law enforcement agencies.

8. Which Google operator is the best choice in searching for a particular string in the website's title?

   A. intext:

   B. inurl:

   C. site:

   D. intitle:

9. An ethical hacker begins by visiting the target's website and then peruses social networking sites and job boards looking for information and building a profile on the organization. Which of the following best describes this effort?

   A. Active footprinting

   B. Passive footprinting

   C. Internet footprinting

   D. Sniffing

10. Which of the following methods correctly performs banner grabbing with Telnet on a Windows system?

    A. telnet <IPAddress> 80

    B. telnet 80 <IPAddress>

    C. telnet <IPAddress> 80 -u

    D. telnet 80 <IPAddress> -u

11. You are examining results of a SYN scan. A port returns a RST/ACK. What does this mean?

    A. The port is open.

    B. The port is closed.

    C. The port is filtered.

    D. Information about this port cannot be gathered.

12. Which TCP flag instructs the recipient to ignore buffering constraints and immediately send all data?

    A. URG

    B. PSH

    C. RST

    D. BUF

13. You want to run a reliable scan but remain as stealthy as possible. Which of the following Nmap commands accomplishes your goal best?

    A. nmap –sN targetIPaddress

    B. nmap –sO targetIPaddress

    C. nmap –sS targetIPaddress

    D. nmap –sT targetIPaddress

14. As your IDLE scan moves along, you notice that fragment identification numbers gleaned from the zombie machine are incrementing randomly. What does this mean?

    A. Your IDLE scan results will not be useful to you.

    B. The zombie system is a honeypot.

    C. There is a misbehaving firewall between you and the zombie machine.

    D. This is an expected result during an IDLE scan.

15. What step immediately follows banner grabbing in EC-Council's scanning methodology?

    A. Check for live systems

    B. Check for open ports

    C. Scan for vulnerabilities

    D. Draw network diagrams

    E. Prepare proxies

16. Which of the following correctly describes the TCP three-way handshake?

    A. SYN, ACK, SYN/ACK

    B. SYN, SYN/ACK, ACK

    C. ACK, SYN, ACK/SYN

    D. ACK, ACK/SYN, SYN

17. The loopback address represents the local host and in IPv4 was represented by 127.0.0.1. What is the loopback address in IPv6?

    A. fe80::/10

    B. fc00::/7

    C. fec0::/10

    D. ::1

18. Angie captures traffic using Wireshark. Which filter should she apply to see only packets sent from 220.99.88.77?

    A. ip = 220.99.88.77

    B. ip.src == 220.99.88.77

    C. ip.equals 220.99.88.77

    D. ip.addr == 220.99.88.77

19. Given the following Wireshark filter, what is the attacker attempting to view?

    ```
    ((tcp.flags == 0x02) || (tcp.flags == 0x12) ) || ((tcp.flags == 0x10) &&
    (tcp.ack==1) && (tcp.len==0) )
    ```

    A. SYN, SYN/ACK, ACK

    B. SYN, FIN, URG, and PSH

    C. ACK, ACK, SYN, URG

    D. SYN/ACK only

20. An ACK scan from an external location produces responses from machines inside the target network. Which of the following best describes the circumstances?

    A. The IDS is not functioning for the DMZ subnet.

    B. The systems are Unix machines.

    C. The systems are Windows based.

    D. The external firewall is not performing stateful inspection.

21. A pen tester connects a laptop to a switch port and enables promiscuous mode on the NIC. He then turns on Wireshark and leaves for the day, hoping to catch interesting traffic over the next few hours. Which of the following is true regarding this scenario? (Choose all that apply.)

    A. The packet capture will provide the MAC addresses of other machines connected to the switch.

    B. The packet capture will provide only the MAC addresses of the laptop and the default gateway.

    C. The packet capture will display all traffic intended for the laptop.

    D. The packet capture will display all traffic intended for the default gateway.

22. Which of the following protocols are considered susceptible to sniffing? (Choose all that apply.)

    A. FTP

    B. IMAP

    C. Telnet

    D. POP

    E. SMTP

    F. SSH

23. What does the following Snort rule accomplish?

    `alert tcp any any -> any 23(msg: "Telnet Connection Attempt")`?

    A. The rule logs any Telnet attempt over port 23 to any internal client.

    B. The rule logs any Telnet attempt over port 23 leaving the internal network.

    C. The rule alerts the monitor of any Telnet attempt to an internal client.

    D. The rule alerts the monitor of any Telnet attempt leaving the internal network.

24. Where is the SAM file found on a Windows 7 machine?

    A. C:\windows\config

    B. C:\windows\system32

    C. C:\windows\system32\etc

    D. C:\windows\system32\config

25. Which of the following commands would be useful in adjusting settings on the built-in firewall on a Windows machine?

    A. The netstat command

    B. The netsh command

    C. The sc command

    D. The ntfw command

26. Which password cracking method usually takes the most time and uses the most resources?

    A. Hybrid

    B. Dictionary

    C. Brute force

    D. Bot-net

27. Which SID indicates the true administrator account on the Windows machine?

    A. S-1-5-31-1045337334-12924807993-5683276715-1500

    B. S-1-5-31-1045337334-12924807993-5683276715-1001

    C. S-1-5-31-1045337334-12924807993-5683276715-501

    D. S-1-5-31-1045337334-12924807993-5683276715-500

28. Which of the following keyloggers provides the greatest risk because it cannot be detected by antivirus software?

    A. Polymorphic

    B. Heuristic

    C. Hardware

    D. Software

29. Which of the following is true regarding LM hashes?

   A. If the left side of the hash begins with 1404EE, the password is less than eight characters.

   B. If the right side of the hash ends with 1404EE, the password is less than eight characters.

   C. There is no way to tell whether passwords are less than eight characters because hashes are not reversible.

   D. There is no way to tell whether passwords are less than eight characters because each hash is always 32 characters long.

30. Which of the following is considered the most secure password?

   A. Ireallyhateshortpasswords

   B. Apassword123

   C. CEHPassw)rd

   D. Ap@ssw0rd123

31. The < character opens an HTML tag, while the > character closes it. In some web forms, input validation may deny these characters to protect against XSS. Which of the following represents the HTML entities used in place of these characters? (Choose two.)

   A. <

   B. >

   C. &

   D. ®

   E.

32. An attacker discovers a form on a target organization's website. He interjects some simple JavaScript into one of the form fields, instead of the username. Which attack is he carrying out?

   A. XSS

   B. SQL injection

   C. Buffer overflow

   D. Brute force

33. An attackers enters the following into a web form: ' or 1=1 --. Which attack is being attempted?

   A. XSS

   B. Brute force

C. Parameter manipulation

D. SQL injection

34. You are discussing different web application attacks and mitigations against them. Which of the following is a proper mitigation against cross-site scripting attacks?

   A. Configure strong passwords.

   B. Ensure the web server is behind a firewall.

   C. Ensure the web server is behind an IDS.

   D. Perform input validation.

35. Which of the following describes a primary advantage for using Digest authentication over Basic authentication?

   A. Digest authentication never sends a password in clear text over the network.

   B. Digest authentication uses multifactor authentication.

   C. In Digest authentication, the password is sent in clear text over the network but is never reused.

   D. In Digest authentication, Kerberos is used to encrypt the password.

36. In HTTP, passwords can be passed in a variety of means—many of them insecure. Which of the following methods is used to encode passwords within HTTP basic access authentication?

   A. MD5

   B. TDM

   C. FDM

   D. Base64

   E. DES

37. After a recent attack, log files are reviewed by the IR team to determine attack scope, success or failure, and lessons learned. Concerning the following entry:

   `SELECT username, password FROM users;`

   Which of the following best describes the result of this command query?

   A. The command deletes username and password fields from a table named *users*.

   B. The command adds username and password fields to a table named *users*.

   C. The command displays the contents of the username and password fields stored in the table named *users*.

   D. The command will not produce any results.

38. An attacker performs reconnaissance and learns the organization's SSID. He places an access point inside a closet, which tricks normal users into connecting, and begins redirecting them to malicious sites. Which of the following categorizes this attack?

A. Replay attack

B. Evil twin attack

C. Closet AP attack

D. WEP nap attack

39. During a pen test, the team lead decides to attempt intrusion using the organization's BlackBerry enterprise. Which tool is used in the blackjacking attempt?

A. Aircrack

B. Kismet

C. BBProxy

D. PrismStumbler

40. Which of the following is a passive wireless discovery tool?

A. NetStumbler

B. Aircrack

C. Kismet

D. Netsniff

41. Which of the following is not true regarding SSIDs?

A. They are used to identify networks.

B. They are used to encrypt traffic on networks.

C. They can be a maximum of 32 characters.

D. Even when not broadcast, SSIDs are easily discovered.

42. Which of the following are true regarding wireless security? (Choose all that apply.)

A. WPA-2 is the best available encryption security for the system.

B. WEP is the best encryption security for the system.

C. Regardless of encryption, turning off SSID broadcast protects the system.

D. SSIDs do not provide any effective security measures for a wireless network.

43. Which command displays all connections and listening ports in numerical form?

A. netstat –an

B. netstat –a localhost –n

C. netstat –r

D. netstat –s

44. Which of the following is true regarding session hijacking?

    A. The session must be hijacked before authentication.

    B. The session is hijacked after authentication.

    C. Strong authentication measures eliminate session hijacking concerns.

    D. Session hijacking cannot be carried out against Windows 7 machines.

45. Which virus type overwrites otherwise empty areas within a file?

    A. Polymorphic

    B. Cavity

    C. Macro

    D. Boot sector

46. Which of the following is not a field within an X.509 standard certificate?

    A. Version

    B. Algorithm ID

    C. Private key

    D. Public key

    E. Key usage

47. Which of the following is a common registry location for malware insertion?

    A. HKEY_LOCAL_MACHINE\SOFTWARE\Microsoft\Windows\CurrentVersion\Run

    B. HKEY_LOCAL_MACHINE\SOFTWARE\Microsoft\Windows\CurrentVersion\RunServices

    C. HKEY_LOCAL_MACHINE\SOFTWARE\Microsoft\Windows\CurrentVersion\RunOnce

    D. HKEY_LOCAL_MACHINE\SOFTWARE\Microsoft\Windows\CurrentVersion\RunServicesOnce

    E. All the above

48. Which of the following is a symmetric cryptographic standard?

    A. AES

    B. PKI

    C. RSA

    D. 3DES

49. Which of the following could be a potentially effective countermeasure against social engineering?

   A. User education and training

   B. Strong security policy and procedure

   C. Clear operational guidelines

   D. Proper classification of information and individuals' access to that information

   E. All of the above

50. Which of the following represents the highest risk to an organization?

   A. Black hat

   B. Gray hat

   C. White hat

   D. Disgruntled employee

51. Jill receives an e-mail that appears legitimate and clicks the included link. She is taken to a malicious website that steals her login credentials. Which of the following best describes this attack?

   A. Phishing

   B. Javelin

   C. Wiresharking

   D. Bait and switch

52. Angie waits by a side door entrance and follows a group of employees inside. She has no visible badge of any kind. Which of the following best describes this action?

   A. Tailgating

   B. Piggybacking

   C. Surfing

   D. Reverse SE

53. Bill is asked to perform an assessment but is provided with no knowledge of the system other than the name of the organization. Which of the following best describes the test he will be performing?

   A. White box

   B. Gray box

   C. Black box

   D. None of the above

54. OWASP provides a testing methodology. Which of the following is provided to assist in securing web applications?

A. COBIT

B. A list of potential security flaws and mitigations to address them

C. Web application patches

D. Federally recognized security accreditation

55. Joe is an IT security consultant, specializing in social engineering. Joe has been given authority to perform any and all tests necessary to audit the company's network security, and no employees know about his efforts. After obtaining a list of employees through company website contact pages, Joe befriends an employee of the company. Soon thereafter, Joe steals the employee's access badge and uses it to gain unauthorized access to the organization offices. What type of insider threat would Joe be considered?

A. Insider affiliate

B. Outside affiliate

C. Inside associate

D. Pure insider

1. D		29. B	
2. A		30. D	
3. A		31. A, B	
4. C		32. A	
5. C		33. D	
6. C		34. D	
7. A		35. A	
8. D		36. D	
9. B		37. C	
10. A		38. B	
11. B		39. C	
12. B		40. C	
13. C		41. B	
14. A		42. A, D	
15. B		43. A	
16. B		44. B	
17. D		45. B	
18. B		46. C	
19. A		47. E	
20. D		48. D	
21. A, C		49. E	
22. A, B, C, D, E		50. D	
23. C		51. A	
24. D		52. B	
25. B		53. C	
26. C		54. B	
27. D		55. A	
28. C			

Total Score: _____

1. ☑ **D.** Zero day means there has been no time to work on a solution. The bad thing is that the discovery by security personnel of the existing vulnerability doesn't mean it just magically popped up—it means it's been there without the good guy's knowledge and could have already been exploited.

   ☒ **A, B,** and **C** are incorrect. Input validation refers to verifying that a user's entry into a form or field contains only what the form or field was designed to accept. The terms *shrink-wrap vulnerability* and *insider vulnerability* are not valid so far as your exam is concerned.

2. ☑ **A.** Controls fall into three categories: preventive, detective, and corrective. In this instance, encryption of data is designed to prevent unauthorized eyes from seeing it. Depending on the encryption used, this can provide for confidentiality and nonrepudiation and is most definitely preventive in nature.

   ☒ **B, C,** and **D** are incorrect. Detective controls are designed to watch for security breaches and detect when they occur. Corrective controls are designed to fix things after an attack has been discovered and stopped.

3. ☑ **A.** The Ethical Hacking methodology laid out by EC-Council flows in five (or six) steps: reconnaissance, scanning and enumeration, gaining access, maintaining access, and covering tracks. In version 7, escalating privileges wasn't a separate step but seems to be looked at as such in version 8. Escalating privileges lives between gaining access and maintaining access, should you be asked.

   ☒ **B, C,** and **D** are incorrect. These do not match the methodology.

4. ☑ **C.** Discretionary access control allows the data owner, the user, to set security permissions for the object. If you're on a Windows machine right now, you can create files and folders and then set sharing and permissions on them as you see fit.

   ☒ **A, B,** and **D** are incorrect. Mandatory access control (MAC) assigns sensitivity labels to data and controls access by matching the user's security level to the resource label. Role-based access control (RBAC) can use either discretionary access control (DAC) or MAC to get the job done. The goal is to assign a role, and any entity holding that role can perform the duties associated with it. Users are not assigned permissions directly; they acquire them through their role (or roles).

5. ☑ **C.** MX records have a preference number to tell the SMTP client to try (and retry) each of the relevant addresses in this list in order, until a delivery attempt succeeds. The smallest preference number has the highest priority, and any server with the smallest preference number must be tried first. If there is more than one MX record with the same preference number, all of them must be tried before moving on to lower-priority entries.

   ☒ **A, B,** and **D** are incorrect. MX records do not require an alias (CNAME), they do not point to name servers, and not every namespace absolutely requires an e-mail server.

6. ☑ **C** is correct. On e-mail headers, you'll most likely be asked to identify the true originator—although there are many other entries to pay attention to. The machine (person) who sent the message in the first place may be impossible to truly decipher, since in the real world attackers have proxies and whatnot to hide behind; however, we can only go off the header provided. From the bottom up (the bottom entry is the first in the line), the originator is clearly shown: "Received: from SOMEONEComputer [217.88.53.154] (helo=[SOMEONEcomputer])."

☒ **A, B**, and **D** are incorrect. These IPs do not represent the true originator of the message. They show e-mail servers that are passing/handling the message.

7. ☑ **A** is correct. From its website, the Computer Security Incident Response Team (CSIRT; www.csirt.org/) "provides 24x7 Computer Security Incident Response Services to any user, company, government agency or organization. CSIRT provides a reliable and trusted single point of contact for reporting computer security incidents worldwide. CSIRT provides the means for reporting incidents and for disseminating important incident-related information."

☒ **B, C**, and **D** are incorrect. These statements don't match CSIRT's purpose.

8. ☑ **D** is correct. Google hacking refers to manipulating a search string with additional specific operators to search for valuable information. The intitle: operator will return websites with a particular string in their title. Website titles contain all sorts of things, from legitimate descriptions of the page or author information to a list of words useful for a search engine.

☒ **A, B**, and **C** are incorrect. The intext: operator looks for pages that contain a specific string in the text of the page body. The inurl: operator looks for a specific string within the URL. The site operator limits the current search to only the specified site (instead of the entire Internet).

9. ☑ **B** is correct. Footprinting competitive intelligence is a passive effort because of competitive intelligence being open and accessible to anyone. Passive footprinting is an effort that doesn't usually put you at risk of discovery.

☒ **A, C**, and **D** are incorrect. This is not active footprinting since no internal targets have been touched and there is little to no risk of discovery. Internet footprinting isn't a legitimate term to commit to memory, and sniffing is irrelevant to this question.

10. ☑ **A** is correct. Telnetting to port 80 will generally pull a banner from a web server. You can telnet to any port you want to check, for that matter, and ideally pull a port; however, port 80 just seems to be the one used on the exam the most.

☒ **B, C**, and **D** are incorrect. These are all bad syntax for Telnet.

11. ☑ **B** is correct. Think about a TCP handshake—SYN, SYN/ACK, ACK—and then read this question again. Easy, right? In a SYN scan, an open port is going to respond with a SYN/ACK, and a closed one is going to respond with a RST/ACK.

☒ **A, C,** and **D** are incorrect. The return response indicates the port is closed. An open port would respond with a SYN/ACK, and a filtered one likely wouldn't respond at all.

12. ☑ **B** is correct. It really does sound like an urgent request, but the PSH flag is designed for these scenarios.

☒ **A, C,** and **D** are incorrect. The URG flag is used to inform the receiving stack that certain data within a segment is urgent and should be prioritized (not used much by modern protocols). The RST flag forces a termination of communications (in both directions). BUF is not a TCP flag.

13. ☑ **C** is correct. A full-connect scan would probably be best, provided you run it slowly. However, given the choices, a half-open scan, as defined by this Nmap command line, is the best remaining option.

☒ **B, C,** and **D** are incorrect. A null scan probably won't provide the reliability asked for since it doesn't work on Windows hosts at all. The –sO (operating system) scan would prove too noisy here. The full scan (–sT) would provide reliable results, but without a timing modifier to greatly slow it down, it will definitely be seen.

14. ☑ **A** is correct. It is absolutely essential the zombie remain idle to all other traffic during an IDLE scan. The attacker will send packets to the target with the (spoofed) source address of the zombie. If the port is open, the target will respond to the SYN packet with a SYN/ACK, but this will be sent to the zombie. The zombie system will then craft a RST packet in answer to the unsolicited SYN/ACK, and the IPID will increase. If this occurs randomly, then it's probable your zombie is not, in fact, idle, and your results are moot.

☒ **B, C,** and **D** are incorrect. There is not enough information here to identify the zombie machine as anything at all (much less a machine set up as a honeypot), and a firewall has nothing to do with any of this. This is also *not* expected behavior during an IDLE scan.

15. ☑ **B** is correct. In order from start to finish, the methodology is as follows: 1. Check for live systems, 2. Check for open ports, 3. Perform scanning beyond IDS, 4. Perform banner grabbing, 5. Scan for vulnerabilities, 6. Draw network diagrams, and 7. Prepare proxies.

☒ **A, C, D,** and **E** are incorrect. These are not the steps immediately following banner grabbing.

16. ☑ **B** is correct. This is bedrock knowledge you should already have memorized from networking 101 classes. TCP starts a communication with a synchronize packet (with the SYN flag set). The recipient acknowledges this by sending both the SYN and ACK flags. Finally, the originator acknowledges communications can begin with an ACK packet.

☒ **A, C,** and **D** are incorrect. These answers do not have the correct three-way handshake order.

17. ☑ **D** is correct. IPv6 uses a 128-bit address instead of the 32-bit IPv4 version. It's represented as eight groups of four hexadecimal digits separated by colons but can be shortened in display by removing leading zeroes (replaced by a double colon). The loopback address, in full, is 0000:0000:0000:0000:0000:0000:0000: 0001, which can be reduced all the way down to ::1.

☒ **A, B**, and **C** are incorrect. These values do not represent the loopback address in IPv6. Fe80::/10 is reserved for link local, FC00::/7 is the unique local (like private addressing in IPv4), and FEC0::/10 is for site local.

18. ☑ **B** is correct. The ip.src xxxx filter tells Wireshark to display only those packets with the IP address xxxx in the source field.

☒ **A, C**, and **D** are incorrect. These are incorrect Wireshark filters.

19. ☑ **A.** You'll see bunches of Wireshark questions on your exam, and EC-Council just loves the "TCP flags = decimal numbers" side of it all. Wireshark also has the ability to filter based on a decimal numbering system assigned to TCP flags. The assigned flag decimal numbers are FIN = 1, SYN = 2, RST = 4, PSH = 8, ACK = 16, and URG = 32. Adding these numbers together (for example, SYN + ACK = 18) allows you to simplify a Wireshark filter. For example, tcp.flags == 0x2 looks for SYN packets, tcp.flags == 0x16 looks for ACK packets, and tcp.flags == 0x18 looks for both.

☒ **B, C**, and **D** are incorrect because they do not match the decimals provided in the capture (2 for SYN, 18 for SYN/ACK, and 16 for ACK).

20. ☑ **D.** A stateful inspection firewall would notice the ACK coming unsolicited and from the wrong side of the fence.

☒ **A, B**, and **C** are incorrect. IDS is passive and reactive, so it would not prevent the packet flow. There is no way to tell, from the information provided, what OS the systems are.

21. ☑ **A and C.** Switches are designed to filter traffic—that is, they send traffic intended for a destination MAC—to only the port that holds the MAC address as an attached host. The exception, however, is broadcast and multicast traffic, which gets sent out every port. Because ARP is broadcast in nature, all machines' ARP messages would be viewable.

☒ **B and D** are incorrect. The switch will filter traffic to the laptop, and MAC addresses will be available from the broadcast ARPs.

22. ☑ **A, B, C, D**, and **E.** All the protocols listed here transfer data—including passwords—in clear text.

☒ **F** is incorrect. SSH can be thought of as an encrypted version of Telnet.

23. ☑ **C.** This rule alerts on Telnet in only one direction—into the internal network. It states that any IP address on any port attempting to connect to an internal client will generate the message "Telnet Connection Attempt."

☒ **A, B**, and **D** are incorrect. A and B are incorrect because they reference log-only rules. D is incorrect because the arrow is in only one direction.

24. ☑ **D** is correct. The SAM file, holding all those wonderful password hashes you want access to, is located in the C:\Windows\system32\config folder. You may also find a copy sitting in repair, at c:\windows\repair\sam.

☒ **A**, **B**, and **C** are incorrect. These folders do not contain the SAM file.

25. ☑ **B** is correct. Netsh is "a command-line scripting utility that allows you to, either locally or remotely, display or modify the network configuration of a computer that is currently running." Typing **netsh** at the command line then allows you to step into various "contexts" for adjusting all sorts of network configuration options, including the firewall. Typing a question mark shows all available commands at the context you are in. You can also execute the command without stepping into each context. For example, typing **netsh firewall show config** will show the configuration of the firewall.

☒ **A**, **C**, and **D** are incorrect. Netstat is a great tool for viewing ports and what's happening to them on the device. Sc is service control. Ntfw isn't a valid command-line tool.

26. ☑ **C** is correct. Brute-force attacks attempt every conceivable combination of letters, numbers, characters, and length in an attempt to find a match. Given you're starting from scratch, it follows you'd need a lot of time and a lot of resources. As an aside, the increase in processing power of systems and the ability to combine multiple systems together to work on problems cuts down on the time portion of this in modern cracking fairly significantly.

☒ **A**, **B**, and **D** are incorrect. Both hybrid and dictionary have a word list to work with and can run through it fairly quickly (in computing time, that is). A bot-net is a series of zombie systems set up by an attacker to carry out duties.

27. ☑ **D** is correct. A security identifier (SID) has five components, each one providing specific information. The last component—the relative identifier (RID)—provides information on the type of account. The RID of 500 indicates the true administrator account on the machine.

☒ **B**, **C**, and **D** are incorrect. The RID values starting at 1000 refer to standard user accounts, so answers A and B can be thrown out. The 501 RID indicates the built-in guest account.

28. ☑ **C** is correct. Hardware keyloggers are the highest risk because they are almost impossible to detect by software analyzers. Their use requires physical access to the target, but they are virtually guaranteed to provide results.

☒ **A**, **B**, and **D** are incorrect. Antivirus systems easily catch most software-based keyloggers. Polymorphic is not a keylogger type. Heuristic reflects to the method in which an antivirus solution functions, not how a keylogger works.

29. ☑ **B.** LM hashes will always have the right side of the hash the same, ending in 1404EE, because of the method by which LM performs the hash.

☒ **A**, **C**, and **D** are incorrect. The left side of each hash will always be different and indicates nothing. Answers C and D are incorrect because the hash value can tell you password length.

30. ☑ **D.** EC-Council cares nothing about the actual length of the password. On this exam, complexity trumps all.

☒ **A**, **B**, and **C** are incorrect. These passwords do not hold all three elements of complexity.

31. ☑ **A** and **B** are correct. Whether attempting to bypass input validation or just having things appear the way you want them to on a web page, HTML entities can be useful. The less-than sign (<) equates to *<*, while the greater-than sign (>) equates to *>*. You can also use their numbered equivalents (*<* and *>*), respectively.

☒ **C** and **D** are incorrect. *&* equates to the ampersand (&), and *®* equates to the Registered symbol, ®. * * is a nonbreaking space.

32. ☑ **A** is correct. Using a script entry in a web form field is cross-site scripting.

☒ **B**, **C**, and **D** are incorrect. This entry does not indicate SQL injection or buffer overflow. Brute force refers to a password cracking effort.

33. ☑ **D** is correct. If you missed this one, please consider taking a break or just starting your study process over again—you're obviously too tired to concentrate or you've never seen this before and are attempting to memorize your way to exam success. This question displays the classic SQL injection example that you'll see on every single practice test you'll take on the subject.

☒ **A**, **B**, and **C** are incorrect. XSS is cross-site scripting and involves inserting a script into a web form entry field to produce an outcome. Brute force is a password cracking technique, using all possible variants to match the encrypted value. Parameter manipulation refers to any parameter within communications being manipulated to force a desired outcome and is most likely displayed on the exam within the URL.

34. ☑ **D** is correct. A typical XSS attack involves an attacker submitting a script in a web form entry field. Input validation—making sure the web form entry field accepts only expected entries—can help prevent this from occurring.

☒ **A**, **B**, and **C** are incorrect. Strong passwords will not protect against XSS, and placing the server behind a firewall or IDS doesn't necessarily do a thing against this attack either.

35. ☑ **A** is correct. There are a couple of different methods a web page can use to negotiate credentials with a web user using HTTP. Digest authentication hashes a password before sending it out, while Basic just sends it out plain text.

☒ **B**, **C**, and **D** are incorrect. The remaining answers do not describe Digest authentication.

36. ☑ **D** is correct. HTTP Basic access authentication is a quick and easy way to pass credentials within an HTTP session; however, it's also easy to intercept. Base64 is a feeble attempt to obfuscate the user ID/password combination, by using 64 bits to represent alphanumeric characters.

⊠ **A, B,** and **C** are incorrect. MD5 is a hash algorithm used in Digest Access Authentication (DAA). TDM is Time Division Multiplexing, and FDM is Frequency Division Multiplexing, both of which are cool topics but do not belong here. DES and encryption algorithm are also not valid here.

37. ☑ **C** is correct. Walking through this command, SELECT retrieves information from a database, and the username and password fields are designated as what to select. Last, using the FROM command, the table holding the fields is identified.

⊠ **A, B,** and **D** are incorrect. DROP TABLE would be used to delete an entire table. ALTER TABLE can add or remove individual fields (columns), among other things.

38. ☑ **B** is correct. A rogue access point is also known as an evil twin. Usually they're discovered quickly; however, there are lots of organizations that don't regularly scan for them.

⊠ **A, C,** and **D** are incorrect. A replay attack occurs when communications (usually authentication-related) are recorded and replayed by the attacker. Closet AP and WEP nap aren't legitimate terms.

39. ☑ **C** is correct. Since BlackBerry devices are basically VPN'd into the corporate network, they can provide a nice back way in, using the proper technique. Blackjacking involves setting up a proxy and bouncing things off and through it into the internal network. BBProxy was presented during a DEF CON conference several years ago as a means to pull off this attack.

⊠ **A, B,** and **D** are incorrect. Aircrack is used to crack WEP encryption keys. Kismet is best known as a passive wireless sniffer. PrismStumbler is a wireless network identifier.

40. ☑ **C** is correct. Kismet works as a passive network discovery tool, without using packet interjection to gather information. Kismet also works by channel hopping to discover as many networks as possible and has the ability to sniff packets and save them to a log file, readable by Wireshark or TCPDump.

⊠ **A, B,** and **D** are incorrect. NetStumbler is an active discovery tool. Aircrack is a WEP cracking program. Netsniff is a false choice.

41. ☑ **B** is correct. The SSID has a singular purpose, which is to identify a network for a client. It can be up to 32 characters long, and you can turn off the SSID broadcast at the access point. However, the SSID is included with most packets leaving the access point and is easily discoverable anyway.

⊠ **A, C,** and **D** are incorrect. These are all true statements regarding an SSID.

42. ☑ **A** and **D.** WPA-2 is the latest encryption standard for wireless. SSIDs do nothing for security other than frustrate casual (lazy) attackers. It's not the intent of an SSID to do anything other than identify a network.

⊠ **B** and **C** are incorrect. WEP is poor encryption (and never the correct answer on this exam for security purposes), and SSID broadcast is nearly irrelevant to security.

43. ☑ **A is correct.** Netstat provides all sorts of good info on your machine. The –a option is for all connections and listening ports. The –n option puts them in numerical order.

☒ **B, C, and D are incorrect.** netstat –a localhost –n is incorrect syntax. netstat –r displays the route table. netstat –s displays per-protocol statistics.

44. ☑ **B is correct.** Session hijacking involves predicting an acceptable sequence number during an exchange of information and taking over the communications channel. By its very nature, authentication must already be completed in order for it to work.

☒ **A, C, and D are incorrect.** Hijacking occurs after authentication, so the measure used is largely irrelevant. Session hijacking can be carried out against all operating systems.

45. ☑ **B is correct.** One thing all malware writers attempt to do is find ways to hide their work. By finding empty spaces in a file and writing to them, a cavity virus can infect a file and not change its size so far as the system is concerned.

☒ **A, C, and D are incorrect.** Polymorphic viruses try mutating themselves to avoid detection. Macro viruses use macros built in to various programs (such as Microsoft Excel). A boot sector virus is exceedingly difficult to get rid of and, obviously, installs on the boot sector of the disk.

46. ☑ **C is correct.** The private key is never shared. Ever. It's not shared via a digital certificate, smoke signal, carrier pigeon, or any other distribution method.

☒ **A, B, D, and E are incorrect.** X.509 is an ITU-T standard defining all sorts of things regarding PKI, including the digital certificate and what it holds. It identifies several components of a digital certificate, including the version, the algorithm ID, a copy of the public key, and the key usage description.

47. ☑ **E is correct.** All of the registry keys listed here are common locations to find malware. The key is that, from here, the malware is continually launched.

☒ **A, B, C, and D are incorrect** as individual choices because they are all viable registry locales.

48. ☑ **D is correct.** 3DES is a symmetric encryption algorithm.

☒ **A, B, and C are incorrect.** PKI, RSA, and AES are asymmetric in nature.

49. ☑ **E is correct.** Social engineering can't ever be fully contained—after all, we're only human. However, these options present good steps to take in slowing it down. A properly trained employee, who not only knows the policies and guideline but agrees with and practices them, is a tough nut to crack. Assigning classification levels helps by restricting access to specific data, thereby limiting (ideally) the amount of damage of a successful social engineering attack.

☒ **A, B, C, and D are incorrect** individually because they all apply.

50. ☑ **D is correct.** It's bad enough we have to worry about the external hackers trying to break their way into a network, but what about all the folks we already let onto it? Disgruntled employees are serious threats because they already have connectivity and, depending on their job, a lot of access to otherwise protected areas.

☒ **A, B,** and **C** are incorrect. A black hat is an external, malicious attacker. A white hat is an ethical hacker. A gray hat doesn't work under an agreement but may not be malicious.

51. ☑ **A** is correct. Phishing is the act of crafting e-mails to trick recipients into behavior they would not otherwise complete. Usually the phishing e-mail contains a link to a malicious site or even an embedded piece of malware.

☒ **B, C,** and **D** are incorrect. The remaining answers are not legitimate attacks and do not apply here.

52. ☑ **B** is correct. If the attacker is not carrying a badge—real or fake—the correct definition is piggybacking.

☒ **A, C,** and **D** are incorrect. Tailgating involves the use of a badge (real or fake) when following employees in through an open door. Surfing and reverse SE have nothing to do with this.

53. ☑ **C** is correct. While there may be some argument in the real-world version of a black-box test, as far as your exam goes it is an assessment without any knowledge provided about the target.

☒ **A, B,** and **D** are incorrect. White-box and gray-box tests both provide information about the target (white is all of it, gray some of it).

54. ☑ **B** is correct. OWASP provides an inside look at known web application vulnerabilities to assist developers in creating more secure environments. From the site, "Everyone is free to participate in OWASP and all of our materials are available under a free and open software license. OWASP does not endorse or recommend commercial products or services, allowing our community to remain vendor neutral with the collective wisdom of the best minds in software security worldwide."

☒ **A, C,** and **D** are incorrect. COBIT is a framework for IT governance and control provided by ISACA. (Previously known as the Information Systems Audit and Control Association, ISACA now goes by its acronym only to reflect the broad range of IT governance professionals it serves.)

55. ☑ **A** is correct. This is one of those infuriating areas of EC-Council's exam that you're just going to have to muddle through. The credential used defines the person carrying out the attack, not the actual human being sitting behind the keyboard. An insider affiliate is a friend or spouse that uses a stolen credential of some sort to access resources. The insider part comes from the credential; the affiliate part comes from being a friend or spouse.

☒ **B, C,** and **D** are incorrect. An outside affiliate represents the hackers— attackers from outside the organization. An inside associate is someone with limited access, generally a cleaning crew member, contractor, or other service personnel. A pure insider would be an employee—someone who already has internal access.

Analyzing Your Results

Congratulations on completing the CEH pre-assessment. You should now take the time to analyze your results with these two objectives in mind:

- Identifying the resources you should use to prepare for the exam
- Identifying the specific topics you should focus on in your preparation

Use this table to help you gauge your overall readiness for the CEH examination:

Number of Answers Correct	Recommended Course of Study
1–25	I recommend you spend a significant amount of time reviewing the material in the *CEH Certified Ethical Hacker All-in-One Exam Guide, Second Edition,* before using this practice exams book.
26–37	I recommend you review the following objective map to identify the particular areas that require your focused attention and use *CEH Certified Ethical Hacker All-in-One Exam Guide, Second Edition,* to review that material. Once you have done so, you should proceed to work through the questions in this book.
38–55	I recommend you use this book to refresh your knowledge and prepare yourself mentally for the exam.

Once you have identified your readiness for the exam, use the following table to identify the specific objectives that require your focus as you continue your preparation:

Chapter	Weight	Objective	Question Number in Pretest
1: Getting Started: Essential Knowledge	8 percent	Identify essential terminology associated with ethical hacking	1
		Understand basic elements of information security	2, 4
		Describe the stages of ethical hacking	3
2: Reconnaissance: Information Gathering for the Ethical Hacker	10 percent	Describe DNS record types	5
		Identify methods and procedures in information gathering	6, 7
		Define and Describe Google hacking	8
		Define footprinting	9

Chapter	Weight	Objective	Question Number in Pretest
3: Scanning and Enumeration	13 percent	Understand enumeration and its techniques	10
		Describe TCP communication	11, 12
		Understand the use of various scanning and enumeration tools	13
		Describe scan types and the objectives of scanning	14
		Describe EC-Council's scanning methodology	15
		Describe TCP communication (three-way handshake and flag types)	16
4: Sniffing and Evasion	13 percent	Describe active and passive sniffing	17
		Sniffing tools and displays	18, 19
		Learn about firewall types, use, and placement	20
		Learn about sniffing and protocols that are susceptible to sniffing	21, 22
		Describe signature analysis within Snort	23
5: Attacking a System	13 percent	Understand Microsoft Authentication mechanisms	24, 27, 29
		Understand Windows architecture	25
		Describe password attacks	26
		Identify various password-cracking tools, keyloggers, and spyware technologies	28
		Describe best effort password complexity and protection	30
6: Web-Based Hacking: Servers and Applications	13 percent	Identify web server and application vulnerabilities	31, 32, 34, 36
		Describe web server and web application attacks	33, 37
		Identify features of common web server architecture	35
7: Wireless Network Hacking	10 percent	Identify wireless hacking methods and tools	38, 39, 40
		Identify wireless network architecture and terminology	41
		Identify wireless network types and forms of authentication	42

Chapter	Weight	Objective	Question Number in Pretest
8: Trojans and Other Attacks	5 percent	Identify Trojan countermeasures	43
		Describe session hijacking and sequence prediction	44
		Define viruses and worms	45
9: Cryptography 101	5 percent	Understand the digital certificate	46
		Identify Trojan deployment methods	47
		Identify cryptographic algorithms	48
10: Low Tech: Social Engineering and Physical Security	5 percent	List social-engineering countermeasures	49
		Describe insider attacks, reverse social engineering, dumpster diving, social networking, and URL obfuscation	50
		Describe phishing attacks and countermeasures	51
		Describe the different types of social-engineering attacks	52
11: The Pen Test: Putting It All Together	5 percent	Define automatic and manual testing	53
		Describe penetration testing, security assessments, and risk management	54, 55

About the CD-ROM

The CD-ROM included with this book comes complete with Total Tester customizable practice exam software with a pool of 300 practice exam questions, enough for three practice exams, and a PDF copy of the book.

System Requirements

The software requires Windows XP or higher and 30MB of hard disk space for full installation. To run, the screen resolution must be set to 1024 × 768 or higher. The PDF copy of the book requires Adobe Acrobat, Adobe Reader, or Adobe Digital Editions.

Total Tester Premium Practice Exam Software

Total Tester provides you with a simulation of the CompTIA Security+ exam. You can also create custom exams from selected domains or chapters. You can further customize the number of questions and time allowed.

The exams can be taken in either Practice Mode or Exam Mode. Practice Mode provides an assistance window with hints, references to the book, explanations of the correct and incorrect answers, and the option to check your answer as you take the test. Exam Mode provides a simulation of the actual exam. The number of questions, the types of questions, and the time allowed are intended to be an accurate representation of the exam environment. Both Practice Mode and Exam Mode provide an overall grade and a grade broken down by domain.

To take a test, launch the program and select Sec+ PE from the Installed Question Packs list. You can then select either Practice Mode, Exam Mode, or Custom Mode.

Installing and Running Total Tester Premium Practice Exam Software

From the main screen you may install the Total Tester by clicking the Total Tester Practice Exams button. This will begin the installation process and place an icon on your desktop and in your Start menu. To run Total Tester, navigate to Start | (All) Programs | Total Seminars, or double-click the icon on your desktop.

To uninstall the Total Tester software, go to Start | Settings | Control Panel | Add/ Remove Programs (XP) or Programs And Features (Vista/7/8), and then select the Total Tester program. Select Remove, and Windows will completely uninstall the software.

PDF Copy of the Book

The entire contents of the book are provided in PDF format on the CD-ROM. This file is viewable on your computer and many portable devices. Adobe Acrobat, Adobe Reader, or Adobe Digital Editions is required to view the file on your computer. A link to Adobe's web site, where you can download and install Adobe Reader, has been included on the CD-ROM.

 NOTE For more information on Adobe Reader and to check for the most recent version of the software, visit Adobe's web site at www.adobe.com and search for the free Adobe Reader or look for Adobe Reader on the product page. Adobe Digital Editions can also be downloaded from the Adobe web site.

To view the PDF copy of the book on a portable device, copy the PDF file to your computer from the CD-ROM, and then copy the file to your portable device using a USB or other connection. Adobe offers a mobile version of Adobe Reader, the Adobe Reader mobile app, which currently supports iOS and Android. For customers using Adobe Digital Editions and an iPad, you may have to download and install a separate reader program on your device. The Adobe web site has a list of recommended applications; McGraw-Hill Education recommends the Bluefire Reader.

Technical Support

Technical Support information is provided in the following sections by feature.

Total Seminars Technical Support

For questions regarding the Total Tester software or operation of the CD-ROM, visit www.totalsem.com or e-mail support@totalsem.com.

McGraw-Hill Education Content Support

For questions regarding the PDF copy of the book, e-mail techsolutions@mhedu.com or visit http://mhp.softwareassist.com.

For questions regarding book content, e-mail customer.service@mheducation.com. For customers outside the United States, e-mail international_cs@mheducation.com.

Complete coverage of today's top IT SECURITY certification exams

0-07-176026-1 • $60.00 • Available now

0-07-183648-9 • $50.00 • May 2014

0-07-183873-2 • $30.00 • Aug 2014

0-07-183557-1 • $70.00 • Oct 2014

0-07-183156-8 • $50.00 • July 2014

0-07-183976-3 • $60.00 • Sept 2014

0-07-183179-7 • $60.00 • Aug 2014

Available in print and as e-books.

 Follow us @MHComputing

Mc Graw Hill Education | Learn more. Do more.™ MHPROFESSIONAL.COM